Soul and Life

MERCER UNIVERSITY PRESS

Endowed by

TOM WATSON BROWN
and
THE WATSON-BROWN FOUNDATION, INC.

Soul and Life

Psyche in Seminal Ancient Greek Thinkers

MARINA MARREN, Ed.

Mercer University Press
Macon, Georgia

MUP/ P692

© 2024 by Mercer University Press
Published by Mercer University Press
1501 Mercer University Drive
Macon, Georgia 31207
All rights reserved

28 27 26 25 24   5 4 3 2 1

Books published by Mercer University Press are printed on acid-free paper that meets the requirements of the American National Standard for Information Sciences—Permanence of Paper for Printed Library Materials.

Printed and bound in the United States.

This book is set in Adobe Caslon.

Cover/jacket design by Burt&Burt.

Cover art: John Craxton, Moonlit Ravine (1970)
© 2023 Artists Rights Society (ARS), New York / DACS, London

ISBN   978-0-88146-925-7
Cataloging-in-Publication Data is available from the Library of Congress

CONTENTS

Acknowledgements / vii

Contributors / viii

Introduction, Marina Marren / ix

PART I

1. "The Soul of Crime and Punishment: Book IX of Plato's *Laws*," by Ronna Burger — 3

2. "Three Accounts of the Soul in Plato's Republic," by Deborah Achtenberg — 25

3. "The Female Drama," by Charlotte Thomas — 45

4. "The Soul, Virtue, and Women's Nature in First-Generation Socratics," by Cinzia Arruzza — 75

5. "Soul, Virtue, and Knowledge: Plato's *Theaetetus* and *Sophist*," by I-Kai Jeng — 98

6. "Herodotus Plays Hide and Seek," Interstitial Essay by Stuart D. Warner — 121

PART II

7. "The Opening of the Ψυχή in Ancient Greek Thought," by S. Montgomery Ewegen — 141

8. "The Teleology of Desire: Nutrition in *De Anima* B.4," by Michael M. Shaw — 164

9. "The Place of Forms," by Daniel P. Maher — 192

10. "Aristotle's Psychology as Fundamental Ontology," by Kevin Marren — 214

ACKNOWLEDGMENTS

This volume came together after an online 2022 *Symposium on the Soul* hosted by the University of Nevada, Reno. The volume would have been impossible without the many excellent papers and conversations that transpired during the event. I would like to thank the UNR Philosophy Department as well as acknowledge the Guy L. Leonard Memorial Fund in Philosophy that sponsored the *2022 UNR Symposium on the Soul*. I am very deeply grateful to all the volume contributors for their rigor and fidelity to the philosophical texts, original thinking, and congeniality as scholars of philosophy and the classical tradition. I also would like to thank the Mercer University Press editorial staff, and especially Marc Jolley.

CONTRIBUTOR LIST

Deborah Achtenberg (achten@unr.edu)
Professor Emerita (Philosophy), University of Nevada, Reno

Cinzia Arruzza (arruzzac@newschool.edu)
Associate Professor (Philosophy), The New School for Social Research

Ronna Burger (ronnaburger@yahoo.com)
Professor (Philosophy), Tulane University

S. Montgomery Ewegen (shane.ewegen@trincoll.edu)
Associate Professor (Philosophy), Trinity College, CT

I-Kai Jeng (ikjeng@ntu.edu.tw)
Associate Professor (Philosophy), Taiwan National University

Daniel P. Maher (dmaher@assumption.edu)
Professor (Philosophy), Assumption University

Kevin Marren (kevin.marrenc@gmail.com)
Independent Scholar

Michael M. Shaw (michael.shaw@uvu.edu)
Professor (Philosophy), Utah Valley University

Charlotte Thomas (thomas_cc@mercer.edu)
Professor (Philosophy), Mercer University

Stuart D. Warner (s.d.warner@hotmail.com)
Professor (Philosophy), Roosevelt University

INTRODUCTION

This volume takes as its point of departure a realization that ψυχή (*psyche*) in ancient Greek philosophy encompasses a meaning that is much wider than the modern idea of an individual soul. Although the latter notion, at least in part, grows out of the canon of ancient Greek and Roman thought, it is not the singular way to understand ψυχή. The essays in this volume seek to recover a more originary account of the soul, which includes an articulation of the relationship between soul and Being; soul and the natural world; as well as soul and the life of a political and ethical community. Thus, the psychological investigation opens unto the questions of πόλις, ἔθός, φύσις, and τὸ ὄν.

The volume is divided into two parts. The essays in Part I focus on political psychology, pursue feminist themes, and problems in ethics in Plato and early Socratics (i.e., contemporaries and followers of Socrates). Analyses that the authors offer in Part II, situate the soul as the principle of nutrition and generation, but also as the underlying structure of the natural world and, furthermore, as an expression of Being as such. The interstitial essay that connects the articulation of the soul, which the authors pursue in Parts I and II, studies ψυχή in its mythological register in Herodotus' *Histories*.

The understanding of the soul that emerges from the contributors' conclusions refigures the relationship between how we think about the soul and the various beings as well as different phenomena in the world—be they natural, mythological, aesthetic, ethical, or political. In the editor's view, it is not the case that the soul has or is an εἶδος or a form (to pass a shot across the bow of the canonical interpretations of Plato). Rather it is the case that ψυχή is a way of living beings and a making of space for life in the world—in all of life's multiplicity.

As such, this collection of essays lays down the groundwork for a rearticulation of ψυχή—be it in the fields of classical studies, ancient Greek literature, history, or philosophy. This volume furthermore makes a valuable contribution to the body of literature on the connection of the soul to politics in ancient thought.

The opening essay of Part I by Ronna Burger advances our understanding of the relationship between penal studies and political psychology in Plato's *Laws*. Burger's insights call us to reckon with and question the origin and nature of the limitations of education that the law confers, and the consequent need for punishment. Deborah Achtenberg's articulation of the soul in the *Republic*, puts pressure on the widely accepted view that the soul emerges as having a tripartite structure, which corresponds to the socio-political arrangement of the city. The destabilization of this schema allows for a rethinking of the meaning of education and virtue. Cinzia Arruzza and Charlotte Thomas make scholarly contributions to the questions of ethics and pedagogy in the *Republic*, from the point of view of feminist studies. Arruzza's focus is the early Socratic treatment of female virtue and the corresponding elements of education appropriate for female psychology. Thomas's nuanced study of the question of women in the *Republic* addresses the dramatic character of the dialogue and, specifically, the "female drama" in order to elucidate the psychology of nurture, procreation, and education. I-Kai Jeng's analysis focuses on education in so far as it relates to the questions of psychology, ethics, and ontology in the *Theaetetus* and the *Sophist*. Stuart D. Warner's contribution pursues questions of rule, power, and tyranny, positioning Herodotus' mythopoetic histories in such a way as to indicate a showing of ψυχή in political action. In the fashion of Aristotle's *Poetics* (which as Michael Davis speculates, could have been entitled *On the Art of Action*), Warner's study leads—by way of a meditation on the plot (which Aristotle says is "like the soul of tragedy" οἷον ψυχὴ ὁ μῦθος τῆς τραγῳδίας, *On Poetics* 1450a40)—to the detection of political ethos, which transpires in our actions and through language; in the deeds and speeches that outline the contours of the human soul.

Part II of this collection contains nuanced articulations of the soul's ontological and world-formative status. The essays by S. Montgomery Ewegen, Michael M. Shaw, Daniel P. Maher, and Kevin Marren broach these questions.

Ewegen's contribution puts Plato's *Phaedrus*—and its concern with the soul—in dialogue with Martin Heidegger's recovery of the ancient Greek meaning of Being and of ψυχή. Ewegen's essay displays the soul, and especially the human soul, in its world-revealing power. However, on Ewegen's presentation, this disclosive power is unthinkable without the support of the non-human, earthly beings, and the intimations of the divine being. Michael Shaw's essay opens avenues for thinking about ψυχή that go beyond the paradigms that are confined to the body-soul dilemma. Shaw investigates the nutritive soul in Aristotle's *De Anima* and argues for a continuity between the physical sustainment of the living being and the desire that reaches toward the divine, eternal life. Daniel Maher's contribution on *De Anima* further takes up the question of reality—or the unfolding of the knowable world—articulated for and through a noetic power of ψυχή. Maher's precision and fidelity to Aristotle's text produce compelling solutions to some of the toughest problems in *De Anima*. Contrary to more anthropocentric or idealist views, Kevin Marren argues that the soul is not an entity at all for Aristotle. On Marren's interpretation, being grows or diminishes through living beings—through becoming. Marren unearths this thesis through an unfolding of *De Anima*, where on his account, the soul announces the meaning of being through various ways and forms of life.

In its aim of working out the meaning of ψυχή, the present volume differs from such collections on the soul that seek to 1) situate the soul in view of the body (Frede and Reis 2009); 2) set the soul within the purview of science and art (Bartoš and King 2020); or 3) offer insights into the Greek thinking about individuated human soul (Davis 2011). The present collection of essays can be seen, on the one hand, as an accompaniment, but on the other hand, as a counterpoint to these and other volumes on ψυχή in the ancient world (e.g., Long 2021; Bremmer 1983; Snell 1975).

This volume will be of interest to specialists and students of the ancient world, and especially of ancient Greek thought (e.g., ancient Greek history and philosophy, ethics, pedagogy, psychology, and ontology, as well as classical studies and feminist readings of ancient Greek philosophy). Those who research and study themes in Plato, Aristotle, and Herodotus will find this volume especially helpful. More generally, all those interested in uncovering an original meaning of ψυχή in ancient culture will benefit from the essays in this book.

PART I

THE SOUL OF CRIME AND PUNISHMENT: BOOK IX OF PLATO'S *LAWS*

Ronna Burger

Introduction

Soul (*psychē*) plays, perhaps, *the* central role in all of Plato's thought, but for that very reason the Platonic treatment of the soul is as varied as the dialogues in which it appears.[1] There is the natural embodied soul of any living being and the metaphysical soul, or mind, imagined separable from the body after death; the cosmological soul of the universe is different from the *psychē* of the individual human, and that in turn shows up in forms as diverse as the erotic soul of the lover and the political soul of the citizen, while even the last displays a special shape in different dialogues appropriate to the particular context.

The tripartite structure of the individual human soul might look like a common account. But the image in the *Phaedrus*—two winged horses led by a charioteer—is not the same as the roles of calculation, spiritedness (*thumos*), and desire in Book IV of the

---

[1] Soul looks like the core of and the key to Plato's exploration of city and cosmos, each as a whole of parts. In his memorial speech for Leo Strauss (1974), Seth Benardete encapsulates the centrality of psychology: "The problem of wholes links the city through the soul with the beings." See *The Archaeology of the Soul: Platonic Readings of Ancient Poetry and Philosophy*, eds. Ronna Burger and Michael Davis (South Bend: St. Augustine's Press, 2012), 377. After noting the importance of *psychē* in Greek thought from Homer on, and especially for Plato, Michael Davis comments on the indirect treatment of soul in every Platonic dialogue, where it always comes to be thematic in connection with another question—justice, love, death. See *The Soul of the Greeks: An Inquiry* (Chicago: University of Chicago Press, 2011), 19.

Republic. The one is meant to illustrate the lover's experience of longing for the beloved and their joint ascent to the idea of the beautiful, the other, the idea of justice in the individual insofar as it is "writ large" in the class structure of the city.[2] Socrates' analysis of the soul in the *Republic*, by analogy with the ruler, auxiliary, and money-making classes of the "best city in speech," is supposed to establish three separate parts, with desire ranked lowest, calculation highest and *thumos* as mediating between them. A close reading, however, indicates a distorted understanding of desire and reason as conceived through the lens of *thumos* and the conflicts meant to separate the central part of the soul from the lower and higher prove to be conflicts within *thumos* itself.[3] While Plato's *Laws* presents another tripartite analysis of the political soul, the distinctive character is determined by its place in Book IX, preparing for the discussion of crime and punishment.

---

[2] After the long central "digression" of Books V–VII, Socrates returns at the beginning of Book VIII to Book IV's analysis of the soul in order to lay out the individual and corresponding political psychology of the series of regimes supposedly inferior to the best city: timocracy, oligarchy, and democracy, finally descending to tyranny and the soul of the tyrannic individual.

[3] Desire, on this account, is engaged only in pulling the individual toward pleasure, like a beast, while calculation, with no goal of its own, is restricted to pulling back bestial desire, and *thumos* only serves to carry out that function by mastering recalcitrant desire. See Burger, "The Thumotic Soul," *Epoché: A Journal of the History of Philosophy* 7, no. 2 (Spring 2003): 151–168. Cf. Deborah Achtenberg, "Three Accounts of the Soul in Plato's *Republic*," in this volume.

The Analysis of the Soul in the Context of Criminal Law

The *Laws* belongs to a subset of dialogues in which the usual role assigned to Socrates is taken over by another, in this case an unnamed Stranger; but the *Laws* is the only dialogue in the Platonic corpus in which Socrates is altogether absent.[4] The Athenian Stranger converses with two old men, the Cretan Kleinias and his Spartan companion Megillus, as they proceed on a lengthy walk to the legendary cave of Zeus, where Minos is said to have worked up the laws of the Cretans with his divine father. Their initial theoretical discussion of the standards for "divine law" (Book I) and law-governed education (Book II) is followed by a consideration of Greek and Persian history, exemplifying the principles of monarchic and democratic regimes (Book III). Book IV suddenly starts over again when Kleinias discloses his involvement in the founding of a Cretan colony, which will need a new set of laws. One other sharp turn occurs at the beginning of Book IX, when the Stranger confronts a task he considers shameful: realizing the limits of the educative law they have been developing (meant to shape the souls of the citizens) he acknowledges the need for a penal code to deal with criminality.

---

[4] In Plato's *Sophist* and *Statesman*, Socrates listens to the conversation conducted by an Eleatic Stranger after assigning him the question whether sophist and statesman are to be understood as two apparitions of the hidden being of the philosopher (*Sophist* 216c–d). In the *Timaeus*, Socrates expresses his interest in seeing the model of the *Republic* "city in speech" set in motion; that task is undertaken by Critias, who retells a story of ancient Athens at war with the island of Atlantis, but only after "the most astronomical" Timaeus provides an account of the generation of the cosmos leading up to the nature of human beings (*Timaeus* 27a–b).

The criminal law begins with temple robbery; it will come back to that mysteriously important crime at the very end.[5] After generalizing to other capital crimes, the Stranger turns to theft and abruptly announces one penalty for all cases; he must intend to provoke Kleinias to ask how this can be right (857b), opening up the digression that leads to an analysis of the soul.[6] The Stranger sets up the discussion by recalling their earlier image of slave doctor and free doctor as two models for legislation (720a–e). He proposes that "If a doctor who practiced medicine simply on the basis of experience ever saw a free doctor in dialogue with his free patient, using arguments, trying to understand the disease from the source, he would mock him: You fool!, You are treating the sick one as if he needed to become, not healthy, but a doctor" (857c–d)![7] The Stranger then offers a defense of the "free doctor," who is "almost philosophizing," at least as a model for their own current undertaking. One of the only two occurrences in the twelve books of the *Laws* of any term referring to "philosophy"

---

[5] See IX. 853e (cf. 869b) and X. 885a–b. The Stranger offers a prelude, addressing someone plagued day and night by the evil desire for temple robbery—a kind of gadfly, which grows out of ancient injustices never purified: "Oh wondrous one, whenever such *dogmata* get hold of you, go as a suppliant to the temples of the gods to partake of the rites of purification" (854b).

[6] The Stranger justifies slowing down for this discussion: they are, after all, only becoming, but are not yet lawgivers (859c)—that, apparently, requires the reflection motivated by the problems of criminal law. Where the translation of the *Laws* differs from Thomas Pangle's translation, *The Laws of Plato* (Chicago: University of Chicago Press, 1988), it is by the author.

[7] Cf. Aristotle's implicit critique of Socrates: "Yet the many do not do [the kind of actions they need to practice to become good]; and seeking refuge in argument, they suppose that they are philosophizing and that they will in this way become serious, thereby doing something similar to the sick who listen attentively to their physician but do nothing prescribed" (*Nicomachean Ethics* II.4.1105b13–16, translated by Robert Bartlett and Susan Collins (Chicago: University of Chicago Press, 2011).

introduces the treatment of criminal law.[8] It proves to be the discussion that shows the Athenian Stranger looking most like a Socratic philosopher, while also suggesting why Plato has put him in Socrates' place.

The Stranger must tackle at the outset two basic issues concerning criminal law and the human soul. First, the practice of punishment exhibits a conflict within morality: everyone believes the just to be noble or beautiful, but however just a punitive act may be, it is not beautiful, either for the one who undergoes it or the one who carries it out (859d–860c).[9] This concern leads the Stranger to a problem at the very heart of the project he is undertaking. He reminds his interlocutors of a principle they had agreed on earlier: no one wants to be bad, but acting unjustly makes one bad, hence it must be involuntary, and if truly involuntary, punishment is unjustifiable.[10] Yet, just when the Stranger endorses, and insists on, this Socratic principle, he seems to violate it by proceeding in the attempt to lay down a punitive legal code.[11] The Athenian Stranger embodies in this endeavor the

---

[8] The other comes in Book XII, in a remark about the poets reviling those who philosophize, looking back to Book X's arguments against atheism (967c).

[9] See especially the story of Leontius, which Socrates presents in *Republic* IV to illustrate the conflict between anger and desire (439e–440b).

[10] The earlier agreement was in Book V, 731c. Now the Stranger insists that anyone who objects to his basic principle would do so out of love of victory or love of honor (860d): the *thumotic* motive for ascribing responsibility for crime is reflected in the argument aiming to support it.

[11] In "The Socratic Principle and the Problem of Punishment," Robert Berman explains: "Abolitionism about punishment is the thesis that there is no justification for criminal punishment…Socratic abolitionism would be that unique version of abolitionism that follows from the specifically Socratic principle—no one commits a criminal wrong voluntarily—based on the premises that everyone wants what is truly his own good, but…doing wrong to another ultimately brings harm to oneself, so it could only be done out of igno-

fundamental clash of philosophy and the city. It remains in question whether he can solve the difficulty by the promise he makes to replace the ubiquitous legal distinction of voluntary and involuntary action with some other basis for dividing two classes of law (861b–d).

The Stranger's starting point is a sharp separation of injustice from injury or harm (861e–862c).[12] Any harm committed must be compensated—insofar as it is possible "to make sound one who has been killed or wounded." We expect the Stranger to turn directly to injustice, but instead he simply maintains that, along with compensation, an attempt must be made to reconcile the perpetrator of a crime and the victim. When he does finally get to injustice, he identifies it as a disease of soul. For cases the lawgiver somehow perceives as incurable, death is appropriate; for the rest, the most beautiful laws would aim, by any means, to bring about hatred of injustice (862d–e). The means the Stranger mentions might indeed motivate a subject to avoid doing injustice with an eye to the consequences; it is far from obvious how they would cure injustice as a disease of the soul.

---

rance….In Book Nine of Plato's *Laws*, the Athenian Stranger…seems to endorse the Socratic principle, while attempting to reconcile it with crime, punishment, and the criminal law. It looks like a rather quixotic attempt, rife with inconsistency. Or is there a sense in which, even if the Socratic principle does entail abolitionism, it is only a station en route to the reestablishment of criminal law and punishment as a political necessity, which political philosophy must recognize?" See Berman's chapter in *The Eccentric Core: The Thought of Seth Benardete*, eds. Ronna Burger & Patrick Goodin (South Bend: St. Augustine's Press, 2018), 125–126.

[12] The Stranger is willing to admit, accordingly, that a benefit, if not done properly, could be a case of injustice. Cf. Aristotle's account of corrective justice: "…the law looks only at the difference that stems from the harm done, and it treats persons as equals" (*Nicomachean Ethics* V.4, 1132a5–6).

The Soul of Crime and Punishment

Kleinias finds the Stranger's remarks well-measured, but he does not understand what the contrast between injury and injustice has to do with a distinction between the voluntary and the involuntary (863c). It is his perplexity that prompts the Stranger's analysis of soul. He singles out, first, the passion or part of the soul we call spiritedness (*thumos*), which is fierce by nature, quarrelsome and violent. But there is something we claim to be different, that is, pleasure, which works through persuasion and "forceful trickery"—note the paradoxical formula. And it would not be false, the Stranger continues, to identify ignorance as a third cause of "faults" (863b–c): it is only with this addition that we learn we are dividing *hamartēmata*, a term whose meaning ranges from error to sin.[13]

The causal role of ignorance in leading us astray proves extremely complex. To begin with, a simple version—just not knowing something relevant—must be distinguished from a double version: ignorance overlaid by an opinion of wisdom (*doxosophia*). This double state of ignorance is familiar to us as the essential target of Socratic examination, for which the fitting correction should be knowledge of ignorance. But the criminal law does not—cannot—endorse that cure. And instead of proposing any other, the Stranger introduces one further distinction: the experience of *doxosophia* if accompanied by strength and force becomes a cause of the greatest faults, while accompanied by weakness it results only in childish or senile forms, which deserve the most forgiving laws (863c–d).

That last distinction echoes the analysis Socrates offers in Plato's *Philebus*, when he uses the psychology of the comic poet

---

[13] See Aristotle on the "flaw" responsible for the downfall of the tragic figure (*Poetics* 1453a7–10).

as a model for the class of mixed pleasures and pains in the soul.[14] The comic poet feels the pain of envy when he recognizes something superior in his friend; but he assuages that pain by arousing laughter at the representation of his friend as a boaster, lacking self-knowledge. Ridicule is possible, however, only as long as the individual targeted is unable or unwilling to take revenge; if his lack of self-knowledge were accompanied by strength, he would be harmful and we would fear him. Of course, laughter can turn into anger if the subject were perceived, not just as ridiculous, but as threatening in some way: Aristophanes' *Clouds* had the whole city laughing at Socrates, but as Socrates claims at his trial, that prepared the ground for the city's eventual condemnation and execution.[15] The political conviction of Socrates suggests that the city itself suffers from ignorance overlaid by a pretense to wisdom, but it is too powerful to be a subject of ridicule. If, however,

---

[14] *Philebus* 48a–50a. See a commentary on this passage by Strauss, *Socrates and Aristophanes* (New York: Basic Books, 1966), 5; Benardete, *The Tragedy and Comedy of Life: Plato's Philebus* (Chicago: University of Chicago Press, 1993), 201; Derek Duplessie, "Socrates' Analysis of Comedy in Plato's *Philebus*," *Review of Metaphysics* 74 no. 1 (Sept. 2020): 243–268.

[15] See Plato's *Apology of Socrates* 18d, 19c. Hearing of Socrates' indictment, Euthyphro sympathizes, knowing what it's like when he speaks of the divine things and the Athenians laugh at him as if he were mad. If only they would simply laugh at me, Socrates responds, but he faces the danger of their punitive spiritedness, aroused when someone is believed to make others like himself (*Euthyphro* 3b–d). Laughter may be transformed into indignation, but it can also serve as a weapon against it. In *Plato and Aristophanes: Comedy, Politics, and the Pursuit of a Just Life* (Chicago: Northwestern University Press, 2021), Marina Marren explores the power of comedy as it serves "the action of the *Republic*," which, in the line she cites from Strauss (11), "can be said to consist in first arousing spiritedness or the virtue belonging to it, that is to say, zeal dedicated to non-understood justice, that is, what we now mean by political idealism, and then in purging it" ("The Origins of Political Science and the Problem of Socrates: Six Public Lectures,' *Interpretation* 23 no. 2 (Winter 1996): 127–207, 192.

Socrates lacked something required to fight back, Plato makes up for that through his art of writing, in his depiction of the comic poet and the city over against *the* philosopher Socrates.

Having laid out three psychic conditions that lead us astray, the Stranger wonders why, in the case of anger or desire, we speak of self-mastery (*enkrateia*) or its lack (*akrasia*), while we don't do so regarding ignorance.[16] But he uses, for now, the difference between them in order to offer his definition of injustice.[17] The tyranny in the soul of spiritedness, fear, pleasure, pain, envies or desires, whether it leads to any injury or not, is proclaimed to be injustice. In contrast, if an "opinion of the best," whatever it may be, masters the soul and brings order to the man, any action done in that condition must be declared entirely just—in fact, not only just, but best for the whole of human life (863e–864a). This is a remarkable claim! To be led by any opinion of the best, no matter how mistaken, is just.[18] The Stranger speaks explicitly of a city or an individual, but he must assume the paradigmatic status of the law, in its function of ordering the community in accord with a common opinion about what is best.[19] The Stranger' surprising

---

[16] Going wrong out of ignorance might not seem to be a matter of inner conflict. If, however, as Socrates would have it, all human beings ultimately desire the good, acting in a state of ignorance could be understood as a condition of conflict, where desire for the good on the deepest level is mastered by bad judgment.

[17] It is not obvious why the Stranger introduces his definitions of injustice and justice as "without complication" (863e).

[18] Indeed, the Stranger adds that many consider "such injury"—presumably resulting from a false opinion of what is best—to be involuntary injustice, though he rejects that (863e, cf. 862a).

[19] The Stranger's definition of injustice and justice sounds like Aristotelian *akrasia* and *enkrateia*. Analyzing in Book III the destruction of the initial power of the Lacedaimonians, the Stranger identifies "the greatest ignorance" with the dissonance between pleasure and pain, on the one hand, and the

definition of justice recalls his description in Book I of the human being as a divine puppet, pulled every which way by the cords of pleasure and pain, urged to follow the cord of calculation (*logismos*), which, however, proves generally too weak to get control without the far stronger cord of the city's law (644d–645a).

The Stranger returns to the three forms of faults or sins, claiming they should be firmly fixed in memory just when he makes certain changes, which introduce further puzzles in his analysis of the soul (864b).[20] Without clarifying those perplexities,[21] the Stranger announces in conclusion the division of laws into two kinds (*gene*, dual), for two classes of action: deeds done

---

opinion that is according to reason on the other (689b). This condition is illustrated by the passions opposing the natural rulers in the soul and likewise the majority in the city opposing the rulers and the laws (689a–c).

[20] The two passions become "the form of pain that we call spiritedness and fear" (864b) over and against pleasure and desires. And while being ruled by an opinion of the best was moments earlier identified as just, the third form of faults now becomes "the striving for expectations and true opinion concerning what is best" (864b). Strauss comments that the Stranger's "not entirely clear" remark points to "the difference between law and respectable opinion on the one hand and the true *logos* on the other" (*The Argument and the Action of Plato's Laws* [Chicago: University of Chicago Press, 1975], 132). On Benardete's reading of this puzzling line, "expectations and opinion truly striving for the best" is a revision that "pulls ignorance into the orbit of desire," while the Stranger's initial classification of the three kinds of error "pulls anger and pleasure into the orbit of ignorance." See his *Plato's Laws: The Discovery of Being* (Chicago: University of Chicago Press, 2001), 270. Hereafter, *Plato's Laws*.

[21] After his perplexing revision, the Stranger concludes with the altogether obscure statement: "When this last is divided into three by two cuts, there come to be five forms" (864b). If he had the initial formulation of the soul structure in mind, two successive divisions could lead to these five sources of going wrong: anger, pleasure, simple ignorance, *doxosophia* with weakness and *doxosophia* with strength. But would that be applicable to the replacement of ignorance by "opinion truly striving for the best" (864b)?

through violence and in the open vs. those done secretly, in darkness and with trickery (864c).[22] This is presumably the division he had promised to provide in place of voluntary vs. involuntary wrong: furtive action does look as if it involves forethought, in a way that action out in the open does not, and that is reflected in the punitive measures that will be assigned to each class. Yet the Stranger calls now for the harshest laws in response to the deeds that combine both: such a combination might sound impossible—unless, perhaps, we remember the description of pleasure operating through "forceful trickery" (863b).

Psychology in the Legal Code of Crime and Punishment

The analysis of soul, with the accompanying definitions of justice and injustice, takes place as a digression on the criminal code.[23] The Stranger had begun his reflections on punishment by affirming the Socratic principle that all wrongdoing is involuntary, hence punishment never justifiable, and his characterization of

---

[22] This is the division Plato's Eleatic Stranger introduces in his search for the sophist when he separates hunting, as furtive action, from combat, which is out in the open (*Sophist* 219d, 222b–223b). This separation shows up in Aristotle's apparently casual set of cases exemplifying corrective justice, which may be more systematic than it first appears: after the original cut between voluntary and involuntary transactions, covert actions in the latter class are distinguished from violent ones (*Nicomachean Ethics* V.2, 1131a5–9). Cf. Burger, *Aristotle's Dialogue with Socrates: on the Nicomachean Ethics* (Chicago: University of Chicago Press, 2008), 98.

[23] When the Stranger resumes laying down laws, he recalls where they left off, with the most serious crimes—plundering the gods, treachery and dissolution of the existing regime (864d). Although all had been designated capital crimes, certain conditions are now said to exempt the perpetrator from any sentence other than compensating the harm he caused—unless he killed someone with his own hands, now polluted (864d–e). And the punishment of exile in that case leads to the treatment of laws for all killing.

injustice as a disease of soul implies that crime calls not for punishment, but for psychic medicine. If he were simply a Socratic, though, he would have restricted the cause of faults to ignorance. Yet, the code he now lays down involves only the other two causes of wrong—anger and desire. Ignorance plays no explicit role: its power as a cause of our going astray is deferred until the analysis of impiety in Book X.[24]

The criminal code will put the preceding psychology to work by distinguishing a class of murder arising from spirited anger in contrast with desire. Yet it highlights a psychological phenomenon that has no obvious place in the original analysis of soul: the notion of pollution. The stain that comes above all with shedding blood appears most vividly in the consideration of accidental killing, the category with which the Stranger begins when he returns to the legal code that had been interrupted. One who has shed blood, even or especially if not legally responsible, may feel himself, or be seen as, a vehicle for the evil outcome, however unwilling.[25] Oedipus, with his unwitting patricide and incest, is the

---

[24] Whether the Stranger's arguments for the existence and goodness of the gods serve to overcome ignorance remains in question. Kleinias, at least, considers those arguments just about the most beautiful and best prelude for all the laws they have been proposing (X. 887b–c).

[25] Robert Parker examines Greek tragedy, Attic law, and other sources to analyze the relation between ritual purification of pollution and legal penalties for homicide. See *Miasma: Pollution and Purification in Early Greek Religion* (Oxford: Oxford University Press, 1993), 104–133. Hereafter, *Miasma*. In the Stranger's code, one who accidentally kills someone in athletic games or war is free from pollution once purified according to Delphic law, but a doctor whose patient dies is held unpolluted according to law (865b). Perhaps doctors must feel confident to proceed with treatment assured of being exempt from pollution if something goes wrong outside their control.

paradigm.[26] Like violating a sacred ritual, causing in some unintended way the loss of a human life produces a sense of being, not unjust, but in some way unclean. This stain is thought, moreover, to be contagious, able to spread to the entire community, but most directly to family members of the victim who allow the killer to remain tainted while continuing to frequent the shared spaces of the city.[27] The experience of pollution goes deeper than the rational calculation of guilt, and the law must find a relief through some rites of purification.[28]

---

[26] Tiresias calls Oedipus an "ungodly pollution" (Sophocles, *Oedipus Tyrannus* 353) and Oedipus' self-blinding in the end is his response to the stain he bears, a man recognized by the gods as unholy (1380–1384).

[27] The Stranger's law for involuntary killing requires the perpetrator to go through rites of purification and then exile, but if he fails to do so, the nearest of kin to the victim should prosecute for murder, otherwise the curse passes on to him and anyone may prosecute him (866a–d). If someone kills in anger but avoids rites of purification and exile, anyone may prosecute, not only the killer, but also the victim's kinsman who let this go (868a–b). In cases of murderous desire, one who kills a fellow tribesman must not pollute the common places; any relative of the victim, as close as a cousin, who fails to proclaim banishment or prosecute the killer acquires the pollution and the enmity of the gods, while being liable to prosecution by anyone willing (871b–c). Plato's portrayal of Euthyphro's confusion under Socrates' examination begins with his explanation of the punitive action he is attempting to carry out, acting on behalf of a victim who is not his kin, while defying filial piety to prosecute his own father. He is surprised to hear Socrates' surprise, when he should realize the only thing that matters is the injustice of the action. But Euthyphro goes on to defend himself by explaining that the pollution of the killer would pass on to him if he knowingly associated with someone who shares his hearth and table without purifying himself as well as the perpetrator (*Euthyphro* 4b–c).

[28] The "ancient and morally ambiguous concept of 'pollution,'" Lorraine Pangle argues, "deepens the seriousness" of the crime, "but also softens society's vindictiveness." The anger of the victim or his family finds some satisfaction when the polluted one makes some expiation, "but once he has done so, he is to be forgiven." And the contagious character of pollution means it must be purged for the sake of the whole community. See "Moral and Criminal

The Stranger adds another feature to the demand for purification when he takes up the involuntary killing of a freeman.[29] That individual must go through the same purifications as when the victim is a slave, but he is also warned of ancient myths: the deceased victim, having lived the life of a free man, feels spirited rage against the killer; and when he sees him in his usual haunts, the dead man elicits memory as his ally and tries to disturb the perpetrator (865d–e). The ancient myth is in fact an explanation of the criminal's conscience, imagined as the product of the victim's anger, however irrational that might be for an involuntary action. Exile of the killer for one year has the primary purpose of calming, in this mythic version, the imaginary anger of the dead victim, for the sake of restoring social order.[30]

From involuntary killing, the code turns to murder done out of *thumos* with a distinction between two classes (866d): killing on sudden impulse and feeling regret afterwards in contrast with intending to kill and feeling no later regret. Recognizing the former as closer to involuntary action, the latter to voluntary, the Stranger starts making a concession to the common view he had rejected on principle.[31] The punishment of exile should help the

---

Responsibility in Plato's *Laws*," *The American Political Science Review* 103 no. 3 (August 2009), 456–473, 466.

[29] It looked as if the criminal code would be based entirely on the preceding analysis of the soul, but the class structure of the city intervenes: punishment for the same action can differ insofar as it is committed by or against citizen or stranger, freeman or slave. See Benardete, *Plato's Laws*, 275.

[30] While acknowledging the natural connection of pollution with the victim's anger, Parker stresses the general sense, reflected in that connection, of pollution as a vehicle of social disruption (see *Miasma*, especially 107 and 121).

[31] The spontaneous cases that resemble involuntary action are to be treated with less harsh penalties than the pre-meditated cases that resemble the voluntary. Kleinias, who must find this sensible, interrupts to affirm the policy (867c). The last time he responded was to accept the Stranger's claim that any deed done both in the open and in secret would merit the harshest

The Soul of Crime and Punishment

killer learn to restrain his own spiritedness (867c). But he could return, the Stranger admits, to commit the same kind of act again and this situation brings out the concern that has dominated all along: purification and exile operate above all, it seems, to assuage the imagined anger of the dead victim in the mythical version, or the experience of his kin in reality.

A special class of *thumotic* murder is that of family members—the material of Greek tragedy. The law lays down a surprisingly mild punishment in the case of a parent killing a child out of spirited rage: after performing rites of purification and going into exile for three years, the father or mother is prohibited from rejoining the family upon return. For the first time, the disobedient are designated impious, and subject to prosecution for impiety: crime within the family belongs to the sphere of the sacred.[32] But the punitive tone intensifies greatly when the Stranger goes on to someone who "becomes so unrestrained in *thumos* toward his parents that he dares, in an insanity of rage, to kill one of his parents" (869a). He must be held responsible for several crimes—assault, impiety, and temple robbing, having plundered the soul of his parent (869b).[33] For the crime of killing a parent, which deserves more than one death, the law has to settle for the death penalty.

---

penalties (864c). He will interrupt once more when the Stranger designates murders out of pleasures and desires as voluntary and totally unjust (869e).

[32] The charge of impiety applies as well to a husband or wife who kills their spouse out of *thumos*, or a brother or sister who kills their sibling (868e). Upon return after undergoing purification and exile, such an individual is never to be part of the hearth or share in sacred rites with his family members.

[33] Temple-robbery, the first crime the Stranger took up, which will be the last (853e–854a, 885a–b), is a symbol here for patricide or matricide. In this case alone, a plea of self-defense cannot legitimate the killing. The Stranger does allow that the victim might voluntarily absolve the perpetrator before he dies; parent and child, then, would presumably be reconciled, and in that case, the killer only undergoes purification as if for an involuntary murder.

Turning, finally, to murders that spring from weakness in the face of pleasures, envies and desires, the Stranger simply assumes that this class involves plotting, and he labels it as a whole "voluntary and totally unjust," which Kleinias quickly affirms (869e). In the psychological analysis, injustice was the tyranny in the soul of anger or desire; in the law code it is only murderous desire that merits this designation. The Stranger describes a soul driven wild by longings, stirred by "tens of thousands of erotic desires"; but just when we might have expected some kind of "crime of passion," the "greatest force" responsible for this condition is said to be love of money: desire is considered merely in its most conventional reflection (870a).[34] Only in the discussion of murder driven by desire are the crimes said to deserve "just punishment according to nature," in Hades and in the next life (870d–e). The belief that a killing is the product of murderous desire must arouse a powerful resentment that is not found in killing attributed to spirited rage. It is assumed, perhaps, that the angry killer is in a state of pain, while the killer moved by desire will or might get a certain pleasure and satisfaction from his action.[35]

This class of murder culminates, again, with the killing of kinsmen, but the Stranger now appeals to "the myth or *logos* or

---

[34] This distorted understanding is confirmed by the two other classes of desire-driven killing: the habit of the honor-loving soul, which breeds envies, and cowardly, unjust fears when the victim knows something that the killer wants to hide (870c–d).

[35] Addressing the question why killing to satisfy desire or from envy is treated more severely than killing in rage, Catherine Zuckert proposes that such crimes appear to be voluntary, and the passion of envy, like desire, tends to be more calculating and longer lasting, without the same hope as in the case of anger for the passion to cool over time and enable reconciliation. See Zuckert's discussion of the *Laws* in *Plato's Philosophers: The Coherence of the Dialogues* (University of Chicago Press, 2009), 119.

whatever it should be called" passed down from ancient priests (872d–e)—the particular animosity against a killing thought to be driven by desire allows a *muthos* to be taken as a rational account. Justice the avenger of kindred blood ordains that the only purification is for the perpetrator to suffer the same things he performed. If a son kills his father, he must undergo the same violent end at the hands of his children; if he kills his mother, he must become a woman in the next life and suffer the identical fate, for there is no other purification for the shared polluted blood.[36] This speech should restrain anyone who fears retributions from the gods. But if anyone is so overtaken that he dares voluntarily, with forethought, to murder a family member, "the law of the mortal lawgiver" requires the servants of the judges to kill him, place his corpse naked outside the city, and each throw a stone at the head to remove impiety from the whole city, then cast the body out of the borders unburied (873b–c). In the case of the patricide or matricide, the death penalty does not bring sufficient satisfaction; the *thumotic* will to punish must be vented through this irrational treatment of the corpse.[37]

---

[36] Only by this "like for like" retribution, the Stranger adds, is it possible to lay to rest the spiritedness of the whole family (873a). This result might seem to be out of place in what was supposed to be a class of murders springing from pleasures and desires, but that designation has been replaced by the characterization "voluntary and totally unjust" (869e). By this point, Thomas Pangle observes, "a strong note of retribution has crept into the Athenian's laws and preludes." The threat of vengeful deities is needed to gratify the indignant demand for punishment not satisfied by human penalties. See *The Laws of Plato*, "Interpretative Essay," 500.

[37] The irrational nature of *thumos* is vividly displayed in Homer's representation of Achilles mistreating the corpse of Hector. Apollo reprimands the gods who do nothing to put a stop to it:

"But this man, now he has torn the heart of life from great Hektor
ties him to his horses and drags him around his beloved companion's
tomb; and nothing is gained thereby for his good, or his honour,

Turning to the killing of what is most of all one's own and dearest, the Stranger adopts a very different tone, granting a broad range to legitimate self-killing: taking one's own life is accepted if ordered by the city's decree (a qualification Socrates' interlocutors in the *Phaedo* seem to ignore), or compelled by pain, bad luck, or some baffling shame. Blame is restricted to self-killing out of lack of effort and unmanly cowardice, and punishment really amounts to a symbol of the action: the person is to be buried without markers on the tomb, in uncultivated and nameless territory (873c–d). In contrast with the punitive anger provoked by other cases of killing, the legal response to suicide reflects a rational assessment of the situation along with compassion. The homicide code does not end, however, on this note, but with another display of *thumos* at work: if someone dies from the attack of a beast, or even from an inanimate object, the victim's kinsmen are to prosecute the "killer" and if it is convicted, cast it out beyond the borders of the country (873e).[38]

The Role of *Thumos* in Crime and Punishment

In several striking ways, the psychology of *Laws* IX recalls the psychology of *Republic* IV. In both cases desire is viewed through

---

Great as he is, let him take care not to make us angry;
for see, he does dishonour to the dumb earth in his fury."
Iliad 24.50–54, translated by Richmond Lattimore (Chicago: University of Chicago Press, 1951).

[38] Actually, the homicide code concludes with cases in which a killer would be unpolluted, and the Stranger then goes on to face the very messy subject of legislating for wounds and maiming (874e). He claims they should be categorized just as murders are—1) involuntary, 2) out of *thumos*, 3) out of fear, 4) voluntarily out of forethought—but it's striking that desire has disappeared altogether.

the lens of *thumos*, with the consequence of a distorted understanding, in particular, the absence of *eros*.[39] The city needs the psychological impulse of indignation against injustice; it cannot afford to diminish the status of *thumos* and elevate desire. In the *Republic*, the strength of spiritedness marks the distinctive nature of soul in the members of the guardian class. In *Laws* IX, it plays an indispensable role in punishment of crime.[40] Of course, this also indicates the need for the city to tame *thumos* or channel it. In the *Republic*, that is the primary task of the music education Socrates outlines in Book III and all the further arrangements meant to direct *thumos* toward a total devotion to the city. But in the *Laws*, it was recognition of the defectiveness of law in its educative function that led in Book IX to the discussion of criminal law. The proposed penalties for crime do appear to be directed above all to calming spirited anger, not so obviously, though, the rage that might have led the criminal to his deed, but rather, the resentment experienced by the victim's family, expressed in the Stranger's mythical version as the *thumos* of the deceased victim himself in Hades.

At the beginning of the discussion of crime and punishment, the Stranger stated that the law, beyond requiring compensation for harm, should aim at reconciling doer and sufferer (862c).

---

[39] The same might be said for the understanding of reason. *Logismos* in *Republic* IV has no natural end of its own, but serves only to hold back desire, with *thumos* as its ally. In *Laws* IX, we hear of ignorance as a cause of wrongdoing, while the role of reason in ruling the passions shows up only as "an opinion about the best" (864a).

[40] In Book V's imagined speech to the new colonists about the most noble life, the one who watches out for the injustice of others is ranked above one who simply refrains from doing injustice himself. Indeed, "the great man in the city, the man who is to be proclaimed perfect and the bearer of victory in virtue, is the one who does what he can to assist the magistrates in inflicting punishment" (730d).

That aim recalls the model for the city that the Stranger introduced in Book I (627c–628e), which proves to be guiding the *Laws* as a whole. They were to imagine a family of brothers, a few just, but most not. The family would be "superior to itself" when the few prevailed; "inferior to itself" in the contrary case.[41] The Stranger then asks: What "judge" would handle them best? Would it be the one who destroyed the wicked and set the better to rule themselves or the one who allowed the worse to live as long as they were willing to be ruled by the worthy? Both options are rejected in favor of a judge who is "third in respect to virtue," who would take over the divided family and without destroying anyone reconcile them by laying down such laws that would secure their friendship for one another (627e–628a). Lawful customs, the Stranger concludes, should aim at peace and friendly feeling (*philophrosunē*, 628c).[42] This choice is confirmed throughout the *Laws*, particularly in Book III, where the Stranger explains the decline of a political regime by the failure of its laws to

---

[41] Soon after the family of brothers, the Stranger introduces his image of the individual as a divine puppet, found to be "inferior to itself" when pulled by the cords of pleasure and pain, but "superior to itself" if able to follow the "golden" cord of calculation, which usually needs the assistance of the strong cord of the law (644e–645b). The whole education through law is then directed to the goal of harmonizing pleasure and pain with reason, training individuals to like and dislike what they should (Book II. 653a–c).

[42] This term appears only in the *Laws*, other than once in the *Critias* (120e3). When the Stranger tries to handle the messy and complicated punitive code for wounding and maiming, he pauses to observe that laws probably come into being partly for worthy human beings, to teach them how to dwell in friendship (*philophronos*), and partly, for those whose tough nature was never softened by education (880d–e).

inculcate in the city moderation, prudence, and especially friendship (693c).[43] The discussion of criminal law in Book IX applies this principle once again. In a regime ruled by law, moral education should aim at harmonizing conflicting elements of the soul; political legislation at harmonizing conflicting elements of the city; and punitive law at reconciling doer and sufferer. Curing the disease of injustice may be a goal inappropriate for the city and its criminal law.

Bibliography

Aristotle. *Nicomachean Ethics.* Translated with an introduction, interpretive essay, and notes by Robert Bartlett and Susan Collins. Chicago: University of Chicago Press, 2011.

Benardete, Seth. *Plato's Laws: The Discovery of Being.* Chicago: University of Chicago Press, 2001.

Benardete, Seth. "Memorial Speech for Leo Strauss." In *The Archaeology of the Soul: Platonic Readings of Ancient Poetry and Philosophy*, 375–377. Edited by Ronna Burger and Michael Davis. South Bend: St. Augustine's Press, 2012.

Burger, Ronna. *Aristotle's Dialogue with Socrates: On the Nicomachean Ethics.* Chicago: University of Chicago Press, 2008.

Berman, Robert. "The Socratic Principle and the Problem of Punishment." In *The Eccentric Core: The Thought of Seth Benardete*, edited by Ronna Burger and Patrick Goodin, 125–142. South Bend: St. Augustine's Press, 2018.

Davis, Michael. *The Soul of the Greeks: An Inquiry.* Chicago: University of Chicago Press, 2011.

---

[43] Kleinias asks for clarification about the lawgiver's aim of friendship, prudence and—in place of moderation—freedom (693c). The Stranger repeats that triad in calling for the need to put together the best features of Persian monarchy and Athenian democracy if there is to be freedom and friendship, together with prudence (693d–e). A seemingly slight but significant revision appears at the end of Book III, with the Stranger's assertion that the lawgiver should lay down laws with three aims: for the city to be free, a friend to itself, and in possession of mind (*nous*, 701d).

Duplessie, Derek. "Socrates' Analysis of Comedy in Plato's *Philebus.*" *Review of Metaphysics* 74 no. 1 (Sept. 2020): 243–268.

Homer. *Iliad.* Translated by Richmond Lattimore with an introduction by Richard Martin. Chicago: University of Chicago Press, 1951.

Marren, Marina. *Plato and Aristophanes: Comedy, Politics, and the Pursuit of a Just Life.* Chicago: Northwestern University Press, 2021.

Pangle, S. Lorraine. "Moral and Criminal Responsibility in Plato's *Laws.*" *The American Political Science Review* 103 no. 3 (August 2009): 456–473.

Parker, Robert. *Miasma: Pollution and Purification in Early Greek Religion.* Oxford: Oxford University Press, 1993.

Plato. *Statesman. Philebus. Ion.* Translated by Harold North Fowler, W. R. M. Lamb. Loeb Classical Library. Cambridge: Harvard University Press, 1925.

———. *Laws, Volumes I and II.* Translated by R. G. Bury. Loeb Classical Library. Cambridge: Harvard University Press, 1926.

———. *Euthyphro. Apology. Crito. Phaedo. Phaedrus.* Translated by Harold North Fowler. Loeb Classical Library. Reprint of 1904 edition. Cambridge: Harvard University Press, 1999.

———. *Republic*, Volumes I and II. Edited and translated by Christopher Emlyn-Jones, William Preddy. Loeb Classical Library. Cambridge: Harvard University Press, 2013.

———. *The Laws of Plato.* Translated with an interpretive essay and notes by Thomas Pangle. Chicago: University of Chicago Press, 1988.

Sophocles. *Volume I. Ajax. Electra. Oedipus Tyrannus.* Translated Loeb Hugh Lloyd-Jones. Loeb Classical Library 20. Cambridge: Harvard University Press, 1994.

Strauss, Leo. *The Argument and the Action of Plato's Laws.* Chicago: University of Chicago Press, 1975.

———. "The Origins of Political Science and the Problem of Socrates: Six Public Lectures." *Interpretation* 23 no. 2 (Winter 1996): 127—207.

Zuckert, Catherine. *Plato's Philosophers: The Coherence of the Dialogues.* Chicago: University of Chicago Press, 2009.

THREE ACCOUNTS OF THE SOUL IN PLATO'S *REPUBLIC*[1]

Deborah Achtenberg

Introduction

We know that split human beings coming back together is not Socrates' final view of love in the *Symposium*, that love as the desire for pleasures in Socrates' first speech in the *Phaedrus* is not his final view of love in that dialogue, and that virtue as true opinion is not Socrates' ultimate view of virtue in the *Meno*. It is easy, though, to think that Socrates' first account of soul in the *Republic*, book IV's tripartite soul is his final and more advanced understanding of soul in that dialogue—especially since it seems to appear again later in book IX. Instead, there are three distinct views of soul in the *Republic* and the tripartite soul least represents what soul is like according to Socrates. For him, soul does not literally have parts but functions *as if* it had parts in the society whose members function on the basis of convention rather than knowledge that is described in books II through IV.

---

[1] Thank you to Alessandra Fussi of the University of Pisa and attendees at the European Philosophical Society for the Study of Emotion conference she held there, Marina Marren of United Arab Emirates University and attendees at the *Symposium on the Soul* she put on at the University of Nevada, Reno, and colleagues at the University of Nevada, Reno, Department of Philosophy's Works in Progress Seminar for comments on earlier drafts of this essay; to David Roochnik who was my *Republic* reading partner when we were graduate students in the 1980s; and to the many students with whom I have read and discussed the *Republic* in classes and independent studies. Translations are Allan Bloom's in *The Republic of Plato*.

In the *Symposium,* the account of *eros* as the pursuit by divided circle people of their archaic missing half is unforgettable but not Socrates' own final account. For him, instead, love aims not at the ancestral or traditional but at the good (*Symposium* 205d10–206a2). In the *Phaedrus,* love as the irrational desire for pleasures which is in intrinsic conflict with acquired opinion that aims at what is best is not Socrates' own view of love but is simply Socrates' clarification of Lysias's views (*Phaedrus* 242d4–7). Instead, for Socrates in his final speech, love and reason are not essentially conflictual but, at their best, aim at the same object, namely, at what is beautiful. Similarly, in the *Meno,* the argument that virtue is true opinion because it guides as well as knowledge in practice is not Socrates' final view of virtue because true opinions without knowledge of why they are true are easily shaken—they run away like the lifelike statues of Daedalus—while virtue is more long-lasting (*Meno* 98a1–4). Virtue, then, is some kind of knowledge instead according to Socrates in the *Meno.*

Similarly, in the *Republic,* the tripartite soul is memorable but not final. As love's ascent to comprehension of the beautiful, the so-called ladder of love, supersedes love as pursuit of what one already is in the *Symposium,* so the soul that has learned all things, all time and all being including the brightest part of being, the idea of the good, supersedes the soul divided into a calculative part and the two basic passions, spiritedness and desire (*thumos* and *epithumia*), in the *Republic.* Striking about the account of the soul as tripartite is that it is the soul of someone whose life is guided by conventional views. As Socrates makes clear in the *Meno* that virtue is not mere true opinion but knowledge, so in the *Republic* he makes the same point by superseding the tripartite soul. The *Republic,* though, has three accounts of the soul, and not just two. I propose that the three-animal soul of books VIII and IX is the soul of a person who does not merely follow conventional views but also does not have the complete or surpassing knowledge attributed to a soul in books V through VII. Unlike the person whose actions are directed by emotions that result from holding conventional views, the person whose soul is described in books VIII and IX has some knowledge of their own, but unlike the person who has seen all time and all being in books V through VII, their knowledge is incomplete. Moreover, like Socrates' own account of love in the *Phaedrus* in which desires and reason aim at the same object, love as described in books VIII and IX has the same object as reason, namely, the good. At its best, reason does not have to control eros in the *Republic* since eros aims at reason's highest or most fundamental object.

In what follows, I will first discuss the signs that the three-part soul is a second-order account of soul; show that reason and passion are separate in it; and argue that *thumos* or spiritedness is central in the account because the three-part soul describes the soul of someone who follows convention. Then I will discuss the first-order account of the soul and show that reason and emotion harmonize in it so that Socrates' claim that virtue is knowledge can be understood to remain true for him in the *Republic*. Finally, I will show that in the intermediate account of the soul, the three-animal soul, reason and emotion are not separate since each aspect of the soul has its own love and as a result love is more central to virtue than spiritedness is. I will establish these claims in part by discussing the significance of the different terms used for the soul as described in the third account of it.

I believe the *Republic* is fruitfully read as having three central parts flanked by the first book and the final book. The central parts are books II through IV; V through VII; VIII and IX. Each part features a different account of soul. Only one of the accounts, the account found in books V through VII, is of first-order virtue, that is, is of virtue in its highest or best form. The account found in books II through IV is of second-order virtue, that is, of virtue that is deficient or second-best. Such second-order virtue is insecure or unstable because it is based not on knowledge but on convention and on a separation between reason and passion. The account of the virtues found in books VIII and IX is neither first-order nor second-order virtue but intermediate between them. Such intermediate virtue is guided by reason that is not separate from passion and, as a result, is better than second-order virtue based on mere convention. Intermediate virtue is based only on some knowledge of the good not on complete knowledge of it and, as a result, is not as good as virtue in the highest or best sense. My exposition of the three distinct accounts of soul in the *Republic* will support the idea of reading major claims in the dialogue in their context, specifically, in relation to the part in which they occur.[3]

I.

The first sign that the tripartite soul is not Socrates' final understanding of it is the terms used for its parts. For example, Socrates uses "calculation" (*logistikē*) in the account of the tripartite soul even though calculation is not the highest kind of reason for him (4.439c9–d8) and our tendency to speak of the rational part of

---

[3] My approach to the soul in the *Republic* is in a similar vein as those of Drew Hyland in "The Animals That Therefore We Were?", Ronna Burger in "The Thumotic and the Erotic Soul," and David Roochnik in *The Beautiful City*. Like Hyland (195), I develop the differences between *epithumia* and *eros* for Plato's Socrates though I do so in relation to the *Republic*. Like Burger (84), I follow out Socrates' suggestion that there is another, longer way to the soul than the account of it as tripartite but I explicate the idea that the longer road is the road to the idea of the good and she, while pointing to such a path, explicates the longer path as one that puts together all the partial or distorted paths. Like Roochnik (97), I see the *Republic* as investigating the tripartite soul rather than positing it but my focus in this essay is on the soul and not on the city and democracy.

the soul in books II through IV is in a way a mistake. Instead, what he speaks of is in fact the calculating or strategizing part of the soul, something like *mētis* in the *Odyssey* (craft or intelligence), reasoning about tactics or ways to achieve a preset end. Socrates' use of that term rather than a term such as *nous* makes sense, though, if the soul described there is the soul of the person who follows convention rather than that of someone who can think on their own. Such a person can strategize means to ends but does not know ends themselves. We know such knowledge is missing in the account of the tripartite soul from the placement of the account in the sections before the education that takes one all the way up to knowledge of forms including the highest form, the form or idea of the good.

Another term that is a sign for us is "desire" or *epithumia* (4.439d6–8). Given that Socrates identifies himself with *eros* in the *Symposium*, we would expect *eros*, not *epithumia*, would be one of the two principal human passions, but in books II through IV it is not. Instead, the two principal passions there are spiritedness (*thumos*) and desire *(epithumia)*, the former a kind of military or policing passion and the other our desire for money and things as indicated by the association of desire with the city's money-making people. There is something appealing about Socrates' discussion of two principal passions, one—spiritedness—that defends boundaries such as friend and enemy and one—desire—that goes beyond boundaries, but the appeal is diminished by the limited nature of desire as compared with some other more expansive emotion such as *eros* or even *philia*.

Another set of signs that the first account of the soul is not Socrates' final account of soul is the definitions of the virtues of the soul that he gives in it. Courage, for example, is defined as the spirited part's preservation, through pains and pleasures, of what has been proclaimed by speeches as terrible or not terrible

(4.442c11). In other words, a courageous person is one whose spirited part retains the idea given in the city's various declarations and images of what is to be feared and what is not to be feared. But then courage would be true opinion! Or, even not true opinion, but authoritative opinion! The point is even clearer in the definition of the city's courage as preservation of opinion produced by law through education about what and what sort of thing is terrible (4.429c7). Courage then is convention produced and secured in us through education and through the action of the defensive part of the soul, the part that defends its own and thwarts enemies, where the enemy in this case is divergent views about what is terrible, and one's own are the views of the city about what should be feared. And what is it that the city teaches about what is terrifying? It teaches some views we know Socrates does not share. It teaches that death is not fearful (3.386a6) something Socrates is unsure of still in the *Phaedo*, and that famous men do not fear (3.387d1), a doubtful view at best.

Similarly, moderation (*sōphrosynē*) is defined as the ruling and two ruled parts—calculation and the two passions, spiritedness and desire—having the single opinion that the calculating part should rule and not raising faction against it (4.442c10). Following what I have just said, this would imply that a moderate soul is one in which not only spiritedness but also desire concurs that the city's lawful or conventional views should be followed. Courage and moderation, then, involve emotions following opinions produced by convention or law and education. And what is that education like in books II through IV? In addition to the teachings above about the fearful, it includes teachings that the gods are good (2.379b1), that they are the cause only of good things (2.379b15), and that the gods do not change (2.381c7). These views, expressed in music and accompanied by gymnastics, are necessary to teach if we are to see that citizens are pious, that is, that they "honor gods and ancestors" (3.386a2), that they are friendly to each other (3.386a3), and that they are courageous (3.386a6) and moderate (3.389d7). This list of the four cardinal virtues at the beginning of book III is another sign that the virtues described in books II through IV are second- not first-order virtues. For it is not quite the standard list of them. It is piety, friendship, courage and moderation instead of wisdom, justice, courage and moderation. What this list indicates is that there is development of the soul in the *Republic*. The wisdom described here is calculation based on a type of piety, rather than wisdom based on knowledge of the good; the justice described is closer to friendship; and the courage and moderation described are conventional courage and moderation not courage and moderation per se.

There are three other clear signs that the virtues and emotions described in books II through IV are second-order, specifically, three statements that clearly indicate this. The first is Socrates' statement cautioning Glaucon not to take the definition of courage proffered by Socrates in book 4 at face value. Socrates gives the definition after he has discussed the fact that education in music and gymnastic dyes the city's opinions about what is pleasant and what painful into people so effectively that the opinions cannot be washed out. Glaucon agrees with the definition, saying, "I accept this as courage." Socrates then cautions him not to accept it as virtue in the strongest sense but instead only as political courage. "Yes, do accept it, but as political courage," he says, and then he goes on to say that later they can "give it a still more beautiful treatment" (4.430c2). There is second-order or second-best courage, then, which Socrates here calls "political courage" (*andreia politikē*).

The account of the afterlife in book X provides a second clear statement of the two orders of virtue. Socrates says there that the person who, living in a good city, practices virtue by habit without philosophy will choose in his next life what turns out to be the greatest tyranny: "the man who had drawn the first lot came forward and immediately chose the greatest tyranny, and, due to folly and gluttony, chose without having considered everything adequately" (10.619b7). "He was one of those who had come [to this part of the underworld] from heaven, having lived in an orderly regime in his former life, participating in virtue by habit, without philosophy" (10.619c6). In other words, he had lived in a good city that instilled virtuous habit in him. At the same time, he did not himself know what was or was not good and was used to acting on habits rather than reflection. As a result, he made his choice of a future life right away, without reflection, and wrongly.

The third clear statement is, again, in book IV. Socrates asks whether the soul actually has the three forms described or not: "Now it's a slight question about the soul we've stumbled upon, you surprising man," Socrates says, "Does it have these three forms in it or not?" (4.435c4). In the context, the question alludes to the difference between the city—in which it apparently is clear that there are three groups in it, the rulers, the guardians and the money-makers—and the soul. Does the soul really have three parts? Or is this simply a manner of speaking? Could it be, to take a cue from Paul Ricoeur on Freud, that the soul here functions *as if* it had parts? Instead, there is nothing but the person and their emotions and emotional dispositions. In addition, are reason (understood as calculation) and the emotions (spiritedness and desire) really separate? It seems that they are since there is a need on this account for reason to rule or control passion, to the extent even that one of the passions, spiritedness, originates in the need to control desire—as in the case of Leontius who desired to look at corpses but was disgusted with himself and forced himself to look away. Spiritedness or *thumos* functions again as the boundary-setter, using force on desire on behalf of reason—where reason still here is understood as calculation of what is best based on conventional views instilled through education.

If the soul does not have parts, then what would be the more precise account of the soul? I imagine it would be one in which a person, a human being, has opinions or emotions that sometimes conflict. Such a person might desire to see corpses, thus indicating an at least implicit or background belief that doing so is good in some way—maybe fascinating or somehow informative about human existence—and another belief that doing so is bad or base; and, in addition, the two views are not harmonized or integrated into some one overarching view that combines and compares them.

This I think indicates Socrates' final view in the *Republic* on whether virtue is knowledge. It is, but knowledge of what? And knowledge of what type? It is not knowledge in the sense of being smart. This is clear from Socrates' remark in the *Meno* that indicates that quick thought or *eumatheia* is not virtue (*Meno* 88a8). Instead, *eumatheia* is listed as one of the states of soul that must be accompanied by or become knowledge if they are to be good, such as courage. Courage if it is not knowledge, Socrates says, is just recklessness (88b3). Calculation, I might say to make sharp the analogy I am drawing, if it is not knowledge is just convention—and is as strong or weak as the city in which it has its home.

An example that shows the significant difference between virtue per se—that is, first-order virtue—and merely conventional virtue is in a later book, book VIII, in which Socrates discusses a son who sees his father allowing injustices to himself due to the father having a high degree of honor and little concern about money. The son is swayed by domestics who tell him to punish the men who do injustice to the father and, in so doing, be a man (8.549e3). The son sees those such as his father who mind their own business being treated as simpletons while others are honored and praised. When he hears and sees such things, he has no knowledge of his own that can counter them. Virtue pales not only in the afterlife if you do not have your own knowledge of what is good, but also in times of what we would call cultural change, in which conventions are in a process of shifting. It also pales in sleep, as we will see in part 3 of this essay. What these three have in common is the weak power of control by convention—whether in some imagined afterlife where any choice is possible; in sleep where—as Freud will say later—ordinary controls can come off; or in times of cultural change in which old conventions are falling away. In sleep, in the afterlife, in times of change, one needs one's own understanding of what is good in order to be virtuous. Convention does not help.

Virtue, for Socrates in the *Republic*, then, is wisdom, not mere strategic intelligence, where wisdom is knowledge of all time and all being all the way up to the forms including centrally the form or idea of the good. Virtue is wisdom, not calculation, where wisdom centrally involves knowledge, for oneself, of what is good. Such knowledge answers the question that many readers of the *Meno* have, namely, if virtue is knowledge, what type of knowledge is it? It also explains Socrates' discussion in the *Statesman* of the measure of the more and less in regard to virtue (*Statesman* 283c11–e6). It cannot mean some numerically quantifiable notion of *more or less*. Instead, it designates the overall assessment of various goods, including knowledge and experience of them, so that one assesses one good in relation to others. The knowledge required for virtue starts with bodily knowledge attained in gymnastics, then the soul's knowledge in music (where gymnastics is understood to tighten us up and music to make us more open and receptive) followed by a long list of more mathematically and formally oriented studies starting, but not ending, with calculation, going from there to geometry, depth, astronomy and harmony, and then to dialectic.

One more point is necessary before discussing the results of such an education on the soul, specifically on emotion. It is that if what I am arguing is, at least in large outlines, a correct interpretation of the *Republic*, then there must be a problem in one of Socrates' arguments in books II through IV. Socrates does, after all, have an *argument* for his claim that the soul has parts—two emotional parts, each separate from the other and both separate from a calculative part. It is the well-known argument based on the law of contradiction, as it came to be called, that Leontius cannot both move toward and away from something at the same time.

As arguments go, it is a fairly strong one. There is, however, an assumption in it that Socrates, in my view, cannot and does not accept.[4] It is the assumption that, for example, thirst is for drink not for good drink: "thirsting itself," Socrates rhetorically asks, "will never be a desire for anything other than that of which it naturally is a desire—for drink alone—and, similarly, hungering will be a desire for food?" (4.437e4). "Now let no one catch us unprepared," Socrates goes on, "and cause a disturbance, alleging that no one desires drink, but good drink, nor food, but good food; for everyone, after all, desires good things; if then, thirst is a desire, it would be for good drink or for good whatever it is, and similarly with the other desires" (4.438a1). Not surprisingly, Glaucon responds with hesitation, "Perhaps the man who says that would seem to make some sense" (4.438a6). Of course

---

[4] Nicholas P. White notes that "there is something merely provisional about the argument that he [Socrates] is about to give" (123) but he attributes the provisionality to the merely hypothetical nature of the law of contradiction (124) while I argue that it is due to the mistaken assumption that there are desires that are not for something perceived to be good.

he would, since this is the view argued by Socrates himself in, for example, the *Meno* where he argues that no one desires anything bad but instead we always desire things perceived to be good.

This argument is the heart of Socrates' overall argument there that virtue is knowledge or wisdom. If we had desire for something other than good, then virtue would not be knowledge but a type of control (or, for later thinkers, will or will power). If, as Socrates himself believes, we only desire what we perceive as or think of as good, then our pursuit of what is not good can be understood as a type of misunderstanding or lack of knowledge or wisdom (*Meno* 77c1). Since we all have the same desire—namely, desire for what appears to be good—then what is needed to see that we pursue what is good is an appropriate type and extent of knowledge of it. That is what the claim that virtue is knowledge means, namely, that once we see what is good—in all its depth and complexity—we will love it and thus do it. Such is the claim of books V through VII of the *Republic*.

II.

What is first-order virtue like? It is a state or disposition of soul in which we see what is good, love it, and therefore do it.[5] The first two indicate a unanimity of reason and passion. When we comprehend what is good, we want it. First-order virtue, in other words, is knowledge. In book VI, Socrates speaks of taking a longer road to get the finest view of the soul and the virtues: "We

---

[5] Charles Kahn argues that Plato has a one-factor explanation of action in which reason is a form of desire. The argument is based in part on the fact that Plato does not distinguish theoretical from practical wisdom. I think instead that, for Socrates, loving the good is not the same as seeing it but necessarily follows from seeing it and that this would explain Plato's non-distinction of theoretical and practical wisdom.

were, I believe, saying that in order to get the finest possible look at these things another and longer road around would be required" (6.504b1). The longer road ends with a greater study—the greatest study—namely the study of the idea of the good: you have heard that "the idea of the good is the greatest study and that it is by availing oneself of it along with just things and the rest that they become useful and beneficial" (6.505a2). The latter claim echoes Socrates' claim in the *Meno*, mentioned earlier, that courage and other so-called virtues are not really virtues if they are not wisdom, or are not accompanied by it. Nothing else is of profit to us if we do not have knowledge of what is good.

The good, for Socrates, is in the realm of being not becoming (7.518c8). This kind of claim in Plato's writings makes us uncomfortable because it seems to suggest an aversion to pragmatism on behalf of an unrealizable ideal. I think such interpretations are misguided, however. Socrates is, in my view, a kind of pragmatist, fully in touch with the non-ideal and ambiguous nature of human existence. This is indicated by his claim that the things around us tumble about between being and nonbeing (5.479c3–5). They are mixed, according to him, not ideal, and they are always changing. What he means by saying that the good is in the realm of being not becoming is that the ontological status of the good is different from the ontological status of entities that exist and therefore come in and out of existence. A tree comes in and out of existence. The idea of tree is not like that. It just is. Moreover, the good is the most fundamental of the things that just are. It is the brightest of the beings: "the instrument with which each learns...must be turned around from that which is *coming into being* together with the whole soul until it is able to endure looking at that which *is* and the brightest part of that which *is*. And we affirm that this is the good, don't we?" (7.518c–

d). I have described the good as most fundamental though Socrates describes it here as brightest (*phanotaton*). My reason for doing so is that the good is the first form in the *Republic* and so, as a result, it is first in intelligibility—that is, brightest—as well, since everything else is, in some sense, understood through it or on its basis.

Following the discussion of the good as the brightest part of being is Socrates' strongest confirmation of the idea of that there is first- and second-order virtue: "Therefore, the other so-called virtues of the soul are probably somewhat close to those of the body. For they are really not there beforehand and are later produced by habits and exercises, while the virtue of exercising wisdom is more than anything somehow more divine, it seems; it never loses its power" (7.518d–e). First-order virtue, wisdom, is permanent, while second-order virtue, virtue produced by habituation and exercise—the second-order virtue we saw described in the book X account of the afterlife—comes and goes. Such virtue is similar to the so-called virtue described as true opinion in the *Meno*. Such "virtue" guides just as well as knowledge in practice (*Meno* 96e1). If you do not know the way from Athens to Larissa but have a true opinion about it acquired from Siri, you will get there just as well. However, if Siri is down or if someone tells you Siri is wrong, you have no resources for finding your way on your own. You may go the wrong way—just as the person who has virtue acquired by habit without philosophy picks the greatest tyranny for his next life. Knowing the good for oneself is what chains down true opinions so that they, unlike the statues of Daedalus, do not run away.

Virtue, therefore, is wisdom understood centrally as knowledge of the good. The one who has it—the philosopher—has all the virtues. The philosopher loves the pleasures of the soul over those of the body and so is moderate. He reaches out for the whole—for everything divine and human—and so is not illiberal or petty. He simply is not concerned about small things. Because he contemplates all time and all being, and is magnificent in doing so, he does not see anything human as great, even death. As a result, he lacks the fear required to be a coward. Finally, lacking such vices, he is not unjust. He lacks vices such as love of money, which is too small for him, and illiberality or cowardice, which generally lead to injustice. In love with learning that discloses being—especially with the brightest part of being, the idea of the good—nothing else has enough value for him in comparison such that he would be drawn to it. He sees what is good, loves it and does it and overlooks doing other things that might to others seem good because to him they are such small values as to be negligible (6.485a–486b).

Two points then are clear about the tripartite soul. First, it is at least an imprecise or figurative account of the soul, if not an inaccurate one. The soul does not really have parts. Instead, a person can have conflicting desires for competing goods which lead to apparently contradictory actions. Such conflict is overcome by having more holistic knowledge in which different goods are assessed in relation to each other and the greatest of them, the idea of the good itself, is seen to be so much greater than the rest that they have no power of compulsion or draw in comparison. Second, the accounts of the emotions and the virtues in the tripartite soul account are false—or at least only true for those who merely follow convention. For such people, *thumos* must be important, since it can say "no" to what is other or enemy and "yes" to what is familiar, while merely calculative reason is separate from the passions and has no power to shape and form them. Put less figuratively, in the parts-of-the-soul account, calculative reason has no comprehension of the good and passions are not in part constituted by perception or awareness of goods.

As a result, reason has no impact on emotion and a defensive, spirited emotion must step in to defend the familiar instead.

III.

The third account of the soul, found in book IX, is an account of a soul that has some but not all of the knowledge required for first-order virtue. One striking thing about the third account is that the terms in it have changed. Though the third account, like the first, has the soul divided into three, we would not so easily think of the three as parts. Once we get to the image Socrates draws of it, we could call it, as I have, the three-animal soul, since he there describes the soul as a human being that has inside itself a human being (reason), a lion (the parallel to book IV's spiritedness) and a many-colored beast with many tame and savage heads in a ring (the parallel to desire) (9.588c7). However, Socrates gives a non-imagistic account as well, one that helps us see how he wishes the image to be understood.[6]

The non-imagistic version of the third account is striking, in comparison to the three-part soul of book IV, because central terms have changed and because love (*philia*) is mentioned in each "part." Most notably, the rational aspect of the soul is called learning-loving and wisdom-loving (9.581b9). The term "calcu-

---

[6] It is not unusual for Socrates to offer an image of something and subsequently give a non-imagistic account of it. In the *Meno* and the *Phaedrus*, for example, he gives both an image of recollection and a non-imagistic account of it. In the *Meno*, remembering what you knew before you were born is followed by securing unstable opinions by reasoning about cause (*Meno* 98a1–4). In the *Phaedrus,* ascending to the place beyond the heavens and seeing the beautiful on a beautiful throne is followed by understanding what is said according to form, moving from many perceptions to what is gathered into one by reasoning (*Phaedrus* 249b6–c4).

lation" drops out, and learning and wisdom take its place indicating the possibility in human beings of real, first-order, virtue that rests on a love both of learning and of the wisdom it can achieve. The spirited "part" of the soul is called victory-loving and honor-loving (9.581b2) and the desiring "part" money-loving and gain-loving (9.581a6).

As Socrates has pointed out, second-order virtues are almost like virtues of the body. The reason for this is that in book IV's tripartite soul, passions are separate from reason. No drive for learning or wisdom is there to reshape passions. Instead, at best on that account, spiritedness controls desire on behalf of convention or what is familiar. Spiritedness, of course, is characterized by defense of what is familiar or friend and harm to what is unfamiliar or enemy. Spiritedness produces second-order virtue, then, by controlling desires that are for what is unfamiliar or unconventional. That convention is not the good, and that philosophy goes beyond convention to the true or the good, is another way of thinking about why the account of the virtues in book IV is problematic or second best.

In book IX, by contrast, philosophy plays a role. Rational soul there is not calculative but instead both loves to learn and loves wisdom (9.581b9–10). The rational soul, in other words, is philosophical. In it, passion and reason go in the same direction. Passion does not need to be corrected by reason or by another passion on behalf of reason. Instead, there is a passion, a love, of reason. On the other hand, passion and reason are not so in sync that reason suffuses all of passion as it does in book VI's first-order account of virtue. There still is love of money and gain (9.581a5–7), and love of victory and honor (9.581b2–3). How do these fit in? And how is this an account of intermediate virtue, virtue that is similar to first-order virtue but achieved to a lesser extent?

First, it is notable that there are two descriptions of each passion in this account. Spiritedness is love of victory and also honor, desire is love of money and also gain. Each pair suggests a kind of progression, from something concrete—victory or money—to something more general—honor or gain. We can see each as moving from concrete and conventional values in the direction of the good itself, that is, to a more general desire for or love of what is good. That is, what is suggested is a development from loving victory, to loving honor to loving the good itself and one from loving money to loving gain to loving the good itself.

Second, in his image, Socrates makes an image of the money- and gain-loving part of the soul as a many-colored beast with many tame and savage heads in a ring. The tame and savage heads, we can assume, are necessary and unnecessary desires. Socrates says that unnecessary desires include some that are hostile to law or convention but that can be checked in three ways (9.971b3–c1). They can be controlled by laws, by better desires, or by the help of *logos*. Sometimes they can even be gotten rid of (9.571b4). The first of the three ways, law, brings books II to IV to mind where convention and law are used to change our emotions. The second way, better desires, reminds us of spiritedness controlling non-conventional desire in the same sections. The third way, reason or *logos*, is new. Reason itself can shape and change desires, this way suggests, at least in some cases. It is important that here reason, not spiritedness, changes desires.

Third, in cases in which the stronger, wild, desires are not, in fact, gotten rid of, we know that they have not been eliminated because they are awakened when the tame part of the soul is asleep and not affected by shame or wisdom—we might say not restrained by shame as in the second-order account of virtue (for example, Leontius' disgust at his own desire) and not shaped by wisdom as in the first-order account or here in the intermediate case. The moderate person, by contrast, awakens and feeds the soul with beautiful *logoi* before going to bed and also soothes the desiring and spirited parts before going to bed so they are not aroused and do not interfere with the wise part (9.571d–e). Reason can, here, have impact on emotion.

These three examples illustrate the fact that the third account of the soul, emotion and virtue is an account of intermediate virtue. Virtues in it are not based on conventional views of what is good. Nor in it are reason and passion separate. Instead, there is a passion—a love—for learning and wisdom and it can and does influence the other passions to a greater or lesser extent. In addition, in this third account of the soul, the soul is not understood on the basis of three parts but, at least figuratively, on the basis of three animals, namely, a human being, a lion and a fictional animal with many heads. The three-animal soul suggests that instead of thinking of the soul as having parts we instead think of beings or even, better, persons with sets of predominant loves that are more or less shaped and informed by wisdom: one who loves money or, better, gain; one who loves victory or, better, honor; and, finally, one who loves learning and the wisdom at which it aims.

Conclusion

In the end, then, for Socrates in the *Republic*, virtue really is knowledge or wisdom because reason and passion can harmoniously aim at what is best. When we have knowledge of the good, it is so beautiful, and so beautiful in comparison with other goods, that we love it and simply do it. For those who cannot achieve wisdom to such a high degree—and that may of course be nearly everyone—various intermediate stages are possible in which reason affects and shapes passion to an extent. For those who cannot go beyond convention, a second-order or second-best state is possible in which spiritedness allies with convention to achieve constraint of unruly or unconventional desires. Such constraint, though, is unstable and temporary since it is dependent on conventions which, of course, themselves are subject to change over time.

Bibliography

Burger, Ronna. "The Thumotic and the Erotic Soul: Seth Benardete on Platonic Psychology" in *The Eccentric Core: The Thought of Seth Benardete*, edited by Ronna Burger and Patrick Goodin, 85–100. South Bend: St. Augustine's Press, 2018.

Hyland, Drew. "The Animals That Therefore We Were? Aristophanes's Double-Creatures and the Question of Origins." In *Plato's Animals: Gadflies, Horses, Swans, and Other Philosophical Beasts.* Edited by Jeremy Bell and Michael Naas, 193–206. Bloomington: Indiana University Press, 2015.

Kahn, Charles. "Plato's Theory of Desire," *Review of Metaphysics* 41, no. 1 (1987): 77–103.

Plato. *Lysis*. In vol. 3 of *Platonis Opera*. Edited by John Burnet. Oxford: Clarendon Press, 1903, 1974.

———. *Meno*. In vol. 3 of *Platonis Opera*. Edited by John Burnet. Oxford: Clarendon Press, 1903, 1974.

———. *Phaedo*. In vol. 1 of *Platonis Opera*. Edited by John Burnet. Oxford: Clarendon Press, 1900, 1985.

———. *Phaedrus*. In vol. 2 of *Platonis Opera*. Edited by John Burnet. Oxford: Clarendon Press, 1901, 1973.

———. *Republic*. In vol. 4 of *Platonis Opera*. Edited by John Burnet. Oxford: Clarendon Press, 1902, 1972.

———. *Statesman*. In vol. 1 of *Platonis Opera*. Edited by John Burnet. Oxford: Clarendon Press, 1900, 1985.

———. *Theaetetus*. In vol. 1 of *Platonis Opera*. Edited by John Burnet. Oxford: Clarendon Press, 1900, 1985.

———. *The Republic of Plato*. Translated by Allan Bloom. New York: Basic Books, 1968.

Roochnik, David. *The Beautiful City: The Dialectical Character of Plato's* Republic. Ithaca: Cornell University Press, 2003.

White, Nicholas P. *A Companion to Plato's* Republic. Indianapolis: Hackett Publishing Company, 1979.

THE FEMALE DRAMA[1]

Charlotte Thomas

Introduction

As Book V of the *Republic* opens, Socrates changes the subject from justice to injustice. The once feverish but now purged city was a fine paradigm, and analyzing it yielded a definition of justice suitable to investigate the comparative value of justice and injustice for a human life. So, Socrates says, the next step should be to consider injustice in the four kinds of deficient cities and souls that their inquiry has pointed them toward. After investigating the four-fold nature of injustice in cities and human beings, Socrates' plan was then to compare the paradigm of justice found in the proper arrangement of the three parts of the purged city/soul with each paradigm of injustice implied by rearranging those parts into other configurations. After comparing the just soul with each of the four unjust souls, they were to have attempted to determine which paradigm was most conducive to happiness in each case. At the end of the comparisons, they were to have attempted to answer to their original question: whether it is better to live a just or an unjust life. Socrates outlines, reviews, and alludes to this plan often; but, of course, things do not go according to plan.

Instead of leaving the just city in speech behind at the beginning of Book V, Adeimantus and Polemarchus insist that Socrates return to elaborate on a matter that they accuse him of

---

[1] Based on Chapter 4 of Charlotte Thomas, *The Female Drama: The Philosophical Feminine in the Soul of Plato's Republic* (Macon: Mercer University Press, 2019). Used here with permission of Mercer University Press.

neglecting: how women and children fit in the city. Glaucon joins with them in arresting (*epilambano*) Socrates and insisting that he continue to elaborate on the constitution of the just city in speech.[2] Even Thrasymachus, who has been silent since shortly after Socrates made him blush in Book I, adds his voice to the cause (450a).

All four of Socrates' most impressive interlocutors in the *Republic* insist that he explain in more detail the role of women and children in the city in speech. Other than the implicit agreement at the beginning of the dialogue that Socrates should stay and talk to them, this is the only time in the dialogue that Glaucon, Adeimantus, Polemarchus, and Thrasymachus are portrayed as agreeing on something. And it is, without qualification, the only thing about which they explicitly agree.

Specifically, Adeimantus, asks to be told more about (1) how arrangements with women and children should be understood as

---

[2] Many scholars have commented on the repetition at the beginning of Book V of the "arrest" scene in Book I and how it sets Books V–VII apart. For example, Laurence Lampert, *How Philosophy Became Socratic: A Study of Plato's Protagoras Charmides, and Republic.* (Chicago: University of Chicago Press, 2010), 279, 306, and 311–12; Stanley Rosen, *Plato's Republic: A Study* (New Haven: Yale University Press), 167–9; Jacob Howland, *The Republic: The Odyssey of Philosophy* (Philadelphia: Paul Dry, 2004), 41; Eva Brann, *The Music of the Republic* (Philadelphia: Paul Dry, 2004), 150; David Roochnik, *The Beautiful City: The Dialectical Character of Plato's Republic* (Ithaca: Cornell UP, 2003), 2–4; Leon Harold Craig, *The War Lover: A Study of Plato's Republic* (Toronto: University of Toronto Press, 1996), 185; Diskin Clay, *Platonic Questions: Dialogues with the Silent Philosopher* (University Park: Pennsylvania State University Press, 2000), 247; Leo Strauss, *The City and Man* (Chicago: University of Chicago Press, 1978), 64, 155; Kurt Hildebrandt, *Platon: Logos Und Mythos* (Berlin: De Gruyter, 1959), 393; Eric Voegelin, *Order and History, Volume III: Platon and Aristotle.* (Baton Rouge: Louisiana State University, 1957), 46–52; and Mark Blitz, *Plato's Political Philosophy* (Baltimore: Johns Hopkins University Press, 2010), 169.

a case of friends sharing everything in common, (2) how procreation will be handled in the city, and (3) how young children will be reared before they begin their formal education (449d). Socrates agrees to work through these questions, but reluctantly. He warns that they will have to start again from the beginning (450a), that they will be unleashing a "swarm" (*esmos*) of arguments (450a), that they are asking him to produce arguments about things of which he is uncertain (450e), and that what they are doing is both frightening (*phoberos*) and treacherous (*sphaleros*) (451a). Socrates says that he is afraid that if he is unsuccessful, he will not only fail himself but also do harm to his friends (451a). He bows to Adrasteia, also known as Nemesis. He asks for forgiveness in advance for what he is about to do (451a).[3]

---

[3] Laurence Lampert describes Socrates prostrating himself to Adrasteia "the most breathtaking image in the whole *Republic*," and calls Socrates' account of it his "most solemn speech in the whole *Republic*." Lampert, who casts Socrates in the *Republic* as a new Odysseus, sets the scene this way: "The solemnity of Socrates' speech derives from the greatness of its occasion: returned Odysseus, having manipulated them into compelling him to do what he alone compels himself to do, now embarks on the introduction of a great novelty into the stream of Greek wisdom and he cannot know whether introducing the rule of the philosopher will succeed. He stands over an abyss unable to know for certain whether it is possible and, if possible, if it is for the best. He must ask himself: is it a prayer? Fearing that he will bring his genuine friends, the few wise, down with him in this boldest of projects on behalf of wisdom, he in fact offers a prayer, the most solemn of prayers and the only one becoming a philosopher: 'I will prostrate myself before Adrasteia.'" He prays the prayer of a philosopher compelled to act on the grandest scale not knowing whether he can succeed; he submits himself to Nemesis, the necessity that rules all, knowing the rashness of his deed while judging that necessity itself calls it forth." Laurence Lampert, *How Philosophy Became Socratic* (Chicago: University of Chicago Press, 2010), 310–311. Whether or not one follows Lampert on the identification of Socrates with Odysseus, the account of Socrates' fear of the consequences of his impiety and the necessity of taking the risk for the sake of philosophy seem precisely right.

I would like to begin to work through some of the arguments of Book V of the *Republic*, especially those leading up to the end of the First Wave, and consider their implications for the further development of the city in speech as a paradigm for the soul. To begin, we will face a swarm of questions implied and expressed in the rich dramatic opening to this new section of the dialogue. My focus will be on the moral psychology of the *Republic*. Chief among my questions are: (1) How do the accounts of women and children in the city in speech illuminate the soul? (2) What do "procreation" (*genesis*) and "rearing" (*trophe*) mean in the context of a soul? And (3) since Socrates offers us a heuristic for this narrative shift, I will also inquire into why he names it as he does, i.e., the "female drama." What might it mean for an inquiry into the moral psychology of the *Republic* that the dialectic within which the city in speech is constructed in Books II–IV is the "male drama"? What light is cast upon this section after Socrates pays his fearful respects to Adrasteia,[4] calling the present inquiry the "female drama?"[5]

---

[4] Jacob Howland notes that the reference to Adrasteia may also be an allusion to Aeschylus' Prometheus. Jacob Howland, *The Republic: A Philosophical Odyssey* (Philadelphia: Paul Dry Books, 2004), 111.

[5] "Female," is my choice of translation for gynaikeion/γυναικεῖον mainly because "the Female Drama" is the conventional translation of what Socrates calls the episode that begins in Book V. But, as Mary Townsend notes, any definitive choice of English words is fraught. "This adjective (γυναικεῖον) has a range of meanings, from 'ladylike,' or 'womanly' in a good sense, to 'womanish' or 'effeminate' in the bad. Socrates uses the word to decry the practice still in use among Greek male soldiers of stripping the corpses of the fallen after a battle; a practice he paints as a womanish custom unworthy of his male and female guardians (469d). I will note that however the reader would wish to gloss this word here, 'feminine' is hardly the right word for tearing valuables away from the dead in a bloody field." Townsend, *The Woman Question in Plato's Republic* (New York: Lexington Books, 2017), 15.

Opening the Curtain on the Female Drama

The dramatic introduction to Book V offers several provocative clues about how Socrates intends to proceed and why he is intimidated by the work that lies ahead. First, Socrates says that they will have to begin again, which suggests that women and children are not a new part of the city in speech that can be tacked on to the account. They may be seen as a version of something that already exists in the city in speech; or as a basic condition that will change the model fundamentally; or as something that pervades the model. Exactly what women and children are to the city in speech is not obvious, but that they are central or fundamental or pervasive seems indisputable given that we have to return to the beginning and retrace our steps in order see where they fit in.[6]

---

[6] Steven Forde provides a helpful survey of interpretations of the role of women and children in the *Republic* ("Gender and Justice in Plato," *American Political Science Review* 92, no. 3 (1997): 657—670. Susan Muller Okin argues that Plato should be credited with a pioneering argument for women's political equality ("Philosopher Queens and Private Wives: Plato on Women and the Family," *Philosophy and Public Affairs*, 6 (Summer 1977): 345–369. While Arlene Saxonhouse ("The Philosopher and the Female In the Political Thought of Plato," *Political Theory* 4 (May 1976): 321–325; Julia Annas ("Plato's *Republic* and Feminism," *Philosophy* 5 (July 1976): 307–321; and Allan Bloom in *The Republic of Plato* (New York: Basic Books, 1968) do not believe that the account women in Book V creates any meaningful equality for women. Jean Bethke Elshtain in *Public Man, Private Woman: Women in Social and Political Thought* (Princeton: Princeton University Press, 1981) argues that Plato creates gender equality, but at the expense of both male and female identity. Since the publication of Forde's piece, a few important variations on these interpretations have appeared, including Catherine Gardner's argument that women play an important role in Kallipolis, but that they are mainly understood as instrumental in its eugenics project. See Catherine Gardner, "The Remnants of the Family: The Role of Women and Eugenics in Republic V," *History of Philosophy Quarterly* 17, no. 3 (July 1, 2000): 217–35. See also Catherine McKeen's argument that women must rule in Kallipolis in "Why Women

Secondly, Socrates tells us that the city in speech that includes a fuller explanation of women and children might appear to be something to be prayed for (*euxos*), rather than something to be worked for (*ergon*) (450c). That is, it might be something that is impossible for human beings to achieve without divine intervention. In Books V and VI, Socrates asks several times whether or not their hopes for the best city/soul are like an *euxos* (450a, 456b, 461a, 499c, and 540d) and the conclusion seems to be clear at 540d, that they are not. The best city would be difficult for human beings to realize.

The idea that what Socrates will present to them might look like a *euxos* is particularly provocative because he seems to be setting it up on the opposite end of a spectrum with *ergon* on the other end. That is, the interlocutors ask over and over again whether or not the city in speech can be a "city in deed," an *ergon*; and Socrates admits at 473a that it cannot be fully instantiated in deed. However, he rejects the conclusion that the unattainability of the fully formed *ergon* of Kallipolis implies that it is just an *euxos*—a lofty dream. Instead it is a paradigm to be strived for, and a thing that is achievable in some sense. And this is a possibility that seems to sit on the line somewhere between *ergon* and *euxos*. The possibility of creating Kallipolis is in deed extremely unlikely, and it would be extraordinarily difficult to do, but Socrates insists that it is not impossible.

These insights into the difficulties of founding a city according to the paradigm of the city in speech point in several directions. They may suggest that Socrates considers the city in speech constructed in Books II–IV to be more plausible than the version

---

Must Guard and Rule in Plato's 'Kallipolis,'" *Pacific Philosophical Quarterly* 87, no. 4 (December 1, 2006): 527–48 and Townsend's recontextualization of the role of women portrayed in Book V in the political and religious culture of Classical Athens. See Townsend's *The Woman Question in Plato's Republic*).

The Female Drama

of the city in speech they are about to investigate. And that would be surprising, at least on the level of political interpretation. If, for the sake of an argument, we bracket the noble lie and even the stringent requirements of qualifying as a guardian, achieving the political order described in the city in speech is still extremely, if not practically impossible. If a suitable guardian were miraculously to emerge, the odds that every citizen would agree to his power and commit wholly to their supporting roles in his regime are extremely long. (This scenario is explored in detail in Book VI.) Other necessary conditions for the well-functioning purged city are just as unlikely.

When Socrates warns that including a fuller account of women and children in the city in speech might make their project seem like an *euxos*, it seems far more likely that he is referring to the city/soul's implications for psychology than politics. Socrates seems to be concerned about whether what they have done and will do to describe the proper arrangement of a human soul will seem to be possible or not. This suggests that Socrates considers the model of the soul in Books II—IV to be apparently more achievable, but that the elaboration on which they are about to embark may less so.[7]

Socrates' concern that he and his interlocutors may be developing their image of justice in an apparently implausible way leads to the third dramatic clue in the narrative frame of Book V. Socrates strongly indicates that adding a fuller account of women and children into the city in speech will be dangerous. The germ

---

[7] Catherine Zuckert, commenting on Leo Strauss's long list of quotations from the *Ecclesiazusae* in the Republic, notes that Plato underlines the "imaginary and non-historical character" of the dialogue by quoting a play that was not performed until after Socrates' death. See Zuckert's, *Platonic Philosophers: The Coherence of the Dialogues* (Chicago: University of Chicago Press, 2009), 353 fn. 134. See further, Leo Strauss, *The City and Man*, 61.

of this danger appears to be Socrates' fear that he might make justice appear to be unachievable. If Socrates makes justice seem unattainable, he will first of all be doing harm to himself because he will look like a fool for devoting himself so completely to something impossible. He says, though, that the threat of appearing ridiculous doesn't trouble him (451a). What seems to worry Socrates deeply is the risk of hurting his friends. What would become of these great-souled, politically powerful men with whom he is having this conversation if Socrates inadvertently convinced them that it is impossible (or radically implausible) to become just? Glaucon, Adeimantus, and Polemarchus (not to mention Thrasymachus) might feel unleashed to a life of injustice—precisely the opposite of what Socrates hopes this conversation (and perhaps every conversation) will encourage.[8] But, he proceeds, nonetheless.

Beginning Again

Socrates' first move in his reluctant, apparently hubristic, attempt to account for women and children in the purged city in speech is to return to his discussion of the proper natures (*physeis*) of the guardians from Book II. Socrates says that "for people born and educated the way we have described, there is no way to acquire and employ women and children other than to follow the path we first set them on" (451c). The Male Drama was not wrong; it was incomplete. So, Socrates says, "let's proceed by giving them

---

[8] According to Debra Nails, the people present at Cephalus's house for the conversation of the Republic represent every sort of person who lived in Athens just before the war, perhaps suggesting that everyone had a stake in what was to come. See Nails's, "Plato's *Republic* in its Athenian Context," *History of Political Thought* 33, no. 1 (Spring 2012): 1–23.

The Female Drama

corresponding rules for birth and rearing, and see whether or not they are fitting" (451d).[9]

The proper place to have introduced women and children in the city in speech would apparently have been the first moment the guardians were mentioned. What Socrates said that they achieved in the argument as they conducted it was to have established the guardians as guard dogs of their flocks. What they need now to consider are the rules for the *genesis* and *trophe* of those guard dogs. It appears that the argument for establishing the guardians as guard dogs was what Socrates is now calling the "male drama," and now as we consider where those guard dogs came from (as well as their *genesis* and *trophe*) we are turning to "the female."

Although much of Books II–IV appears to be about education, I do not think an argument about the proper form of education is actually presented there. What is presented in Book II through the beginning of Book IV is an argument for the *telos* of *logismos* in a just soul, i.e., this is the culmination of a proper education.[10] The full actualization (*telos*) of the calculating part of the soul (*logismos*) is an important and necessary part of an account of education, but it is far from a sufficient one.[11] Because

---

[9] "ἀνθρώποις γὰρ φῦσι καὶ παιδευθεῖσιν ὡς ἡμεῖς διήλθομεν, κατ' ἐμὴν δόξαν οὐκ ἔστ' ἄλλη ὀρθὴ παίδων τε καὶ γυναικῶν κτῆσίς τε καὶ χρεία ἢ κατ' ἐκείνην τὴν ὁρμὴν ἰοῦσιν, ἥνπερ τὸ πρῶτον ὡρμήσαμεν... ἀκολουθῶμεν τοίνυν καὶ τὴν γένεσιν καὶ τροφὴν παραπλησίαν ἀποδιδόντες, καὶ σκοπῶμεν εἰ ἡμῖν πρέπει ἢ οὔ" (451c–d).

[10] As Strauss puts it, "The question of possibility came to the fore only at the beginning of the fifth book as a consequence of an intervention initiated by Polemarchus. The two earlier comparable interventions—that of Glaucon after the description of the healthy city and that of Adeimantus after the abolition of private property and of privacy altogether—were limited to the question of desirability" (*The City and Man*, 122).

[11] Eva Brann gives a remarkably economical summary of what was established about the soul in Book IV. "There are then, to begin with, two parts,

the *telos* of *logismos* includes authority over the other parts (*thumos* and *epithumia*) of a just soul, understanding it involves also understanding a great deal about the whole soul, but it cannot answer at least one essential question: How does one develop a fully formed soul? Or, in simpler terms, how does one become just?

What we have in Books II and III under the guise of the education of the guardians is really an account of their proper characteristics—the full actualization of all their characteristic determinate potencies. If we were to carry the image of dogs into the contemporary context of breeding and dog shows, we could think of it as their "conformation." Beagles and Great Danes are held to different conformation standards, and breeders need to understand what each aims to be before they can undertake a plan to breed a dog to approach those standards. They need an account of what is desirable before they will be in a position to consider the conditions necessary for making the desirable actual. With apologies for the crass example, Books II–IV does the work of specifying (most of) the standards according to which a guardian should be judged (i.e., what is desirable); but it is not until Book V that Socrates begins to inquire into what would need to happen for such a guardian to come into being, (i.e., the conditions for actualizing what has already been determined desirable).

Because of the elaborate accounts of music and gymnastic in Books II and III, we know what needs to be true of the guardians and auxiliaries if they are to be capable of ruling and protecting

---

the rational part (*logistikon*) 'with which man calculates' (*logizetai*), and the desiring part (*epithymetikon*) which is unreasoning (*alogiston*) and in which desire (*epithymia*) is located (49d). Between these two, the forms (*eide*) that are ordinarily recognized, Socrates inserts a pivotal third, the spirited part (*thymoeides*)...Finally, these three parts are arranged within us as the "three terms of a musical proportion" (443d6), and *thymos* becomes "the in between power" (479d8), which, while itself obedient to reason, can in turn govern the body (403d, 411e6)" (*The Music of the Republic*, 162).

The Female Drama

the city in speech. And it is these same arguments in Books II and III that show us in Book IV what needs to be true of *thumos* and *logismos* if they are to be capable of ruling and protecting a just soul. But, neither the arguments of Books II and III nor their alignment with the soul in Book IV show what must be true of *thumos* and *logismos* in order for the soul to become just. That is the business of the Female Drama.

Books II–IV give us a target to shoot for, but no instruction in archery.[12] Socrates' answer to that question comes in Book VII and is a continuation of the accounts of the *genesis* and *trophe* that begin in Book V. All three of these modes of development (*genesis*, *trophe*, and *paideia*) are a part of what Socrates is here calling the Female Drama, and they were left out of the city/soul of Book IV.

My argument, in the briefest terms, is that the Male Drama is an account of the being and actualities of the just soul, and the Female Drama is an account of the becoming and potencies of the just soul (which open into a consideration of the activity of the most just soul, philosophy). What we know at the end of Book IV is what all of the parts of the soul need to look like in order for that soul to be just. What we begin to consider in Book V is what needs to be true of each part of the soul in order for it

---

[12] While I will later in this study consider the relationship between *logismos* and *nous* in the *Republic* in detail, it is important to notice that Socrates is careful only to refer to the former in Book IV. Once again, Brann's account is extremely helpful. "Why then does Socrates call it the *logistikon*, connecting it explicitly with *logizesthai*, to reckon or to calculate (439d5), rather than with the *logos* of *dialegesthai* (511b4, 534c)? It is because the *logistikon* is a restricted power, a power of planning, whose specific work later does turn out to be calculation (cf. *Nicomachean Ethics* 1139a13), measuring, and weighing—in short, whatever corresponds only to the lower level of knowing power, to that power of mathematical thinking which Glaucon will discover later on as a mean between opinion and knowledge; it will be called *dianoia*" (*The Music of the Republic*, 163–164).

to become what Book IV tells us it needs to be. And, as the Female Drama illuminates the Male Drama dialectically, the Male Drama, itself, will require revision. That is, the account of the *telos* of the just soul prompted the inquiry into the origin (*genesis*), nurture (*trophe*), and education (*paideia*) required to approach that *telos*. But when the *genesis*, *trophe*, and *paideia* of the just soul come into focus, they will illuminate things about the *telos* of justice that were not clear before. Generically, this is how Platonic/Socratic dialectic often operates. Specifically, it is the process by which the inquiry into the nature of justice turns toward the inquiry into the nature of philosophy in the *Republic*.

Socrates marks the beginning of the Female Drama by saying that we must return to the beginning of our account of the guardians and consider their *genesis* and *trophe* (451d). I think this is exactly what he does in Books V and VI. There are three sorts of possibility or becoming that are systematically presented in Books V–VII: *genesis*, *trophe*, and *paideia*, and these three are, for the most part, taken up in Books V, VI, and VII respectively. What this implies for the soul is straightforward, in principle, but extremely complicated in practice. Books V–VII will take up the potencies of soul necessary for the possibility of becoming just. The processes of becoming just will then move those potencies into actuality.

Socrates takes the conversation back to the beginning and turns our attention to what it would look like to introduce women and children into the city in speech. So, we find ourselves considering once again the dog-like disposition appropriate to potential guardians; but now we are prompted to consider the case of the female dogs. First, we are asked whether female dogs should be considered capable of becoming guard dogs. The answer is a quick yes, they should. This first point about female dogs is not argued, but merely just affirmed. The first claim to be scrutinized is the second one to be made. It constitutes an apparent implication of the capacity of the female dogs to become guard dogs, i.e., to become such female dogs whose nature should share everything with similarly disposed males (including their rearing or *trophe* and education or *paideia*, 451e).

The first principle of this further elaboration on the city/soul is that women and men can do the same work, and the first implication of this principle for the city in speech is that they should. This principle is no more argued than any of the principles that led to the organization of the cities constructed in Books II and III (i.e., insufficiency, efficiency, and desire). An immediate implication of the assertion that women can and should do the same work as men is that they should be prepared to do this work, just as men are. They should share the same rearing (*trophe*) and education (*paideia*), despite the fact that women are generally weaker than men.

When Socrates says that he must go back to the beginning to account for the role of women and children, he does not go back to the most necessary city or the healthy city or even to the structure of the feverish city. He goes to the first moment of the discussion of the nature of the guardians, which is the beginning of the construction of the purged city. This is the beginning of the account of women and children. This is where the distinction between male and female first matters.

Not every dog, male or female, will be born with a nature suited to be trained and educated as a guard dog, but some will. Therefore, by implication, maleness and femaleness cannot be categories Socrates uses to explain the *genesis* of justice. Whatever maleness and femaleness are to the soul, they are both compatible with the nature (*physis*) of the guardians. We should be prepared to see that the proper *genesis* of the guardians may distinguish guardians from auxiliaries and workers, but it will not distinguish males from females. In terms of moral psychology, the question then is: which parts or versions of the calculating[13] part of the soul (analogous to the guardians) are male and which are female; and what does maleness or femaleness mean in relation to *logismos*?

When Socrates said what would have to be done to give a fuller account of women and children in the city in speech, he said that he would have to go back and consider birth and rearing (*genesis* and *trophe*, 451d). Now, he says that female guard dogs (which will immediately be altered, by analogy, into human female guardians of the city in speech) should share completely in the upbringing and education (*trophe* and *paideia*) of the male guardians (451e). Taken together, these two passages indicate the formal relationship of maleness and femaleness to the three categories of potentiality and becoming (*genesis*, *trophe*, and *paideia*) that run through Books V–VII. *Genesis*, which would seem to mean "origin" in terms of procreation or breeding in this context, precedes the maleness and femaleness of the progeny. However,

---

[13] "Calculating" is the conventional translation for λογιστικός, and I will use it consistently. "Planning" or "logical" might be better, except that "calculating" has become so well-known, especially insofar as logic is understood to deal with validity (or internal consistency) and not with soundness. The *logismos* of the mind is what calculates the best set of arrangements, given some set of given conditions or premises. *Nous* is the power of mind to apprehend the truth or well-foundedness of those conditions or premises (and thus the soundness of those arrangements), but the psychology of Book IV does not include *nous*. The soul of Book IV is capable of knowing that its arrangements are valid, but is completely cut off from knowing if they are sound because it has no access to a reference point for determining whether or not something is true, i.e., it has no access to the Good. When I use "calculating" to describe a psychological power, I mean something very much like, perhaps precisely like, its logical capacity to determine the validity, but not the soundness, of a psychological arrangement. It is the part that can optimize a plan given a set of elements, but it cannot evaluate those elements except according to how well they fit together.

the specifications of *genesis* relevant to the potential to become guardians is shared by women and men. Moreover, when it comes to *trophe* and *paideia*, female guardians should be treated just like males and included in every way.

The Risk of Eristic

The next two sections of the argument happen in reverse order. First, Socrates moves to what I take to be the crucial problem of this section of Book V: the apparent ridiculousness of the proposal to educate men and women the same and together (452a–d). Secondly, the dialogue returns to defend the original organizing principle of this elaboration on the city/soul, i.e., that women and men can and should do the same work. (452e–456c). Then, after establishing that what they are proposing is possible, the interlocutors move to the question of whether sharing all work between women and men is best (456c–457a). Only then does Socrates return to the claim that because the proposal for women and men to be educated together is both possible and best, one should ignore those who say it is ridiculous (457a–b).

Much of the argument of this section takes the form of Socrates responding to an objection that he himself raises. The way the objection is presented suggests that Socrates is unwilling to proceed until it is answered, even though none of the interlocutors raised it.[14] The objection is that since men and women are

---

[14] David Wolfsdorf argues that the imaginary interlocutor Socrates engages in this section is less metaphysically sophisticated than Glaucon and must be convinced by arguments that do not rely on the distinction between ideas and those things that participate in them. For Wolfsdorf, the reason for introducing the imaginary interlocutor is to give Socrates a reason to use a form of argument that would be inappropriate for Glaucon. This does not seem right to me. The room is full of interlocutors, and Plato's mind is full of people with whom he could have populated the room. There must be some other reason to introduce an imaginary interlocutor, and I think it is to signal

different, and since we established in Book II that different citizens were suited for different sorts of work (the principle of efficiency, introduced at 370c), it must follow that men and women should do different work (453c). This is a centrally important objection because, so far, the interlocutors have only added to the model of the city/soul through their conversation; they have not reversed themselves substantially regarding the nature of any of its structural elements. If a more thorough explanation of the role of women and children in the city/soul ends up contradicting what has already been established, the interlocutors will be in trouble. Socrates admits, in fact, that they are lost at sea, but that perhaps they can hope for an unlikely rescue; maybe by a dolphin or that perhaps their little ship might withstand the storm (453d).[15]

Socrates' response to his own objection has two parts: first, Socrates investigates the nature of the differences between women and men; secondly, he asks what relevance these natural

---

that this is an issue that is particularly important to Socrates. See Wolfsdorf's "Plato's Conception of Knowledge," *The Classical World* 105, no. 1 (Fall 2011): 57–75.

[15] It is interesting that Socrates mentions a dolphin specifically in his account of what their possible rescue might look like. This could be an allusion to Apollo, since he took the form of a dolphin to escape the island where he was born, Delos, and make it to his sanctuary on the mainland, hence its name, "Delphi." It could also be an allusion to the dolphin that rescued the invisible goddess, Aphaia, whom, though obscure, Plato would have known well if he spent some of his childhood on Aegina, as some believe he did. See Diogenes Laertius. *Lives of the Eminent Philosophers*, James Miller, ed. and Pamela Mensch, trans. (New York: Oxford University Press, 2018), 3.1. The story of Arion from Herodotus might be in play here, as well, as Townsend suggests (*The Woman Question in Plato's Republic*, 35). There could be a Homeric allusion to this shipwreck, as well, although Leukothea, not a dolphin, rescued Odysseus from the sea in Book 5 of the *Odyssey*. All of these possibilities are provocative, but since the dolphin does not appear again, it is difficult to know what work it is doing in the dialogue.

differences have to the sort of work that women and men can and should do in the city in speech. It is in the first part of his response to his own objection that Socrates offers his famous and important distinction between *dialectic* and *eristic* (454a). In *dialectic*, interlocutors engage in conversation to get to the truth. They may be impassioned and deeply committed to their positions, but ultimately they would rather be proven wrong than maintain a false opinion. In *eristic*, interlocutors just want to win; they are more attached to winning than to finding out the truth. At the moment, and according to Socrates, they are in danger of falling into *eristic* if they do not look behind the words they are using to recall the meaning of those words and the role they play in the inquiry. This warning operates on two levels: first, it helps the interlocutors respond successfully to Socrates' objection that giving women and men the same work violates the principle of efficiency. But, secondly, it also serves as a warning to the interlocutors (and to Plato's readers) regarding the dangers of this section of the *Republic*. The larger warning will be clearer if we deal with the smaller one first.

If one operates on the surface of the two claims that are opposed in the objection Socrates raises, then one faces a big problem. We established in Book II that citizens with different natures are suited to different work. We asserted in Book V that women and men should do the same work (even though women and men have different natures). Therefore, it seems we can either hold fast to the old principle (different natures imply different work) or the new principle (women and men, despite their different natures, should do the same work), but not to both. But if one asks what sorts of differences are relevant to one's work, then there appears to be a way out of the dilemma. If we are attempting to determine whether citizens should be shoemakers or guardians (454b–c), then surely it doesn't matter whether citizens are bald or have long hair. If the natural difference between women and men is like the natural difference between long haired people and bald people, then the problem posed in the objection is merely semantic and not worth our concern (if we are committed to *dialectic* rather than *eristic*).[16]

Socrates then turns to the second part of the argument, which asks: are the differences between men and women relevant to the work they pursue (454e)? And the answer is: apparently not. The commonplace that all the interlocutors agree to in this passage is that even though there may be certain arts (*techne*) such as baking and weaving that we could quibble about, and even though there may be individual exceptions, in general, men are better at everything than women (455c–d). But, the argument continues, it does not make sense for men to do everything in the city and for women to do nothing, so the principle of male superiority in all things actually supports the position of educating women in all things. Plus, women are competent in all things, even if they are not equal to men (456b). For these reasons, Socrates concludes that they were right to say that women and men should be educated together.[17]

---

[16] This part of Socrates' argument is sometimes used to credit Plato with being the first feminist, a claim Julia Annas, among others, rejects outright. She argues that "his arguments are unacceptable to a feminist, and that the proposals made in Republic V are irrelevant to contemporary debate." See Annas's "Plato's Republic and Feminism," *Philosophy* 51 (1976): 307–321.

[17] Several commentators have noticed that Socrates' revision to the status of women does not make them equal to men so much as it makes them identical to them, and yet inferior. Arlene Saxonhouse frames it this way: "Sexual equality is tied to the destruction of what is separate, what is other. On the one hand, in Greek thought the female had always stood for what is private and other. By equating the male and the female, the public and the private are made one. There is no 'other.' But, more basically, the female suggests the divisiveness of the human species, that we are indeed not all the same, that there *is* something that is other. In order to create the unified city, Socrates

The Female Drama

There is a larger issue operating in this section, though. The interlocutors do not only risk falling into *eristic* on the question of whether or not the differences between men and women demand that they do different work. They risk the whole inquiry devolving into *eristic*. Socrates has been clear since the introduction of the city/soul in Book II that the purpose of the model is to aid in their inquiry into the nature of the human soul, the place of justice within it, and the relative choice worthiness of justice and injustice for a human life. But the question posed at the beginning of Book V that Polemarchus, Adeimantus, Glaucon, and Thrasymachus insisted Socrates answer does not seem to be motivated by their interest in the soul. They thought a full account of women and children had been left out of the city in speech, but was their concern based on the usefulness of an account of women and children to their inquiry into the nature of justice for individuals, or were they focused on a concern for the paradigm itself? The latter seems to be more plausible.

Not only do none of the interlocutors mention the soul explicitly when they insist Socrates compose what he calls the Female Drama, but none of their arguments even seem to allude to the soul by analogy or otherwise. One of the reasons that it is so difficult to see what women and children signify for the structure

---

must destroy the female as female, the female as a threat to the unity of the human species. She is integrated into the political community not as herself, as one with distinctive talents or distinctive experiences, but as an inferior male, a physically weaker male." See Arlene Saxonhouse, *Women in the History of Political Thought: Ancient Greece to Machiavelli*. (Westport: Praeger Publishers, 1985), 47–48. Townsend puts it like this: "All this puts women in a very strange metaphysical position, no less strange than their resulting political one; it demotes them even as it raises them. Their situation is not that of women whose goodness is finally acknowledged as justice might demand; rather they have been given the status of lesser men, people who possess all the qualities of men but in a lesser degree" (*The Woman Question in Plato's Republic*, 38).

and activity of the soul in the *Republic* is that it is nowhere made explicit in the beginning of Book V how a more detailed explanation of women and children in the city in speech will contribute to the psychological inquiry they agreed to undertake together. Those accounts do not begin to emerge until late in Book VI. All four of Socrates' most powerful and vocal interlocutors in the *Republic* seem to be in danger of falling from *dialectic* to *eristic* by attaching themselves to the literal meanings of the elements of the city in speech and forgetting or neglecting what makes them relevant to their shared inquiry.

Socrates' warning against devolving into *eristic* is explicitly aimed at his imaginary interlocutor who claims to have found an internal contradiction in the constitution of the city in speech, but I also read it to be an implicit warning to Adeimantus, Polemarchus, Thrasymachus, and especially Glaucon. I understand it to be a warning to the readers of the *Republic*, as well. If we want to continue to engage in *dialectic*, which may lead us to the truth, and not *eristic*, we must remember the meanings of our terms and what roles they play in our inquiry. We must try not to get lost in semantics, surface meanings, or side concerns.

The Dangerous Turn Toward What's Best

Socrates' warning about what could divert us from dialectic may serve as a heuristic for approaching the *Republic*, and especially its most confusing arguments. When we seem to be talking about ridiculous or implausible things, it will serve us well to recall how we got to that part of the argument, from where its terms were derived, and what work we were supposed to be doing. But I believe there is another heuristic of sorts introduced in this section, as well, and it is even more subtle. At 456c, Socrates claims to have shown that it is possible for women to do the same work as men and, therefore, for men and women to be educated together.

Immediately afterwards, he shifts his focus to a consideration of whether educating men and women together is best. This seems like a sensible and obvious argumentative development: first show that education in common is possible, then show that it is optimal. But this is not how any of the elements in the city in speech have been established before. Throughout Books II, III, and IV we considered the desirability, but not the possibility of each institutional arrangement. Is it possible to constitute a city with only four or five individuals? Probably not. Could we find the perfect balance of citizens with natural talents for each task in the city—each of whom does his work and only his work so that we could constitute a healthy city? Almost certainly not. If we let desires run amok (as in the fevered city) could we set up institutional arrangements and find sufficiently wise leaders to moderate and balance that city into a purged, harmonious whole? Also extremely unlikely.

But even though the cities in speech of Books II through IV are as implausible as the city in speech emerging in Book V, the possibility of constituting them was never at issue in the dialogue. What explains this, I believe, is the relative plausibility of the souls analogous to the cities in speech in Books II–IV versus the soul analogous to the city in speech that is beginning to emerge in Book V. If we shift our focus to the soul, the prescriptions for shaping up a life of justice are certainly demanding, but they are not implausible. One must cultivate *logismos* so that it is capable of determining the proper internal balances between itself, *thumos*, and *epithumia*. *Logismos* and *thumos* must be allied so that *epithumia* can be controlled and directed toward the good of the whole. These are no small tasks, but they are intelligible and even, to a degree, manageable.

There is also no expectation of a perfect achievement of virtue in the city/soul of Books II through IV. The model seems to suggest that the more you achieve the proper interrelationships and internal balances of soul that come to be known as the virtues, the better. The work one should be doing to become virtuous seems fairly clear and the hope for progress seems fairly reasonable. This is a workable model of the soul on its face, regardless of how far-fetched the political analogues might be. In that sense, there is no need for Socrates to defend its possibility.

The city/soul of Book V is different not because the political arrangements it describes are less plausible but because their psychological analogues are. Despite the specter of Sparta that always seems to float around descriptions of the city/soul in the *Republic*, it is indeed difficult to imagine how even these first institutions of the city in speech that will come to be known as parts of the Kallipolis will be established and maintained. All of the practical problems of the earlier cities in speech persist, e.g., such as how one could accurately and consistently determine what sort of nature and thus education each baby proto-citizen would best be suited for. Another problem is that given the fact that our legislative goal is to create a happy city and not necessarily happy citizens (although this will follow if the happiness of the city is perfectly instantiated), then it is unclear how the potentially unhappy people will continue to work well at and focus solely on their exclusive tasks. This is just the low-hanging fruit. The practical problems inherent in this political model are multitudinous. However, the problems inherent in the psychological model introduced in Book V are worse.

Unlike the city/soul of Books II through IV, where the political arrangements were far-fetched but the psychological analogues were more plausible, Kallipolis is less plausible as a soul than as a city.

As I have already noted, at 451d Socrates casts the task of giving a fuller explanation of women and children in the city in speech as the challenge of accounting for the *genesis* and *trophe* of the guardians. And as he begins this account, he immediately adds education *paideia* to the list of things about the guardians that this elaboration on the city in speech will have to include. So, we must ask: What is the disposition or original condition (*genesis*) of a soul capable of becoming just? What sort of rearing (*trophe*) prepares such a well-disposed soul for education? And, what sort of education (*paideia*) will move a well-disposed, well-formed soul to the actualization of justice?

When we ask about conditions for the possibility of something coming into being, we bring the definition of the thing for which they are the conditions into our consideration; at least implicitly. The conditions for the actualization of a thing is a teleological consideration, which implies at least a provisional or inchoate idea of the *telos* of that thing. This dynamic created by the connection in our minds between the minimal conditions specified in a definition and the *telos* those conditions imply plays a central role in the constitution of Kallipolis—the noble and beautiful city in speech that is begun after the interruption at the beginning of Book V. The consideration of conditions opens up, by implication, a consideration of the thing for which those conditions are conditions. Now that the interlocutors have begun to consider the minimal conditions for the possibility of justice, the conversation opens to a consideration of the *telos* of justice.

The risk that Socrates seems to fear most acutely at the beginning of Book V is the danger of corrupting his friends. If Glaucon or the others see Kallipolis for what it is—a paradigm that could orient their ambitions to become just—and if they commit themselves to an attempt to approach the Good, then their successes and failures in that pursuit are not likely to be terribly dangerous. The model of the best life, like the model constructed in Books II through IV, will serve as their target, but there may be nothing inherently problematic about a life that misses the mark while keeping it in sight and attempting to get closer to it with every "shot," regardless of how one might lament one's failures.

On the other hand, if Socrates' interlocutors (or Plato's readers) see that the realm of conventional justice is not truly authoritative, and moreover, if they do not (for whatever reason) attach themselves to any higher authority, then they will be both politically powerful and morally unfettered. Socrates' attempts to contribute to the improvement of his interlocutors' souls cannot help but risk corrupting them in, perhaps, the worst possible way. If they cannot see the authority of the Good for their lives, or if they willfully choose to ignore it, they could be diverted from the project of trying to live a good and reasonable life approximating virtue. They could veer toward a life that embraces injustice, vice, and dissipation. They might not see or care to acknowledge that such a choice would bear any substantial costs, and they might not scratch beneath the veneer that makes such a choice appear to carry with it obvious benefits. The great is often the enemy of the Good, and Socrates knows it only too well. By taking the risk of having great ambitions for the souls of his interlocutors, Socrates might make the more modest, less dangerous, and more conventional ambitions that approximate goodness in human life appear less choice-worthy and perhaps even unacceptable.

The threat of war and Athens' inevitable defeat looms in the background of the *Republic*.[18] The ghosts of Alcibiades and Critias, Socrates' most infamous followers, lurk not too deeply in the shadows, as well. As Socrates shows, Glaucon, Adeimantus, Polemarchus, and Thrasymachus (who certainly already knows) how to detach themselves from convention in order to attach

---

[18] See Debra Nails, *The People of Plato* (Indianapolis: Hackett Publishing, 2002), 324–326 for a summary of debates regarding the dramatic dating.

themselves to the Good. Socrates shows the way for them to become psychologically and politically tyrannical. Perhaps, this is what happened to Alcibiades and Critias. Therefore, and as Plato appears to suggest, the promise of educating them for philosophy seemed to be worth the risk.

Weathering the First Wave

The risks of composing the Female Drama are significant, but they are also necessary. Socrates cannot keep faith with his interlocutors without responding to their questions about women and children, and there is an important part of the story of the soul that has not yet been told. Socrates returns, after his brief excursus on *dialectic* and *eristic*, to the claim that women and men should train and be educated together. Or, more specifically, he returns to a consideration of what an instituting of this principle will look like and how one should react to those who will oppose it.

When Socrates introduced the idea that women and men should pursue their physical training together, the first prompt he gave to Glaucon was to admit that what he was proposing seemed ridiculous (452a). In fact, Socrates didn't just ask for an affirmation from Glaucon that he shared the view that the instantiation of this principle would look ridiculous, he pressed him to think through what its *most* ridiculous implications would be. This is not a question that was asked about any of the previous cities in speech, although it could have been. For example, there would have been nothing absurd about Socrates asking: "what would be the most ridiculous aspects of trying to constitute a city with only four or five men?" or "could we really expect each person to do precisely the work they were best at and only that work?" Why is Socrates bringing forward these apparently ridiculous implications of trying to instantiate the city in speech? Why now?

If the Female Drama tells the story of how a soul may become just, then it should begin with the sort of conditions that must exist in order for that process of becoming to commence. This is what I believe is beginning to happen when Socrates asks Glaucon to focus on the ridiculousness of the proposal that women and men should train together. In every society, the conventions of public behavior tend to be formidable. Practices that may once have been a matter of choice or legislation become ingrained over time and enacted unselfconsciously by many members of that society. Others may be more self-conscious but believe there are rational justifications for maintaining conventional practices whether or not they find them rational. Resisting ingrained conventions tends to be difficult and to come at a high social cost.

If one aspires to be just in the city or the soul, then one must be capable of resisting convention intellectually and in practice. Intellectually, one must be able to see conventions for what they are; affirm them when they serve the good; and resist them when they do not. In practice, one must be able to withstand the resistance that inevitably will come from those for whom convention is more powerful. In the soul, that resistance comes from habit. In the city in speech, it might come from those who found unconventional behaviors ridiculous.

Socrates' point appears to be that a soul that will be capable of training and education for virtue will be the soul that can manage, among other things, the difficult business of being unconventional. This is precisely the lesson that Socrates emphasizes to Glaucon in their consideration of women and men exercising together. That is, in what will soon be named "the first wave"

(457a). If training men and women together is the best thing for the city in speech, then one must not be deterred by those who call it ridiculous. Nor should one be moved by the part of oneself that sees it as ridiculous. The part of oneself that understands it to be right must be in control.

In large part this provision is clear in Book IV where Socrates emphasized the nature of the guardians and *logismos*, and virtue's requirement that it rule in the city/soul. This account in Book V is entirely harmonious with what was presented in Book IV, but it shows the dynamic from a different angle. In Book IV, Socrates elaborated on the necessity of the rule of the calculating part of the soul. Here, in Book V, the emphasis is on the capacity of the other parts of the soul to be ruled. Successfully controlling the desire to laugh at the ridiculousness of old men and women exercising together is Socrates' image for surviving the first wave. Psychologically, it depicts *logismos* properly containing *epithumia*, which implies both a sufficiently strong calculating faculty (which was treated in the Male Drama) and a sufficiently containable appetitive faculty (which is what is now added to the account by way of the Female Drama).

It is possible to know what is good and yet not to act on it when there are parts of your soul that are stronger than the part that knows what is good. Here, Plato anticipates what, in Book VII of the *Nicomachean Ethics*, Aristotle calls *akrasia*. One can both know the right thing and be dissipated beyond the capacity to act on that knowledge. There are many ways to become one for whom right reason, or even knowledge, is insufficient to guide action. Drug addiction is the easiest example. It is a commonplace that addicts can talk sensibly about their misguided choices; can lament their dissipation; can decide to do what they know to be right; but can then succumb over and over again to urges that overwhelm their resolve. For addicts the lesson is clear: knowing what is good is a necessary condition for virtue, but it is not always sufficient for putting it into practice.[19]

Knowing that it is best to create a training regimen for men and women together is not sufficient for institutionalizing that arrangement in the city in speech. Having the most knowledgeable person in charge of instituting the right plan is also not sufficient. In addition, the rest of the city must be capable of being led toward arrangements that they may find ridiculous. The psychological analogue to this is that one who hopes to be trained and educated for virtue must be capable of overcoming those instincts and habits that are not virtuous, according to the calculating part of the soul, and in such a way that would be best for the whole. One's *thumos* must be willing to align itself with *logismos*. One's *epithumia* must be containable. This is the first lesson of the Female Drama. We have weathered the first wave.

Bibliography

Annas, Julia. "Plato's Republic and Feminism," *Philosophy* vol. 51 (1976): 307–321.

Blitz, Mark. *Plato's Political Philosophy*. Baltimore: John Hopkins University Press, 2010.

Bloom, Allan, "Interpretive Essay" in Plato's Republic. New York: Basic Books, 1968, 307–436.

Brann, Eva. *The Music of the Republic*. Philadelphia: Paul Dry, 2004.

Clay, Diskin. *Platonic Questions: Dialogues with the Silent Philosopher*. University Park: Pennsylvania State University Press, 2000.

Craig, Leon Harold. *The War Lover: A Study of Plato's Republic*. Toronto: University of Toronto Press, 1996.

Diogenes Laertius, Pamela Mensch, and James Miller. *Lives of the Eminent Philosophers*. Edited by James Miller. Translated by Pamela Mensch. New York: Oxford University Press, 2018.

---

[19] For an account of how the structure of the tripartite soul in the *Republic* implies the existence of *akrasia*, see Michael Morris "Akrasia in the Protagoras and the Republic," *Phronesis* 51, no. 3 (2006): 195–229.

Elshtain, Jean Bethke. *Public Man, Private Woman: Women in Social and Political Thought*. Princeton: Princeton University Press, 1981.

Forde, Steven. "Gender and Justice in Plato." *American Political Science Review* 92, no. 3 (1997): 657–670.

Gardner, Catherine. "The Remnants of the Family: The Role of Women and Eugenics in Republic V." History of Philosophy Quarterly 17, no. 3 (July 1, 2000): 217–235.

Hildebrandt, Kurt. *Platon: Logos Und Mythos*. De Gruyter, 1959.

Howland, Jacob. *The Republic: The Odyssey of Philosophy*. Philadelphia: Paul Dry, 2004.

Lampert, Laurence. *How Philosophy Became Socratic: A Study of Plato's Protagoras Charmides, and Republic*. Chicago: University of Chicago Press, 2010.

McKeen, Catherine. "Why Women Must Guard and Rule in Plato's 'Kallipolis.'" Pacific Philosophical Quarterly 87, no. 4 (December 1, 2006): 527–548.

Morris, Michael. "*Akrasia* in the *Protagoras* and the *Republic*." *Phronesis* vol. 5, no. 3 (2006): 205–206.

Nails Debra. *The People of Plato*. Indianapolis: Hackett Publishing, 2002.

———. "Plato in its Athenian Context." *History of Political Thought*, 33, no. 1 (Spring 2012): 1–23.

Nussbaum, Martha. *The Fragility of Goodness*. Cambridge: Cambridge University Press, 1983.

Okin, Susan Miller. "Philosopher Queens and Private Wives: Plato on Women and the Family." Philosophy and Public Affairs, 6 (Summer 1977): 345–369

Roochnik, David. *Beautiful City: The Dialectical Character of Plato's Republic*. Ithaca: Cornell University Press, 2003.

Rosen, Stanley. *Plato's Republic: A Study*. New Haven: Yale University Press, 2005.

Saxonhouse, Arlene W. "Comedy in the Callipolis." *American Political Science Review* 72, no. 3 (September 1978): 888–901.

Saxonhouse, Arlene W. *Women in the History of Political Thought: Ancient Greece to Machiavelli*. Westport: Praeger Publishers, 1985.

Strauss, Leo. *The City and Man*. Chicago: The University of Chicago Press, 1978.

Townsend, Mary. *The Woman Question in Plato's* Republic. New York: Lexington Books, 2017.

Voegelin, Eric. *Order and History, Volume III: Plato and Aristotle*. Baton Rouge: Louisiana State Press, 1957.

Wolfsdorf, David. "Plato's Conception of Knowledge." *The Classical World*, 105, no. 1 (Fall 2011): 57–75.
Zuckert, Catherine H. *Plato's Philosophers: The Coherence of the Dialogues*. Chicago: University of Chicago Press, 2009.

THE SOUL, VIRTUE, AND WOMEN'S NATURE IN FIRST-GENERATION SOCRATICS

Cinzia Arruzza

Introduction

In book 1 of the *Politics* (1260a20–31), Aristotle attacks the view that the virtue of man and woman is the same, holding instead that virtue is intrinsically tied to both the nature and the status of the different constituents of the household and the city. Approvingly quoting Sophocles' Ajax, he comments that "silence is an appropriate ornament for a woman," but that "this is not the case for man" (1260a30–31). Aristotle's distinction between virtues based on social role was fundamentally in line with traditional popular understandings of virtue. From Plato's *Meno* (73a–e), we also gather that Gorgias may have endorsed and systematized this popular view. In the passage mentioned above, Aristotle ascribes the contrary thesis, that the virtue of man and woman is the same, to Socrates. Moreover, his reference to Gorgias' position suggests that the discussion of this issue in Plato's *Meno* must have been one of the polemical targets of his critique.

Yet, the thesis that the virtue of man and woman is the same was not defended only by Plato's Socrates. We find it explicitly ascribed to Antisthenes by Diogenes Laertius[1] and, despite the absence of fragments or testimonies reporting this claim, we can

---

[1] For Antisthenes I provide reference to the ancient source reporting the fragment or testimony and —between brackets—to Gabriele Giannantoni's edition in *Socratis et Socraticorum Reliquiae*, (Naples: Bibliopolis, 1991). Here: Diogenes Laertius, 6.12 (= V A 134.15). All translations from the Greek are mine.

gather that Aeschines shared this same belief from the extant fragments of his lost dialogue *Aspasia*, in which Socrates provides examples of women endowed with rhetorical, political, and military excellence.[2] In Xenophon's *Symposium* (2.9 and 2.11–12), we find the claim that women are not inferior in nature and are endowed with the same capacity for learning as men. Finally, in *Oeconomicus* 7 we find that women have an equal capacity for self-control and rulership as men (although, in the case of women, this ability is exercised in the *oikos*). While there are significant differences in these thinkers' development and defense of it, the underlying claim that virtue is the same for men and women appears to have been shared by several first-generation Socratics. Consequently, although this cannot ultimately be proved, it is plausible that the claim was part of the historical Socrates' own teachings.

In the passage from the *Politics*, Aristotle indicates that this Socratic claim is tightly connected to the thesis that virtue consists in the good condition of the soul (ὅτι τὸ εὖ ἔχειν τὴν ψυχὴν ἀρετή, 1260a26), which he also rejects as deceptive. Aristotle's diagnosis is correct: the Socratics' internalization of virtue, conceived of as a property of a *soul* distinct from the body, enabled them to develop highly unconventional views about women's nature and their ability to acquire the same virtues as men. Thus, the Socratics' revaluation of ethical values countered the traditional distinction between man's and woman's virtue by decoupling virtue from the status and social function one played within the household and city and attaching it to the soul. To put the preceding point in another way, the key Socratic innovation that made it possible to think that virtue is not a function of social

---

[2] In support of this reading of the dialogue, see Heinrich Dittmar, *Aischines von Sphettos: Studien zur Literaturgeschichte der Sokratiker* (Berlin: Weidemann, 1912).

position is their reconceptualization of what counts as inner (i.e., a person's soul) and its sharp distinction from the body and from external goods and circumstances (now reconceptualized as the "outer" or even as the "alien"). By carving a new conceptual space for thinking of interiority, the Socratics could rethink moral agency by ascribing virtues to the soul independently of assigned social status or function. Moreover, as bodily sexual difference became irrelevant to the consideration of what virtue is, they could then claim that virtue is the same for men and women. The connection between these unconventional views about women and the conception of the soul as the seat of moral agency distinct from the body is explicit in the discussion of the inclusion of talented women into the class of guardians in book 5 of the *Republic* (453a–455a). We do not have the same degree of clarity in the textual evidence concerning the other Socratics. Yet, in this article, I argue that the internalization of ἀρετή as a property the soul ought to be taken as the implicit assumption of Antisthenes' and Xenophon's thinking on the topic of women. I first briefly discuss popular understandings of ἀρετή in the fifth century. Then I turn to an analysis of Antisthenes' attack on conventional morality and reconceptualization of virtue in general, which offers one of the clearest examples of the Socratic internalization of virtue. Against this background, I then assess his claim that virtue is the same for men and women. Finally, I turn to Xenophon to argue that, although his theory of sexual complementarity and his consideration for the role played by the body and its relation to the soul lead him to retain distinct predispositions and roles for men and women, he does not think this entails an in-kind distinction between male and female virtue, insofar as virtue is still conceptualized as a property of the soul.

Virtue and the Soul in Fifth-Century Literature

Broadly speaking, the fifth-century popular conception of ἀρετή before Socrates was characterized by two key aspects: First, ἀρετή was not primarily referred to as a state of a "soul" that was sharply distinguished from the body. Second, ἀρετή was predicated upon the social and political status of its presumed bearers. With the emergence of the classical *polis*, the standard exemplar of ἀρετή became the male citizen who contributed to the wellbeing and prosperity of the κοινωνία of citizens by virtue of his roles as a landlord and a warrior.[3] A future citizen would be educated to the ἀρετή specific to his social and political position through his socialization within the city's institutions. This socialization was achieved through practices such as military drills, observance of civic laws, participation in religious festivals, and everyday association with adult citizens in public spaces such as the *gymnasia*. As Simonides put it: "The city is man's teacher" (πόλις ἄνδρα διδάσκει)."[4] Protagoras' speech in Plato's eponymous dialogue (320c–323a) is illustrative of this imbrication between ἀρετή and civic life. Plato's Protagoras presents a foundational myth for the Greek *polis* in which the universal distribution of the virtue of justice and of the emotion of respect (αἰδώς) is presented as the necessary condition for associated life. In this speech, the city's laws and institutions are conceptualized as teachers of ἀρετή.[5]

---

[3] See Joseph Bryant, *Moral Codes and Social Structure in Ancient Greece: A Sociology of Greek Ethics from Homer to the Epicureans and Stoics* (Albany: SUNY Press, 1996), 190–191 and Margalit Finkelberg, "On the City-State Concept of Arete," *The American Journal of Philology* 123, no. 1 (2002): 35–49.

[4] Simonides, f. 15, in West, M. L. (ed.) *Iambi et elegi Graeci ante Alexandrum cantati. 2: Callinus. Mimnermus. Semonides. Solon. Tyrtaeus. Minora adespota* (Oxford: Clarendon Press, 1972).

[5] On the politicized morality of fifth-century Athens, see chapter 3 in Mario Vegetti's, *L'etica degli antichi* (Rome-Bari: Laterza 2007).

The link between ἀρετή and social benefit tied its conceptualization inextricably to the social roles of its bearers. According to this fifth-century view, ἀρετή was primarily the prerogative of free citizens based on their distinctive contribution to the *polis*. While other constituents of the city could also contribute to the wellbeing of the community, their contribution was mediated by their subordinated social status. Thus, the ability of women, foreigners, and slaves to capably fulfill their function amounted to a form of ἀρετή that was considered to be fundamentally different in kind from the ἀρετή expected from a citizen.

The conceptual linkage between social role and ἀρετή in the popular fifth-century understanding facilitated the identification of ἀρετή with external goods and actions while precluding its conceptualization as a purely inner state. εὐδαιμονία was also associated with wealth, political power, honor, and household prosperity, rather than an inner state of bliss. The close connection between the possession of excellence and competitive success characteristic of the fifth century's ethical outlook is exemplified in the standard definition of justice voiced by Polemarchus in book 1 of Plato's *Republic*: "to harm one's enemies and benefit one's friends" (*Rep.* 332d). As argued by Bruno Snell, pre-Socratic literature never decoupled ἀρετή and ἀγαθός from the notions of the advantageous or of profit: ἀρετή and ἀγαθός denoted the qualities that a man must possess in order to achieve success within the community. Crucially, this success was measured by external markers, with wealth and good reputation among the most relevant.[6]

Although there are some relevant internal differences in the way individual Socratics reconceptualized virtue, by and large, the Socratic philosophers opposed both the identification of

---

[6] See chapter 8 in Bruno Snell, *The Discovery of the Mind: The Greek Origins of European Thought* (Cambridge: Harvard University Press, 1953).

ἀρετή with external goods or circumstances and its specification according to social roles. *Contra* the popular fifth century understanding, the Socratics internalized virtue as a property of the soul. This revisionist undertaking was predicated on their elaboration of a robust notion of the soul (ψυχή) as both distinct from the body and as the seat of moral agency.

By the last decades of the fifth century, the term ψυχή had already taken on a variety of nuanced meanings.[7] Alongside its traditional meaning of life-force or after-life shadow, the term had come to indicate the seat of strong emotions (such as grief and anger) and of desires (such as the desire for food).[8] Additionally, ψυχή was identified with the seat of courage[9] and the bearer of moral qualities, and was used as a synonym for character.[10] Eschatological Pythagorean[11] and Orphic doctrines may have contributed to the attribution to ψυχή of features characterizing personality through their doctrines of the immortality and transmigration of the soul.

The soul/body (ψυχή/σῶμα) couple appeared prominently for the first time in early medical treatises and in Democritus' ethical fragments, both of which articulated a psychosomatic therapy of the soul.[12] As David Claus argues, this therapeutic

---

[7] For a study of earlier meanings of ψυχή, see D. J. Furley, "The early history of the concept of soul," *Bulletin of the Institute of Classical Studies*, 3 (1956): 1–18; Jan N. Bremmer, *The Early Greek Concept of the Soul* (Princeton: Princeton University Press, 1983); and David Claus, *Toward the Soul: An Inquiry into the Meaning of Ψυχή Before Plato* (New Haven and London: Yale University Press, 1981).

[8] Euripides' *Ion*, 1170 and Aristophanes' *Birds* vv. 1557–98.

[9] Pindar, *Pythian*, 1.47–8; the view of the soul as the seat of courage is especially prominent in the Hippocratic *Airs, Waters, Places*, chapter 23.

[10] Thucydides, 2.40.3; Pindar, *Second Olympian* 2.68–70.

[11] Xenophanes, fr. 7, KR&S 260.

[12] The distinction ψυχή/σῶμα also appears in Lysias 24.3 and Antiphon 5.

project was predicated upon the ontological continuity between soul and body and placed the general health of soul and body (rather than merely that of the soul) as its goal.[13] Granting Claus's argument, these doctrines represent the soul as the subject of moral admonition and as the locus of genuine *eudaimonia*.[14] Such a view marks a sharp divergence from the conventional association of *eudaimonia* with external goods and characterization of the soul as a mere animating life-force. This insight, as we will see, was radicalized by first-generation Socratics, who elaborated a view of ethics distinct from popular fifth-century views of civic virtue and replaced the prosperous citizen with the unassailable and self-sufficient sage as a moral exemplar.

Virtue is the Same for Man and Woman: Antisthenes' Revaluation of ἀρετή and εὐδαιμονία

The Socratic critique of popular understandings of virtue is particularly evident in the fragments and testimonies we have of Antisthenes' works and teaching. Antisthenes' thought is characterized by his disregard of convention, the idealization of the self-sufficient sage, and a staunch critique of Athenian politics. In Antisthenes' ethical theory, the pursuit of virtue through toil, endurance, and the search for truth is the highest activity in life and the only human access point to the higher pleasures and *eudaimonia*. Antisthenes distinguishes these higher pleasures from the enjoyment of material and conventional goods, which can destroy the virtuous person's freedom when unguided by reason. For ex-

---

[13] See Claus, *Toward the Soul*, 142–148.
[14] Democritus fr. B 170; B171.

ample, in Xenophon's *Symposium*, Antisthenes favorably contrasts the pleasure of drawing from the treasure of his soul to bodily enjoyment through material possessions.[15]

While Antisthenes emphasizes the prominence of the soul over the body, as already noted by Susan Prince, the status of ψυχή in his thought remains unclear.[16] In particular, it is unclear whether Antisthenes conceived of ψυχή as separable (rather than merely distinct) from the body. Such a view would posit an ontological difference between soul and body absent from medical treatises and from Democritus' fragments. It would, furthermore, imply the soul's immortality. Despite these ambiguities, it can be safely argued that Antisthenes' soul is the moral agent within us through which we attain knowledge, wisdom, and virtue. While exercising the body does appear as an integral part of the acquisition of virtue, the latter is conceived of as a state of the soul. In addition to virtue, *eudaimonia* is also conceived as a condition of the soul. In sum, the goal of Antisthenes' ethical theory is the wellbeing of the soul and its achievement of an unassailable state.[17]

Like his Socratic inspiration, Antisthenes emphasizes the key role wisdom (φρόνησις) plays as an infallible guide in orienting the life of the virtuous sage. While some of the sayings

---

[15] Xenophon, *Symposium*, 4.41 (=V A.31–32).

[16] Susan Prince, "Antisthenes' Ethics" in *Early Greek Ethics*, (ed.) David Conan Wolfdorf (Oxford: Oxford University Press, 2020), 356.

[17] "Those who wish to become good must exercise the body with gymnastic and the soul with education": Stobaeus, II 31.68 in Curtius Wachsmuth, Otto Hense, *Ioannis Stobaei Anthologium*, 2, (Berlin: Weidmannsche Buchhandlungmm 1909): (=A 163); see also H. D. Rankin, *Anthisthenes [sic!] Sokratikos* (Amsterdam: Adolf M. Hakkert, 1986), 111.

reported by Diogenes Laertius may seem to associate Antisthenes' view with the later Cynics' anti-intellectualist stance,[18] there is ample evidence against such an interpretation. The catalogue of Antisthenes' many writings devoted to the exegesis of Homeric poems, the logical investigation of truth and proper names, and the development of his theory of language evince Antisthenes' positive estimation of intellectual enterprises.[19] For Antisthenes wisdom is acquired through a process of learning which includes the search for truth carried out through logical and linguistic investigation.[20]

Antisthenes describes φρόνησις as an unassailable fortress whose walls are constructed through reasoning.[21] These military images highlight the dramatic difference between popular fifth-century conceptualizations of ἀρετή as civic virtue (that is, as a function of the citizen's contribution to communal wellbeing) and Antisthenes' relatively individualistic and internalized notion of ἀρετή. For Antisthenes, φρόνησις enables the sage to resist the assaults occasioned by the very necessity of living in a society. Thus, Antisthenes contrasts the inner excellence of the soul (based on reasonings and practical wisdom) with external excellence (which depends on worldly success and its recognition within the community).[22] His φρόνησις, moreover, enables the

---

[18] Diogenes Laertius attributes to Antisthenes the saying according to which virtue pertains to deeds and does not need a great number of discourses and learnings; Diogenes Laertius, 6.11 (=V A 134.4–5).

[19] On the role of wisdom in Antisthenes' ethics and against readings of Antisthenes' view as anti-intellectualist, see Aldo Brancacci, *Oikeios logos: La filosofia del linguaggio di Antistene* (Naples: Bibliopolis, 1990), ch. 3 and Aldo Brancacci, "'Episteme' and 'Phronesis' in Antisthenes," *Méthexis* 18 (2005): 7–28.

[20] See Brancacci, *Oikeios logos*, 96.

[21] Diogenes Laertius, 6.13 (=V A 134.17–19).

[22] See Prince, "Antisthenes' Ethics," 338.

virtuous man to correctly recognize what belongs to him and what is alien to him so as to take care only of what belongs to him, namely his own virtue: "Consider all evil things as foreign."[23]

This radical internalization of ἀρετή is accompanied by a staunch critique of conventions and, accordingly, a corresponding criticism of the importance afforded to conventional goods as the marker of a gentleman's goodness: wealth, honor, and noble birth. Antisthenes' long speech in Xenophon's *Symposium* articulates such a critique of the pursuit of material goods.[24] When asked what makes him most proud, Antisthenes responds that it is his own wealth. This statement—both paradoxical and provocative considering Antisthenes' humble social condition and willfully ostentatious poverty—offers him the opportunity to develop an anti-conventional view on the nature of genuine wealth: "For I think, gentlemen, that human beings have wealth and poverty not in their household but in their souls."[25] The soul's treasures from which Antisthenes draws are Socrates' very teachings.[26] These teachings render Antisthenes free of want, while enabling him to enjoy higher pleasures than those provided by material goods.

Other fragments and testimonies attest to Antisthenes' disparaging attitude toward the pursuit of material benefits or

---

[23] Diogenes Laertius, 6.12, in Tiziano Dorandi (ed.) *Lives of Eminent Philosophers* (Cambridge: Cambridge University Press, 2013): (=V A 134.16).

[24] Xenophon, *Symposium*, 4.34–44 (=V A. 82). According to Fernanda Caizzi, the speech was probably composed by Xenophon, but with the intent of giving an overview of Antisthenes' main ethical tenets: see Fernanda Caizzi, "Antistene," *Studi urbinati di storia, filosofia e letteratura*, 38, no. 1/2 (1964): 48–99.

[25] Xenophon, *Sym*posium, 4.34, in Edgar C. Marchant (ed.) *Xenophontis Opera Omnia* (Oxford: Clarendon Press, 1900–20).

[26] Xenophon, *Symposium*, 4.43–44 (=V A. 82.39–47).

honor.[27] Diogenes Laertius radicalizes this point by attributing some punchy sayings concerning ill-repute to Antisthenes: "ill-repute is good and the same as toil."[28] In this statement, toil (πόνος) is understood as the labor or effort necessary for the acquisition of virtue. To develop the preceding point, the contempt of society is part of the educational and self-transformative process through which a human being endowed with the necessary intellect can become virtuous. This view sharply separates the student of virtue from society.[29] Finally, in a saying attributed to him by Diogenes Laertius, Antisthenes evinces a total disregard for noble birth and reconceptualization of what counts as nobility: "only the virtuous are noble."[30] This does not mean that natural endowments are altogether irrelevant to Antisthenes' moral thinking. Rather, the only natural endowment that plays a decisive role for the possibility of acquiring virtue is the possession of an adequate intellect (νοῦς), which has nothing to do with blood nobility.

Hopefully, this short discussion of Antisthenes' notion of ἀρετή elucidates the import of his claim that virtue is the same for men and women and, consequently, that there is no "women's virtue" distinct from virtue in general. There are at least two possible readings of the preceding claim. As Antisthenes denies in-

---

[27] On Antisthenes' contempt for material wealth see also Diogenes Laertius 6.8 (=V A 15.1–3). For a critique of the pursuit of mortal goods in general see Themistocles, *On the Soul*, 43 Mach (=V A 96). For an analysis of the critique of the pursuit of honor in Odysseus' speech, see Susan Prince, "Antisthenes' Ethics," 325–360.

[28] Diogenes Laertius, 6.11 (=V A 134.6–7). See also Diogenes Laertius, 6.3 (=V A 28): "it is the lot of a king to do good deeds and be ill-spoken of," and Diogenes Laertius, 6 .7 (=V A 90).

[29] See H. D. Rankin, *Anthisthenes [sic!] Sokratikos*, 122–123.

[30] Diogenes Laertius, 6.11 (=V A 134.2–3).

termediate states between virtue and its lack, either women cannot access virtue because they lack the necessary intelligence and endurance for its acquisition, or women possess the natural endowments requisite for the acquisition of virtue. The second interpretation accords with the views of Antisthenes' Socratic peers. In addition to Plato's *Republic* 5 453a–455a, Xenophon's Socratic writings explicitly defend the claim that women can be taught virtue. Moreover, in both Xenophon's and Plato's writings this claim is generally either attributed to or approved by Socrates. Crucially, we find no trace of any controversy regarding the preceding point between Antisthenes and his peers in the extant testimonies and fragments. Given that the tradition paid close attention to polemics within the Socratic circle, it is likely that Antisthenes' views on the education of women coincided with the general Socratic line.[31]

In his commentary on Aristotle's *Nicomachean Ethics*, Aspasius ascribes an argument to the Socratics that may have originated from one of Antisthenes' writings and that had the following structure.[32] The argument started with the claim that if it is right that a man is just, it cannot be right that a woman is unjust. The same claim was then repeated for each of the other virtues, leading to the conclusion that the virtue of men and women in general must be the same.[33] A similar argument is also attributed

---

[31] See, for example, Antisthenes' polemics against Plato on the status of concepts and Forms: Diogenes Laertius, 6.7 (=V A, 27) and Simplicius, *In Aristotelis Categorias Commentarium*, 208.28–32. Antisthenes is also credited with having written a book polemically titled *Sathon* (a pun on the name Plato) on the impossibility of contradiction: Athenaeus 5.220 D-E (=V A 147) and Diogenes Laertius, 3.35 (=V A 148).

[32] As suggested by Jonathan Barnes, "An Introduction to Aspasius," in *Aspasius: The Earliest Extant Commentary on Aristotle's "Ethics,"* (eds.) Antonia Alberti and R. W. Sharples (Berlin: De Gruyter, 1999), 29.

[33] Aspasius, In *Ethica Nicomachea quae supersunt commentaria*, 177.3–7.

to the Cynic Hipparchia by Diogenes Laertius.[34] In considering these sources, Prince suggests that Antisthenes' full argument may have been that the same nature would acquire the same virtue when given the same education.[35] If we accept that Antisthenes agreed with the tenet that women can learn virtue, our discussion of Antisthenes' ethical revolution provides both the underlying assumptions of his claim that the virtue of man does not differ from that of woman and the far-reaching implications of the claim. As argued above, Antisthenes individualizes and internalizes virtue. Virtue can be taught and its acquisition demarcates the virtuous person (i.e., the sage) from society. In addition to mental and physical exercises, the teaching of virtue includes the study of philosophy, i.e., the search for truth through logical and linguistic analysis. The implication then is that a talented woman can in principle become a sage. She can study philosophy, endure toil, and exercise in order to build a fortress within her soul through the possession of φρόνησις. In this light, the Socratic reconceptualization of virtue as the inner excellence of the soul, in contrast with the popular fifth-century view (i.e., a view that ties civic virtue to an individual's specific social and political role), is precisely what may have enabled Antisthenes to include women as potential philosophers and sages.

Women's Virtue and the Soul in Xenophon's Socratic Writings

Xenophon is less critical of existing social conventions than Antisthenes. For example, as we will see, he offers a philosophical and religious justification for the gendered division of labor between indoor and outdoor tasks (*oikos* and *polis*). Moreover, his

---

[34] 6.97

[35] Susan Prince, *Antisthenes of Athens: Texts, Translations, and Commentary* (Ann Arbor: University of Michigan Press, 2015), 68.

thought places more emphasis on the role played by the body in its union with the soul. Despite these differences, Xenophon does assert the priority and distinctiveness of the soul in contrast with the body, conceptualizes virtues as properties of the soul, and maintains that virtue does not differ in kind for men and women.

The claim that women can be taught the same virtue as men can be found in Xenophon's *Symposium*. At 2.9, after observing a girl acrobat, Socrates argues that her performance is proof that a woman's nature is not inferior to a man's except in regard to might and strength (ῥώμης δὲ καὶ ἰσχύος δεῖται).[36] Socrates also argues that women are teachable. Then, he concludes by inviting his fellow symposiasts to set about teaching whatever they wish to their wives. Socrates further insists on women's ability to acquire virtues a few lines later: at 2.11–12, upon observing the dancer's somersaults through a hoop with upright swords, he argues that ἀνδρεία is teachable, given that the dancer obviously displays it *despite being a woman*. Socrates' remark implies that women are not naturally inclined to ἀνδρεία, which, as the term already conveys, was traditionally considered to be the exclusive province of men. Thus, the acrobat's example indicates that courage is a *teachable* virtue, and the existence of brave women indicates that women can, after all, learn to be courageous through the proper training.

Further discussion of women's virtue can be found in Ischomachus' description of the education of his young wife in Xenophon's *Oeconomicus*.[37] This discussion has much to offer for

---

[36] I accept Lange's conjecture replacing γνώμης with ῥώμης in *Xenophontis Symposium: Textu recognito in usum lectionum seorsum*, (ed.) Guilielm Lange (Halle a.S: Kümmel, 1825), *ad loc*. For a discussion of this conjecture, see Prince, *Antisthenes of Athens*, 69.

[37] Against Leo Strauss's interpretation of the text as an exercise in Socratic irony, I follow Sandra Taragna Novo in seeing Ischomachus as a representative of a propertied gentleman, who falls short of the philosophical life

our analysis of the Socratics' views on women, virtue, and sexual difference and their connection to the elaboration of a notion of the soul as the seat of moral agency distinct from the body. Ischomachus' conversation with his wife articulates a conception of sexual difference as complementarity that compares men and women with regard to their virtue and natural vocations. This theory is predicated upon this soul-body distinction and the ascription of virtue to the soul.

In order better to assess this distinction for the sake of our discussion, it may be helpful to briefly consider Xenophon's notion of the soul. The terms ψυχή and σῶμα are often coupled in his Socratic writings. However, the status of ψυχή relative to σῶμα—whether it is separable or ontologically discontinuous from the body—is never completely clarified. In *Memorabilia* 1.4.9–14, we find the most explicit treatment of the relation between soul and body and the most explicit statement of the soul's supremacy over the body. In this passage, Socrates explains that the gods have given prominence to human beings over other living beings by endowing them with an upright position, hands, a tongue capable of articulating speech and, most crucially, with a soul uniquely capable of apprehending the existence of the gods,

---

but has managed to put his material possessions to good use for both himself and the members of his *oikos*. See Leo Strauss, *Xenophon's Socratic Discourse: An Interpretation of the* Oeconomicus (Ithaca: Cornell University Press, 1971) and Sandra Taragna Novo, *Economia ed etica nell'*Economico *di Senofonte* (Torino: G. Giappichelli, 1968). As evidenced by Louis-André Dorion, moreover, there are several significant similarities between Ischomachus' views and Socrates' moral tenets. Notably, they both share the same foundation insofar as they take self-control to be the necessary condition for *oikonomia* and rulership. Louis-André Dorion, "Socrate oikonomikos" in *Xénophon et Socrate: Actes du Colloque d'Aix-en-Provence (6-9 novembre 2003)* (ed.) Michel Narcy and Alonso Tordesillas (Paris: Vrin 2008), 253–281.

worshipping them, planning, and acquiring knowledge. The harmonious combination of the soul's capacity for knowing and deliberation and the body's capacity of carrying through the soul's designs is unique to humans. Despite this passage's emphasis on the combination of body and soul, the soul clearly has a dominant position. The soul has mastery over the body (τοῦ σώματος κυρία ἐστίν,)[38] and its power is human beings' most important endowment (ὅπερ μέγιστόν ἐστι, καὶ τὴν ψυχὴν κρατίστην τῷ ἀνθρώπῳ ἐνέφυσε).[39]

To go back to the *Oeconomicus*, Ischomachus first mentions his wife while accounting for his ability to spend all his time outdoors: "my wife is entirely capable of managing the affairs in my household even by herself."[40] This division of labor between outdoor and indoor tasks governs Ischomachus' views about the natural capabilities of women. For Ischomachus, the gods have yoked males and females together in a mutually beneficial partnership (κοινωνία). This partnership is necessitated by the needs of biological reproduction and by the requisite specialized work humans perform to maintain their shelters.[41] The god has distributed similar and dissimilar capabilities to men and women because of the specialization required for indoor and outdoor tasks. Despite the differing demands of indoor and outdoor labor, intellectual capabilities such as memory (μνήμη) and attention (ἐπιμέλεια) are allotted by the gods equally and no sex has a greater share of them.[42] In fact, Ischomachus later agrees with Socrates when the latter exclaims: "By Hera, Ischomachus, you

---

[38] Xenophon, *Memorabilia*, 1.4.9, in E. C. Marchant (ed.), *Xenophontis Opera Omnia* (Oxford: Clarendon Press, 1900—20).

[39] Ibid., 1.4.13.

[40] Xenophon, *Oeconomicus*, 7.3, in E. C. Marchant (ed.) *Xenophontis Opera Omnia* (Oxford: Clarendon Press, 1900-20).

[41] Xenophon, *Oeconomicus*, 7.18–21.

[42] Ibid., 7.26.

The Soul, Virtue, and Women's Nature

are showing that your wife has a masculine mind" (ἀνδρικήν ... τὴν διάνοιαν).[43]

Significantly, the moral capacity for self-control (ἐγκράτεια) is also distributed equally between the two sexes. In fact, while the god has made both men's soul and body more capable of enduring (καρτερεῖν) adverse conditions such as extreme temperatures, harsh journeys, and military campaigns in order to equip them for outdoor work,[44] it is possible for women to acquire more self-control than men.[45] The attribution of an equal capacity for self-control to women counters traditional depictions of women as naturally prone to incontinence. Moreover, it indicates a novel moral status afforded to women given the pivotal role Xenophon attributes to ἐγκράτεια in his moral thinking. According to Dorion, the notions of self-control (ἐγκράτεια), endurance (καρτερία), and self-sufficiency (αὐτάρκεια) represent a foundational triad in Xenophon's writings. This marks a profound difference with other Socratic authors. For Xenophon, ἐγκράτεια rather than wisdom (σοφία or φρόνησις) is the ground for all other virtues and for a moral agent's undertakings.[46]

Self-control and endurance are tightly bound with the ideal of self-sufficiency (αὐτάρκεια). A discussion of self-sufficiency as the outcome of self-control and endurance can be found, for example, in the conversation between Socrates and Antiphon. Moreover, Socrates' and Antiphon's conversation contrasts the

---

[43] Ibid., 10.1.
[44] Ibid., 7.23.
[45] Ibid., 7.27.
[46] Louis-André Dorion, "Xenophon's Socrates," in *A Companion to Socrates*, (ed.) Sara Ahbel-Rappe and Rachana Kamtekar (Oxford: Wiley-Blackwell, 2009), 93–109.

possession of material riches with the genuine wealth of self-sufficiency. In response to Antiphon's disparagement of Socrates' impoverished lifestyle and clothing,[47] Socrates argues that he is not poor insofar as he always has more than enough to satisfy his own needs. This relative wealth is a product of Socrates' constant training of his body to endure adverse conditions and the most strenuous efforts,[48] rendering him the least in need of anything. As Socrates concludes, to have as few needs as possible is god-like.[49]

To return to Ischomachus' discussion of women, while women have an equal capacity for ἐγκράτεια (which equips them to play a queenly role and govern others within the *oikos*), they are less endowed with καρτερία (rendering them in need of a more sheltered way of life). Given that, elsewhere, καρτερία is treated as a precondition for self-sufficiency, it seems that women do not have access to a god-like life. However, several considerations mitigate this conclusion. First, Ischomachus is using a comparative term (i.e., μᾶλλον, at *Oeconomicus*, 7.23) and therefore does not deny the natural capacity for καρτερία in women altogether. Second, as evinced from Socrates' conversation with Antiphon, καρτερία depends as much on training as on natural disposition. Socrates' exceptional endurance is as much a product of his constant exercise in the face of adverse conditions and physical urges as it is of his nature.

It remains to be clarified whether women's comparative deficit of καρτερία refers to the body-soul couple or only to the body. When first introducing this difference Ischomachus claims that the god has made both man's soul *and* body more capable of endurance in order to equip him for outdoor tasks. However, a

---

[47] Xenophon, *Memorabilia*, 1.6.2–3.
[48] Ibid., 1.6.7–8.
[49] Ibid., 1.6.10.

few lines later, he only mentions women's bodies and not their souls. Women have a *body* that is less capable of enduring outdoor tasks and efforts (τῇ δὲ γυναικὶ ἧττον τὸ σῶμα δυνατὸν πρὸς ταῦτα).[50] I take it that the elucidation of the psychological difference of women's capacity for endurance comes in the following passage, in which Ischomachus argues that women are more naturally fearful than men.

> And since the god had also assigned to the woman the task of guarding the goods that have been brought indoors, knowing that a fearful soul (φοβερὰν … τὴν ψυχὴν) is not a bad thing for guarding things, he distributed a greater share of fear (πλέον μέρος καὶ τοῦ φόβου ἐδάσατο) to the woman than to the man. But knowing that, on the contrary, the one responsible for the outdoor work would need to ward off any wrong doer, he distributed to him a greater share of courage (πλέον μέρος τοῦ θράσους).[51]

If I am correct, women's fearfulness contributes to explain their reduced capacity to endure typically male activities, such as military campaigns or travels. Therefore, the natural predisposition to either courage (θράσος) or fear represents the main difference between men and women's souls.[52] Yet, it is important to keep in mind the comparative terms of this discussion so as not to take this discussion to claim that courage is an exclusively male virtue. As already seen, in the *Symposium* Socrates ascribes courage (ἀνδρεία) to an acrobat girl hopping on knives[53] and uses this example to argue for the teachability of courage. Given that his implicit assumption is that women are not naturally inclined to

---

[50] Xenophon, *Oeconomicus*, 7.23.
[51] Ibid., 7.24–25.
[52] Ischomachus also ascribes to women a greater natural affection for newborn babies: Ibid., 7.24.
[53] Xenophon, *Symposium*, 2.11–12.

courage, the presence of this quality in them must be the outcome of training and education. Interpreted in this way, the passage is entirely compatible with Ischomachus' claim and implies a more nuanced consideration of it. Ischomachus does not claim that women are either devoid of courage or barred from its acquisition. Rather, he claims that they are naturally *less* inclined to it than men. The combination of their lesser bodily capacity for endurance and weaker psychological inclination to courage ultimately justifies gendered division of labor in Ischomachus' eyes. Aside from these differences, men and women have equal natural endowments and, crucially, an equal capacity for learning and education. Given these natural differences, men and women are best when yoked in complementary couples, "for one is capable where the other is deficient."[54] In this respect, Ischomachus finds nature and convention in agreement rather than opposition. "For the woman it is finer to remain indoors than to be outside, while for the man it is more shameful to remain indoors than to take care of things outdoor."[55] Ischomachus still maintains a modicum of sexual difference that is necessary to justify existing social conventions as far as the distinction between private and public, *polis* and *oikos*, and the respective roles of men and women within this divide, are concerned. His views on sexual difference, therefore, combine conservatism and innovation.[56] On the innovative side, Xenophon (through Ischomachus) ascribes the same capacities of learning the same virtues to women and men. These capacities include the ability to rule others, albeit with a comparative deficiency in women's natural predispositions to endurance and cour-

---

[54] Ibid., 7.28—29.
[55] Ibid., 7.30—31.
[56] See Jean Luccioni, *Les idées politiques et sociales de Xénophon* (Paris: Ophrys, 1953), 7—77.

age. Most importantly, whether men and women have comparatively greater or lesser natural predisposition to certain virtues, the virtues they acquire are not different in kind. They are the same and pertain mostly to the soul. As I hope I have shown, this innovation is made possible by Xenophon's emphasis on the soul and consideration of virtue as its property.

Conclusion

Several Socratics shared the view that virtue is the same for men and women. Focusing on Antisthenes and Xenophon, in this article I have argued that the more general philosophical assumptions underlying this claim in its various iterations are the conceptualization of the soul as the seat of moral agency and the internalization of virtue as its property. Popular understandings of virtue in fifth-century Athens did not consider it as an inner state distinct from, and possibly opposed to, external goods and circumstances such social status, nobility, or wealth. In this conventional moral outlook, the virtues of men and women were essentially different. Some virtues were considered to be the exclusive purview of specific constituents of the *oikos* and of the *polis*, while others acquired an altogether different meaning and shape depending on the moral agent in question. Consequently, according to the conventional view, a woman's self-control was not the same as a man's self-control.

The Socratics embarked on a comprehensive critique of such conventional moral outlook. Antisthenes' thought offers a more radical version of this critique in its comprehensive attack on both convention and the pursuit of material goods, and in its sharp opposition between inner and outer (i.e., what belongs to a moral agent and what is alien to it). Xenophon's critique is less radical and the relationship he posits between soul and body focuses less sharply on their opposition. Despite these differences, I have argued that both authors differentiate between body and soul, assert the soul's priority, and attach virtue to it. This shared philosophical outlook underlies their discussions about women and virtue and enables their anti-conventional argument that women and men share the same virtue.

Bibliography

Barnes, Jonathan. "An Introduction to Aspasius." In *Aspasius: The Earliest Extant Commentary on Aristotle's "Ethics."* Edited by A. Alberti and R. W. Sharples. Berlin: de Gruyter, 1999, 1–50.

Brancacci, Aldo. *Oikeios logos: La filosofia del linguaggio di Antistene.* Naples: Bibliopolis, 1990.

Brancacci, Aldo "'Episteme' and 'Phronesis' in Antisthenes." *Méthexis* 18 (2005): 7–28.

Bremmer, Jan N. *The Early Greek Concept of the Soul.* Princeton: Princeton University Press, 1983.

Bryant, Joseph. *Moral Codes and Social Structure in Ancient Greece: A Sociology of Greek Ethics from Homer to the Epicureans and Stoics.* Albany: State University of New York, 1996.

Caizzi, Fernanda. "Antistene," *Studi urbinati di storia, filosofia e letteratura* 38, no. 1–2 (1964): 48–99.

Claus, David. *Toward the Soul: An Inquiry into the Meaning of Ψυχή Before Plato.* New Haven and London: Yale University Press, 1981.

Dittmar, Heinrich. *Aischines von Sphettos: Studien zur Literaturgeschichte der Sokratiker.* Berlin: Weidemann, 1912.

Diogenes Laertius. Lives of Eminent Philosophers. Edited by Dorandi, Tiziano. Cambridge: Cambridge University Press, 2013.

Dorion, Louis-André. "Socrate oikonomikos." In *Xénophon et Socrate. Actes du Colloque d'Aix-en-Provence (6-9 novembre 2003).* Edited by Michel Narcy and Alonso Tordesillas, Paris: Vrin 2008, 253–281.

Dorion, Louis-André. "Xenophon's Socrates." In *A Companion to Socrates.* Edited by Sara Ahbel-Rappe and Rachana Kamtekar. Oxford: Wiley-Blackwell, 2009, 93–109.

Finkelberg, Margalit. "On the City-State Concept of Arete." *The American Journal of Philology* 123, 1 (2002): 35–49.

Furley, David J. "The Early History of the Concept of Soul." *Bulletin of the Institute of Classical Studies*, University of London, 3 (1956), pp.1–18.

Giannantoni, Gabriele, Editor. *Socratis et Socraticorum Reliquiae*, 4 vols. Naples: Bibliopolis, 1991.
Luccioni, Jean. *Les idées politiques et sociales de Xénophon*. Paris: Ophrys, 1953.
Prince, Susan. *Antisthenes of Athens: Texts, Translations, and Commentary*. Ann Arbor: University of Michigan Press, 2015.
Prince, Susan. "Antisthenes' Ethics." In *Early Greek Ethics*. Edited by David Conan Wolfdorf. Oxford: Oxford University Press, 2020, 325–360.
Rankin, H. D. *Anthisthenes [sic] Sokratikos*. Amsterdam: Adolf M. Hakkert, 1986.
Snell, Bruno. *The Discovery of the Mind. The Greek Origins of European Thought*. Cambridge, MA: Harvard University Press, 1953.
Stobaeus. *Ioannis Stobaei Anthologium*, 2. Edited by Curtius Wachsmuth and Otto Hense. Berlin: Weidmannsche Buchhandlungmm 1909.
Strauss, Leo. *Xenophon's Socratic Discourse: An Interpretation of the* Oeconomicus. Ithaca: Cornell University Press, 1971.
Taragna Novo, Sandra. *Economia ed etica nell'Economico di Senofonte*. Torino: G. Giappichelli, 1968.
Vegetti, Mario. *L'etica degli antichi*. Rome-Bari: Laterza 2007.
West, L. Martin. Editor. *Iambi et elegi Graeci ante Alexandrum cantati*. Oxford: Oxford University Press, 1989–1992.
Xenophon. *Xenophontis Symposium: Textu Recognito in Usum Lectionum Seorsum*. Edited by Guilielm Lange. Halle a.S: Kümmel, 1825.
Xenophon. *Xenophontis Opera Omnia*. Edited by Edgar C. Marchant. Oxford: Clarendon Press, 1900–20.

SOUL, VIRTUE, AND KNOWLEDGE: PLATO'S *THEAETETUS* AND *SOPHIST*

I-Kai Jeng

Introduction

In this paper I examine the soul's pursuit of knowledge as depicted in Plato's *Theaetetus* and its sequel the *Sophist*. In the *Sophist*, the main speaker, the Stranger, argues that both motion and rest must be real (250a11) to guarantee the possibility of knowledge, in a passage commonly called "the philosopher's prayer." But he does not further explain how motion and rest relate to each other so that knowledge results.[1] The drama of the *Theaetetus*, I argue, enacts a possible solution to that puzzle. Theaetetus's soul, as he comes to know his ignorance with the help of Socrates, is a blending of motion and rest.

Section one discusses the dramatic puzzle of the *Theaetetus*. Socrates is initially supposed to make Theaetetus more courageous, but at the end, he says that Theaetetus will behave *sōphronōs* in the future (210c3). *Sōphronōs*, a word of rich meaning, here suggests intellectual modesty and sobriety. I show that Theaetetus's initial courage and modesty were in tension, and Socrates aims to blend them into a unity. Section two interprets the philosopher's prayer in the *Sophist*. I argue that the prayer is less about how beings in general can both move and rest than about how the soul moves and rests in relation to beings. Such a

---

[1] Stephanus page numbers are based on Burnet's OCT. See John Burnet, *Platonis Opera I* (Oxford: Oxford University Press, 1900; 20th reprint, 1992). Translations are my own unless otherwise noted. When unclear, *Theaetetus* and *Sophist* will be cited as *Tht.* and *Sph.* respectively.

reading readily shows why Socrates' education of Theaetetus exhibits an answer to that question. Section three reflects on what this reading implies for the doctrine of recollection, the Socratic view that virtue is knowledge, and that human wisdom is knowledge of ignorance.

The Pedagogical Drama of the *Theaetetus*

The *Theaetetus* investigates what knowledge is, and the relevant issue of Theaetetus's courage is raised right away.[2] Euclides recalls Socrates' conversation with Theaetetus when he hears of Theaetetus's valor on the battlefield (142b7–8, c4–8). Back then, Theaetetus was in his teens, and Socrates explained that courage is needed for the inquiry into knowledge. We soon discover that young Theaetetus was timid and needed prodding from Socrates before their inquiry could begin.[3] The cultivation of Theaetetus's intellectual courage, of which his military valor is implied to be

---

[2] Lewis Campbell, *The "Theaetetus" of Plato* (Oxford: Oxford University Press, 1861), liii; Kenneth Dorter, *Form and Good in Plato's Eleatic Dialogues: The "Parmenides," "Theaetetus," "Sophist," and "Statesman"* (Berkeley: University of California Press, 1994), 72. The theme of courage has been treated in detail by Ruby Blondell in *The Play of Character in Plato's Dialogues* (Cambridge: Cambridge University Press, 2002), Chapter 5 and Jill Gordon, *Plato's Erotic World: From Cosmic Origins to Human Death* (Cambridge: Cambridge University Press, 2012), Chapter 4. I will draw upon their works below.

[3] Theaetetus's timidity is indicated in the following ways. He was afraid of not living up to Theodorus's high opinion of him (145b10–c1; 148b8). He hesitated to voice his thoughts until Socrates repeatedly urged him to try. Socrates talked about his art of midwifery in order that Theaetetus "behave like a man (*andrizēi*)" (151d5). And once the definition of knowledge as perception is proposed, Socrates uses a tricolon crescendo to emphasize the importance of courage: "be confident (*tharrōn*), be very steadfast (*karterōn eu*), and answer courageously (*andreiōs apokrinou*) whatever appears to you about whatever I ask" (157d3–5).

the outgrowth, therefore forms the pedagogical drama of the dialogue.[4]

At the end of their inquiry, without any positive results, Socrates remarks that Theaetetus will now become "less harsh and tamer to others, in modestly (*sōphronōs*) thinking that you no longer know what you do not know" (210c2–4). This is designed to surprise. Socrates is not only silent about courage, but even mentions tameness and modesty, qualities usually in tension with courage.[5] For example, in the *Statesman*, the Stranger states that the courageous and the moderate (*sōphronika* 307a7; *sōphron* 309e6) tend to be opposed (309d10–311b9). Similarly, in *Republic* 375a2–c9 Socrates remarks that courageous people tend to be harsh, the very opposite of being gentle (*praion*). Since both passages suggest that a courageous temperament must be curbed to become tame, gentle, or modest, Socrates' departing remark seems to contradict the initial task of the *Theaetetus*. How does a training in courage result in more modesty and tameness, not less? And since Theaetetus initially seemed too tame for his own good, why would he need to be more modest? This, I submit, is the educational riddle of the *Theaetetus*.[6]

To answer the riddle, I begin with Theodorus's assessment of Theaetetus:

> I have never seen anyone who is so marvelously good in nature. Because, being good at learning—something difficult for anyone else—he is outstandingly gentle (*praion*), and on

---

[4] As Gordon puts it, Theaetetus's "courage as a young man...augured well for his courage later in life" (*Erotic World*, 125).

[5] Seth Benardete, *Being of the Beautiful*, notes that the ending is the only place in the whole dialogue where modesty is mentioned. See Benardete, *The Being of the Beautiful: Plato's "Theaetetus," "Sophist," and "Statesman"* (Chicago: University of Chicago Press, 1984), I.182.

[6] Commentators generally do not see the ending as problematic, but to neglect this is a mistake.

> top of that, he is courageous compared to anyone...those who are sharp, quick of mind, and have good memory like him are suddenly quick to anger very often, and they dart forth, moving like ships without anchor, and grow up (*phuontai*) crazier than courageous. And then again, the more ponderous ones move towards learnings somehow sluggishly and are full of forgetfulness. But he goes to learnings and searchings smoothly without stumbling; efficiently with much gentleness, like the flow of olive oil flowing without sound. (*Tht.* 144a2–b5)[7]

To be intellectually courageous means to react fast, to anticipate where a lesson is going, and to recall past lessons with ease. Theodorus does not appear to have good things to say about the "ponderous" ones, considering them to be rather slow, clumsy learners. But he still implies that there is a good kind of slowness, one that manifests as gentleness. While the gentle ones learn more slowly and passively than the courageous types, they are steadier and more orderly, less prone to losing temper in discussion.

In Theodorus's experience, most students are only one or the other, and Theaetetus is one of a kind because he has both. In being both courageous and gentle, he is neither mad nor sluggish. Gentleness makes him think twice before speaking, and he listens (thus "without sound"; compare *Tht.* 183d6–7) before rushing to conclusions. But courage or gentleness alone cannot sustain themselves. The natural development (as indicated by *phuontai*, "they naturally grow into") of courage is madness and makes it a defect instead. Hence an ideal learner must balance courage with

---

[7] Although Theodorus does not speak of tameness and modesty as Socrates does, Gordon notes that gentleness, *praios*, expresses the same idea (*Erotic World*, 129). As I will suggest below, Socrates' use of different terms could indicate a transformation of Theaetetus's inchoate character into something more mature.

gentleness. Theodorus envisions the ideal student using the strength of one to counteract the weakness of the other. The result is a psychic state of being in between, of being neither too quick nor too slow, of staying between recklessness and circumspection. Hence the best learner is steady and self-assured but does not lose the vigor (suggested by the association of olive oil with life) needed to learn difficult topics.[8]

As a young man, Theaetetus is still growing. Thus, his courage is incomplete. He is courageous enough to tackle a mathematical problem with a friend when their teacher lacks an answer (*Tht.* 147c7–148b2). But he panics and retreats when he has to answer what knowledge is by himself. In short, his natural courage is inadequate for philosophical discussion.[9]

Both Theodorus and Socrates would probably agree that Theaetetus's courage is not fully mature. However, as the conversation moves on, Socrates develops his courage in a direction that must appear mad by Theodorean standards, and we begin to suspect that Socrates will not educate Theaetetus in the way envisioned by Theodorus. Socrates recommends, and sometimes even demands, "craziness" or what I call "radical courage" in at least three ways.

First, he encourages Theaetetus to tarry in the improbable. Rosemary Desjardins, commenting on the first definition of

---

[8] Benardete criticizes Theodorus's simile as a mathematician's clumsy attempt at poetry (*Being of the Beautiful*, I.90). Even so, the simile nevertheless indicates what characteristics in Theodorus's eyes qualify someone as an ideal learner.

[9] There are good reasons to think that Theodorus, in the above quote, has not fully grasped the inchoate character of Theaetetus's courage, even though he does speak of that courage as "natural." Cf. Gordon on the limitations of Theodorus, and my remarks on Theaetetus's "hidden harshness" below (*Erotic World*, 135). Blondell tellingly characterizes the dialogue as a "coming-of-age drama" (*Play of Character*, 281).

knowledge as perception, wonders "Why on earth will Plato… become so caught up in what is obviously an unpromising proposal?"[10] Even if this definition is more promising than she thinks, surely the later ones are at least equally if not more promising, yet their treatment is disproportionally short. Moreover, one must explain why Socrates postpones the knock-down argument (*Tht.* 184b5–186e12) against knowledge as perception for such a long time. Why go through all the trouble, even producing some sophisms of questionable value (such as the argument in 163c5–164d2) before dismantling it?

At least part of the answer is that Theaetetus was insufficiently mad. If Theodorus thought Theaetetus superior because he is less mad than other courageous students, Socrates thought he should be more so. Radical courage requires *self-reliant risk-taking*. Desjardins's question actually misrepresents the dramatic situation. In fact, Socrates initially makes Theaetetus's definition appear extremely promising by claiming that almost all wise poets and philosophers teach that knowledge is perception (or that there is only becoming). Theaetetus is emboldened as expected (160d7–e2, 180c7–d3; cf. 157c4–6). The definition only turns out to be "obviously unpromising" after Socrates crushes Theaetetus's confidence. In refuting the definition, Socrates by implication debunks all those supposed authorities in wisdom as well. In other words, a major goal in examining the first definition is to make it impossible for Theaetetus to appeal to authority later on. This likely explains why no authorities are named in

---

[10] Rosemary Desjardins, *The Rational Enterprise: Logos in Plato's "Theaetetus"* (Albany: SUNY Press, 1990), 16.

support of the last two definitions.[11] The examination of the first definition effectively isolates Theaetetus, compelling him to rely on himself.

There are both philosophical and pedagogical reasons to examine the "knowledge is perception" definition in excruciating detail. Philosophically, it has a strong grip on us—attractive enough that a mathematician, someone whose knowledge seems to be or involve non-sensible elements, still nonetheless thinks of perception as a promising answer to what knowledge is. A comprehensive examination of it would then be necessary as an inoculation against future attractions to it. The pedagogical reason is that intellectual courage (understood as the willingness to defend a seemingly hopeless position) is a virtue, which is still out of Theaetetus's reach.[12] Therefore, Socrates assists in playing both sides, challenging Theaetetus to distinguish the real from sophistic objections, on the one hand, and coming up with responses on Protagoras's behalf, on the other.[13] Socrates is giving Theaetetus a practice run in how to stand his ground when facing a

---

[11] Homer is mentioned (194c7–8) to support not the definition that knowledge is true judgment, but the imagery of the mind as a wax tablet. Hesiod is mentioned as well, but only as an illustration of a possible candidate for knowledgeable account, *logos* (207a3–4).

In scholarship, there is much discussion about the author of the "dream" in the final definition of knowledge, "true opinion accompanied by *logos*." On my reading, there are good dramatic reasons to keep it anonymous: Theaetetus, by this point, has learned how to examine a philosophical position on its own merits, without regard for *who* proposed it.

[12] See Gordon for important remarks on why joint inquiry is compared to wrestling, which is practiced naked in ancient Greece (*Tht.* 169a9–c3 and Gordon, *Erotic World*, 139–141). Nakedness makes one vulnerable and fearful, and overcoming it requires courage.

[13] One extraordinary feature of the examination of the first definition is the breathtaking speed with which one argument follows another, as if Socrates himself cannot stay still while examining the doctrine that nothing stays still (cf. *Tht.* 180b8–c6).

barrage of objections. The decisive takedown argument is postponed because Socrates seems to understand that fruitful philosophical discussion requires that opponents not back down too soon and too meekly. The goal is to make Theaetetus generate from within himself the kind of speech that Socrates can summon on Protagoras' behalf.

The kind of intellectual courage cultivated here recalls Laches's first two definitions of courage, namely "willing to stay in rank and defend against enemies" (*Laches* 190e5–6) or "a certain steadfastness (*karteria tis*) of the soul" (192b9). While Socrates refuted those definitions in the *Laches*, they are encouraged here as conversational principles (*karteria*, for example, shows up in verb form in *Tht.* 157d4 *karterōn*). And Socrates does not ask Theaetetus to be steadfast only when it is safe to do so, but to be almost importunately steadfast. He makes Theaetetus insist on something ludicrous for the sake of appearing consistent (163e13–164a1). Thus, at 164c1–2, it appears that the refutation of the first definition of knowledge is over. However, Socrates suddenly resumes the examination, because he wants to win fair and square, like an honorable warrior (169c8–d1, 171c9–10). Steadfastness thus emerges as a commendable trait in philosophical discussion. (One cannot help but wonder if Socrates' cultivation of Theaetetus's intellectual courage made him too courageous on the battlefield, which in turn, led to his premature death.)

If intellectual courage is a kind of steadfastness, and steadfastness can be foolish (*Laches* 192d1–12), then evidently the kind of character Socrates cultivates is too excessive for Theodorus. We witness his annoyance at Theaetetus's gradual change (*Tht.* 183d3–4). This brings me to the second feature of radical courage, the willingness to transgress, expressed by the verb *tolmaō* or "to dare" to do something. Generally it is used negatively, pointing at the threshold that the ordinarily courageous person must not transgress. All seven occurrences of this term in the *Theaetetus* concern daring to say or think something. Four of those seven (172b1, 177d3, 190b6 and c1) indicate undesirable transgressions. Socrates refers to certain ideas that are so mad to even entertain that the mere mention of them is enough to count as a refutation. Courage is a concern with being noble; daring is an unconcern with being shameful or ugly.[14] To be courageous therefore ordinarily means to refrain from *tolmaō*.

The other three occurrences of this term, however, all occur in a single passage and subvert this negative estimate. After their unsatisfactory attempt to explain false judgment through the wax tablet imagery, Socrates suggests that "since one must dare (*tolmēteon*) everything—what if we try to be shameless?" (196d2–3) He demands that they lose their sense of shame. They shall try "to say what sort of thing 'to know' is" (196d5, 197a4) and propose the aviary as an image to explain the difference between possessing and activating knowledge. This is shameless because they are speaking as if they understand what "to know" means before successfully defining knowledge. Socrates notes in passing that they have been doing this all along. Namely, conversing in words about which one lacks clarity. That is, they were conversing impurely (*tou mē katharōs dialegesthai*, 196e1–2). Unlike the other four instances, "*tolmaō*" here becomes desirable. It is imperative—as indicated by the *-teon* suffix—to dare everything. Unlike Theodorus, Socrates willfully exposes himself to ridicule. Such persistence appears even more stubborn than the heroic steadfastness admired by Laches.

---

[14] The verb and its noun form *tolma* are often associated with shamelessness in the literature, for example Plato, *Apology* 38d7; Sophocles, *Antigone* 370–1; Euripides, *Bacchae* 636.

The irony should not be missed. Socrates acts as if this is the first and only time that they are conversing impurely. But, actually, he has already compelled Theaetetus to define knowledge despite the latter's protest that he does not know (148e1–4). Philosophical conversation concerns topics so foundational, primordial even, that it cannot but be impure. It is compelled to use the very terms under investigation. Philosophizing thus requires overcoming the sense of shame that guides ordinary courage. *Tolmaō* is the soul's precondition for philosophizing.

The third and final feature of radical courage is excess. *Deinos*, equally "terrible" and "clever," refers to any quality that frightens or alarms due to its being unfamiliar or exceeding what is ordinary.[15] Thus, to think someone can know the syllable *SŌ* without knowing its constituent letters sigma and omega is a *deinos* thought. Such an idea exceeds what discourse can communicate and is not at home in intelligible discourse (*alogos*, *Tht.* 203d6). *Deinoi* thoughts force the inquirer to either withdraw or overcome the fear. If one can conquer the excessive or the unfamiliar, and make it familiar or appropriate it for oneself, then the outcome itself is also *deinos*. It would be an extraordinary response to an extraordinary situation.

Not all responses are appropriate. If one fixes attention on words instead of the thoughts behind them (154e2–4, 164c7–d2), acting like an orator or sophist, that too can be seen as *deinos*,

---

[15] Sean Kirkland in *The Ontology of Socratic Questioning in Plato's Early Dialogues* (SUNY Series in Ancient Greek Philosophy. Albany: SUNY, 2012), gives an eye-opening reading of *deinos* in Plato's early works (48–51). He argues that *deinos* indicates a phenomenological "excess" and shows the truth of virtue already present in everyday experience; namely something disruptive and discomfiting. Socratic questioning merely "excavates" that truth and makes it come to light. While Kirkland does not discuss the *Theaetetus*, since it is not an early work, his interpretation of *deinos* applies here as well, as we will soon see.

albeit not truly so. By contrast, there is a true and philosophical showing of a *deinos* character. Socrates claims that "the true *deinotēs* of a man and worthlessness and lack of manliness (*anandria*)" (175c3–4) is not whether one achieves victory over others but whether a person resembles god in word and deed. True *deinotēs* means to transcend one's humanity, to become more godlike and wiser. Note that *deinotēs* is contrasted with *anandria*; the contrast implies that *deinotēs* is the word for true courage (*andreia*). This quality of being *deinos* is Socrates' understanding of radical, philosophical courage.

Socrates characterizes himself as *deinos* in two places in the *Theaetetus*. Midway through the conversation (when Theodorus refuses to participate, citing the shame of showing his body in old age) Socrates claims that he is gripped by "a certain terrible passion" (*tis erōs deinos*, 169c1) for intellectual exercises. Later, Socrates mocks his own attempts at solving the problem of false judgment, saying that his garrulity is a *deinos* thing (195b9), since he accomplished nothing but a false account of false judgment (cf. 189d4). In both cases, the term indicates an outpouring of speech. Socrates has an overflowing, excessive love for talking (146a6). Overwhelming difficulties require extraordinary responses, responses that may very well fail and make oneself appear ridiculous. While excess alone is not sufficient to solve philosophical problems, without it one cannot offer even a solution to be examined and refuted. Radical courage or *deinotēs* manifests here as the excessive love of dialogical examination spurred by the drive to transcend one's human limitations.

In short, in urging Theaetetus to defend seriously what is difficult to defend, to dare to discourse impurely, and to do so passionately and excessively, Socrates radicalizes Theaetetus's courageous nature into something that verges on madness. The effect of such practice, I argue, *transforms Theaetetus's initial knowledge of ignorance into a genuine knowledge of ignorance.* Theaetetus professes knowledge of ignorance at the very beginning of the conversation, perhaps unique among Socrates' interlocutors (148e1–5). But his knowledge of ignorance and Socrates' are not the same. Theaetetus's knowledge of ignorance made him concerned with the question of knowledge: it motivated and began inquiry. But there is also a knowledge of ignorance that is an accomplishment of inquiry. This latter knowledge of ignorance is a discursive awareness of the insights and difficulties in each proposed definition of what is examined, of the weaknesses that plague each and can be exploited by sophistic arguments. And the transition from the initial awareness of one's lack to this more comprehensive clarity about what exactly is lacking requires radical courage. In this sense, Theaetetus now "knows his ignorance better."[16]

Socrates and Theodorus have different diagnoses of Theaetetus's soul. Theodorus thinks that Theaetetus's natural gentleness is good because it curbs his natural courage from becoming mad. But Socrates judges that gentleness to be bad, as it avails Theaetetus of the excuse to not offer any definitions of knowledge. It allowed him to escape from a true examination of himself. It even made his gentleness disguise a harshness, as he risks the danger of becoming prideful towards those who lack that initial awareness of one's ignorance. Socrates thus replaces that gentleness with something different. That something is not meant to check or balance courage as in Theodorus's vision, but

---

[16] In this respect, to say that "the dialogue fails to achieve any positive results, despite Theaitetos's superiority as an interlocutor" (Blondell, *Play of Character*, 260) is only partly correct. It is also *because* of Theaetetus's superiority that the dialogue ends aporetically. The lack of positive results in this dialogue is an achievement. Aporetic endings could imply the failure of Socratic education; it could also signal the interlocutor's improvement.

rather, it emerges as the result of radical courage. Initially Theaetetus's soul balanced between the restlessness of courage and the slowness of gentleness. Socrates unifies the two by "blending" them into an extraordinary unity. In view, courage and gentleness are opposed to each other and stand in an inverse relation. The Socratic view instead grasps that the more *deinos* one responds to philosophical questions, the more gentle one will become. Perhaps in order to mark the difference between the initial and the resulting gentleness, Socrates ends up talking about becoming modest and tame.[17] Gentleness finds excuses to avoid examination; modesty and tameness offer reasons to not be prematurely satisfied with any account. Through Socrates' deliberate silence about courage at the end of the conversation, Plato draws the reader's attention to how Theaetetus's new modesty resulted from the enhancement of his natural courage.

Motion, Rest, and the Possibility of Knowledge in the *Sophist*

Theodorus associated courage with action, speed, and restlessness. Conversely, gentleness is associated with caution, steadiness, and therefore akin to psychic rest (compare the first definition of *sōphrosunē* in *Charmides* 159b1–6). One can readily see, then, that the pedagogical drama of the *Theaetetus* is related to the philosopher's prayer in the *Sophist*, namely how motion and rest must "both together [be] being and the whole" (*to on te kai to pan sunamphotera*, 249d4) so that knowledge is possible (248d4–249d5; also *Tht.* 180c7–e4). The prayer, however, is sometimes interpreted as concerned with Forms, the objects of knowledge,

---

[17] Benardete's remark that "Socrates was apparently unable to enhance Theaetetus's natural gentleness without sacrificing his manliness" (*Being of the Beautiful*, I.90) is mistaken. It is only through enhancing his manliness that Socrates makes Theaetetus truly gentle or *sōphrōn*.

instead of the soul, namely the knower.[18] Because of this, this section argues for two points. First, the overall trajectory of the *Sophist* shows a clear concern with the soul. Second, although the Stranger presents positive doctrines (251a5–264b8), he does not explore how to actually fulfill the prayer and explain the possibility of knowledge. The reason for his silence, I suggest, is that Socrates' education the day before already provides the answer.

The Stranger's discussions of the five greatest Kinds and parts of Otherness are indeed about Forms, not the soul. But it is more accurate to say that the *Sophist* as a whole deals, not with Forms as such, but with Forms *as they appear to the soul*. Scholarly discussion of Motion and Rest in this dialogue often begins from 246a3, the *gigantomachia* section that concluded in the philosopher's prayer.[19] But motion and rest appear early on in 228a4–c8, where noble sophistry or elenchus is defined. Elenchus purifies bad things in the soul, but there are two kinds of psychic badness (226d1–7, 227d6–13). Illness is defined as psychic *stasis*, a conflict between parts of the soul (228a7–8, e2–5). Although here *stasis* is often rightly translated "faction," the connotation of "rest" is still there, since a soul, being pulled in different directions, is paralyzed and comes to a standstill. Moral vices, such as injustice

---

[18] For example, one sometimes claims that the Forms move insofar as they change from being not known to being known. For a short summary and crucial objection to this reading, see Lesley Brown, "Innovation and Continuity: The Battle of Gods and Giants, *Sophist* 245–249" in *Method in Ancient Philosophy*, Jyl Gentzler ed., 181–207 (Oxford: Clarendon Press, 1988), 198–199. For other interpretations of this highly debated passage, one should consult Kristian Larsen's "The Virtue of Power: The Gigantomachia in Plato's *Sophist* 245e6–249d5 Revisited," *The New Yearbook for Phenomenology and Phenomenological Philosophy* 13 (2015): 306–317.

[19] Below, I shall capitalize "Motion" and "Rest" when they are clearly about the Forms, but will use "motion" and "rest" when they refer to an instance of motion or rest, or a moving or resting particular.

and hubris, are instances of psychic *stasis*. Elenchus cures a specific kind of illness: it exposes an interlocutor's conflicting opinions (230b7–8, c4–d2) and makes their soul *sōphrōn* (230d5). However, elenchus cannot remove ugliness (230d3–4). Psychic ugliness is defined as wayward motion (*kinēsis*), or the inability to hit the target of truth (228c1–6). Conversely, psychic beauty would be getting answers right and acquiring knowledge. Motion and rest thus first emerge in the *Sophist* as concerning the soul's virtues and vices (227d4), which presupposes or is related to the pursuit of knowledge (230d6–e4).

I now turn to the final argument in the *gigantomachia* against the friends of Forms. The friends claim that only what is knowable is real, but only what is at rest is knowable (246b7, 248a11, 249b11–c1). Thus, only the stable and eternally self-identical Forms are real. The Stranger argues against this in 248e6–249c9. This argument opens with the sudden intrusion of the phrase, *to pantelōs on*, the referent of which is notoriously controversial. The gist of the rest of the argument, however, is tolerably clear. Knowledge requires not only what is intelligible (the Forms) but also what is intelligent, *nous*. Intelligence is always the intelligence of a living being; thus, there is no *nous* without soul or life; but soul or life is motion. Therefore, knowledge requires motion. At first glance, this suggests a straightforward way of understanding the ensuing philosopher's prayer. When the Stranger says: "all that are immoveable and have moved" (249d3) are real, it is simply an abstract way of saying that *both Forms and soul are real*. He characterizes this assertion as a prayer (d3) for two reasons. First, it is hypothetical: *if* knowledge is possible, then both soul and Forms must qualify as *on*. But we do not yet know whether the antecedent is true. Indeed, the philosopher must believe in it because he honors knowledge and intelligence (249c10). Second, even if the antecedent is true, an account of how restless soul can partake in immovable Forms is still required.

The philosopher's prayer guides the Stranger's subsequent inquiry (249e7–257a12). In that stretch of the text he speaks of how they ought to "posit [some Form] in the soul" or think of Forms (250b7, 251d7–8, 255b8, c1, c6, c9–10). The procedure is to move from how we talk and think about Forms to their actual constitution; the latter is often indicated by *physis* (nature) or *anagkaios* (necessary). One example will suffice. The Stranger asks Theaetetus whether they should think that every being mixes with every other being; or none of them mixes with any; or "some mix with some but others do not" (251d9).[20] He then shows that the first two possibilities lead to internal contradictions for many philosophical positions. By elimination, only the last possibility, partial mixing, allows for coherent thinking. Since this is the only non-contradictory option in thought, it must (*anagkaion*, 252e1) be how beings actually relate to each other as well.

If one's thought about Forms is what they are by nature, then one has reached the truth and thus has beautified their soul. And since the Stranger presents positive teachings about Forms, he seems to envisage his conversation with Theaetetus as complementary to Socrates' the day before. Socrates is the noble sophist who makes Theaetetus's soul healthy, but only the Stranger's beautifying speeches guide Theaetetus towards truth.

But are his speeches successful? I would argue that they are both problematic and inadequate. The philosopher's prayer concerned how to articulate the essential mobility of soul and stability of Form. The Stranger elides this issue by no longer talking about soul and Forms, but about Motion and Rest. What was

---

[20] The *Sophist* seems to use a variety of terms to denote partaking relations: *koinōneō* ("to commune with"), *metechō* ("to partake"), or *(sum)meignumi* ("to (co-)mix"). In this paper I shall treat them as synonyms.

originally an issue about the relation between the knower and the known is transformed into a question concerning the relation between objects of knowledge. Such talk obscures the issue, since soul is not Motion, but rather a peculiar kind of mobile being.

Even if the shift from soul and Forms to Formal relations themselves is justified, the Stranger still falls short of answering the prayer. Knowledge must be a *partial blending between Motion and Rest without violating the rule of non-contradiction.* The rule of non-contradiction cannot be violated, because it is the basis of elenchus.[21] A partial blending or communion is required so that certain motions of the soul, to qualify as knowledge, in some way partake in rest. But the *Sophist* assumes throughout that Motion and Rest are opposites (250a8, 255a12), that is, incompatible, and in the Stranger's language, that means they do not mix or partake in each other. The Stranger's doctrines tacitly deny the condition for the possibility of knowledge.

It would be hasty to conclude, however, that his doctrines fail for this reason. A more charitable reading is that he deliberately simplifies things. On this reading, "Motion and Rest are opposites" is a helpful if inaccurate way to carry their inquiry into Forms. As the Stranger himself suggests at 254c7–d2, their procedure might fall short of the highest rigor. Such a simplification does not warrant a wholesale rejection of what he otherwise says about Forms. But it remains the case that no adequate answer to the prayer is offered in the *Sophist*. The Stranger actually draws attention to this in a much-discussed passage.

> ES. So, even if somehow Motion itself shared in Rest, wouldn't it be not at all out of place to address it as stationary?

---

[21] Olga Alieva, "Elenchus and Diaeresis in Plato's *Sophist*," *Hermathena* 189 (Winter 2010): 71–92 and *Sph.* 230b6–8.

Tht. Most correctly so, at least if we agree that some Kinds are willing to mix with each other and others not.

ES. And surely we have arrived at the demonstration of that before the discussion at hand, namely showing that it is that way in accordance with nature.

Tht. Definitely. (256b6–c4)

Scholars debate the interpretation of the counterfactual statement on b6–7. It seems to me that Mary-Louise Gill must be right that the Stranger adopts the counterfactual to keep up the appearance that Motion and Rest cannot blend.[22] The very fact that he interrupts his own presentation and alerts Theaetetus to this possibility suggests his awareness of the disparity between his presentation and the requirements of the prayer. In this respect, it is noteworthy that Theaetetus, who mostly remains passive, contributes in 252d4–11 by precisely appealing to the alleged fact that Motion and Rest do not mix. There are thus good reasons, contra Gregory Vlastos, to think that the Stranger simplifies matters for Theaetetus's sake.[23]

"Motion and Rest do not mix" is therefore not simply true, but the *Sophist* fails to explain under what conditions they could mix. The Stranger's silence might be for a good reason: Socrates' transformation of Theaetetus's soul illustrates such a partial blending. Psychic motion consists in the daring exhibition of *deinotēs*, and the result of such motion is modesty (i.e., a state of rest) because one has become imperturbable by sophistry and the seductions of seemingly promising accounts. This power to not be tripped up, *a-sphaleia*, makes the soul immovable and secure

---

[22] Mary-Louise Gill, *Philosophos: Plato's Missing Dialogue* (Oxford: Oxford University Press, 2012), 227.

[23] See Vlastos's chapter on "An Ambiguity in the *Sophist*," *Platonic Studies*, 2nd printing (Princeton: Princeton University Press, 1981), 270–322.

(*asphalēs*) in understanding (*Sph.* 229c6, 231a7, 242e1). This extraordinary unity of courage and modesty serves as a model for thinking about how Motion and Rest can by nature partially blend.

Soul, Virtue, and Knowledge of Ignorance

In sum, the drama of the *Theaetetus* relates to the philosopher's prayer in the *Sophist* in two ways. On the one hand, Socrates prepares Theaetetus so that he becomes receptive to the Stranger's philosophical doctrines. On the other hand, the model of the soul operative in that preparation also becomes a *paradigm and goal* that the Stranger's inadequately formulated doctrines aspire to become. On this reading, Socrates and the Stranger are not Plato's mouthpieces in different guises as some scholars assume, nor are the two characters antagonistic as others suggest, but complementary. In addition, they are not complementary only in the sense that Socrates destructs and the Stranger constructs, but Socrates' negative destructions are also in a deeper sense higher than the Stranger's positive constructions.

I conclude by elaborating on this complex interplay in Plato's depiction of the soul pursuing knowledge, where the negative is both lower and higher than the positive.

Some scholars think that "learning is recollection" is a view that only belongs to "middle Plato." They note its absence in the *Republic* and later works, and argue that some discussions in the *Theaetetus* (notably the model of the aviary) imply its denial.[24] But on my reading, recollection is submerged and deepened in the *Theaetetus* and the *Sophist*, not abandoned. Perhaps Plato no

---

[24] See, for example, David Bostock, *Plato's "Theaetetus"* (Oxford: Clarendon Press, 1988), 22, 190–2.

longer assumes pre-natal knowledge. But the basic idea of learning as recollection is that having an experience and understanding it are different things, and learning is the discovery of the significance of what one previously experienced. The *Theaetetus-Sophist* suggests such a recollective structure, since what answers to a perplexity in the *Sophist* is already contained in its prequel. In other words, Theaetetus's soul underwent a change with Socrates, but he did not understand his experience, and the Stranger's speeches are designed to stimulate that (re)discovery. This is why he withholds from explicitly spelling out a possible answer to the philosopher's prayer: the answer is in a sense already there. A non-mythical version of learning as recollection is embedded in the dialogical unfolding of these two dialogues.[25]

My reading also has bearings on the Socratic view that virtue is knowledge. Although I spoke of "intellectual" courage or modesty when discussing the *Theaetetus*, Theaetetus's resulting character is on display in the non-intellectual activities of his life as well. He exhibits one and the same courage on the battlefield and in mathematics. Here, "virtue is knowledge" means that the two are inseparable, and Socratic education is never "purely academic." By contrast, the Stranger appears more Aristotelian than Socratic in implying a distinction between morality (psychic health) and knowledge (psychic beauty). Accordingly, his education of Theaetetus, both in form (technical training in *diaeresis*)

---

[25] In the *Phaedo*, recollection works by perceiving something sensible and noetically grasping the Form it instantiates. Recollection seems to work here in the reverse, since the Stranger speaks of the Forms Motion and Rest, while Theaetetus is expected to recall how his own soul was moving and resting with Socrates' guidance. On the other hand, however, learning as recollection also implies that knowledge is within oneself, and therefore the pursuit of knowledge and the achievement of self-knowledge are one and the same. And that is just what Theaetetus is expected to do; namely, to solve the problem of knowledge through self-knowledge.

and content, appears detachable from the non-intellectual aspects of life. Even though there is no *nous* without soul and life, *nous* seems to operate independently of them.

However, since Socratic education enables a restless soul to partake in secure knowledge, perhaps the distinction between psychic health and beauty must be similarly grounded in an account of virtues that transcends that dichotomy. If the Stranger's division between morality and knowledge is derivative, then maybe the ground for his division would exhibit a deeper connection between the two. This possibility is further supported by the observation that the Stranger's dichotomy is inherently unstable. Elenchus aims to remove folly (*amathia*), but folly is alternately described as ugliness (229a1–2, c5–10) and disease (230b8, c4–5), which upsets the neat division drawn by the Stranger.

The Stranger required an account of Motion and Rest that made knowledge possible. But Theaetetus's soul exhibits, not knowledge simply, but knowledge *of ignorance*. The two are not quite the same. Knowledge is directed towards reality; its object is "what is." Knowledge of ignorance is reflexive, directed at one's state of mind; it is to know what one has and lacks in relation to reality. Moreover, knowledge does not err and is final, but knowledge of ignorance is by nature open to future revision and enrichment. How can the reflexivity and openness of knowledge of ignorance be a model for knowledge, which seems to be non-reflexive and closed in its finality?

I can do no more than sketch what I think is the answer to this question. Properly understood, the Stranger's doctrines do not overcome knowledge of ignorance, but rather constitute its obverse, as it were. His teachings and Socrates' perplexities are two sides of the same coin. Knowledge is impossible if there is only motion or only rest. The Socratic follow-up to this is "being neither moves nor rests;" the Stranger's is "being both moves and rests." The conjunction of these two claims generates the perplexity of being (250c6–d3), which gives the Stranger the basis for developing his doctrines. He presents *aporiai* in a positive key, but they do not stop being *aporiai* because of that. Just as courage results in modesty, the soul's beautification turns out to be no different from its convalescence. The bifurcation of virtue and knowledge in the soul emerges as a roundabout way towards their hidden unity.

Bibliography

Alieva, Olga. "Elenchus and Diaeresis in Plato's *Sophist*." *Hermathena* 189 (Winter 2010): 71–92.

Benardete, Seth. *The Being of the Beautiful: Plato's "Theaetetus," "Sophist," and "Statesman."* Chicago: University of Chicago Press, 1984.

Blondell, Ruby. *The Play of Character in Plato's Dialogues*. Cambridge: Cambridge University Press, 2002.

Bostock, David. *Plato's "Theaetetus."* Oxford: Clarendon Press, 1988.

Brown, Lesley. "Innovation and Continuity: The Battle of Gods and Giants, *Sophist* 245–249." In *Method in Ancient Philosophy*. Edited by Jyl Gentzler, 181–207. Oxford: Clarendon Press, 1988.

Burnet, John. *Platonis Opera I*. Oxford: Oxford University Press, 1900. 20th reprint, 1992.

Campbell, Lewis. *The "Theaetetus" of Plato*. Oxford: Oxford University Press, 1861.

Desjardins, Rosemary. *The Rational Enterprise: Logos in Plato's "Theaetetus."* SUNY Series in Ancient Philosophy. Albany: SUNY Press, 1990.

Dorter, Kenneth. *Form and Good in Plato's Eleatic Dialogues: The "Parmenides," "Theaetetus," "Sophist," and "Statesman."* Berkeley: University of California Press, 1994.

Gill, Mary-Louise. *Philosophos: Plato's Missing Dialogue*. Oxford: Oxford University Press, 2012.

Gordon, Jill. *Plato's Erotic World: From Cosmic Origins to Human Death*. Cambridge: Cambridge University Press, 2012.

Kirkland, Sean. *The Ontology of Socratic Questioning in Plato's Early Dialogues*. SUNY Series in Ancient Greek Philosophy. Albany: SUNY Press, 2012.

Larsen, Kristian. "The Virtue of Power: The Gigantomachia in Plato's *Sophist* 245e6–249d5 Revisited." *The New Yearbook for Phenomenology and Phenomenological Philosophy* 13 (2015): 306–317.

Vlastos, Gregory. *Platonic Studies*, 2nd printing. Princeton: Princeton University Press, 1981.

HERODOTUS PLAYS HIDE AND SEEK

Interstitial Essay

Stuart D. Warner

Herodotus, the *muthologos*...
—Aristotle, *The Generation of Animals* 756 b7

Half the art of storytelling is that of keeping it free of all explanations during the telling. In this respect, the ancients, Herodotus above all, were the masters.
—Walter Benjamin, "Little Tricks of the Trade"

Introduction

Herodotus's *Histories*, whatever else it is, is a work about time—about origins and beginnings, about the corruption and generation of all manner of beings over time. Much of the proem of the work, Herodotus's beginning, is devoted to what we can glean as a Persian demythologized understanding of how the conflict between Greeks and barbarians began. But after relating this with some specificity, Herodotus remarks that he will refrain from commenting on whether things happened to Io, Europa, Medea, and Helen in the way the Persian *logioi* say they did—that is, he is not going to remythologize the Persian view. Instead, he will set those figures aside and set his mark on Croesus—the man he claims to know began to act unjustly against the Greeks. From there he will go forward to great cities and small cities alike, revealing, in something of a Heraclitean fashion, how those that were once great became small and those that were once small became great. More colloquially, he might be said to indicate that nothing fails like success, and nothing succeeds like failure...which brings us to *our* beginning proper, Herodotus's story involving Candaules, Gyges and, most significantly, the conspicuously nameless wife of Candaules—a story which, on the surface, aims at explaining how it happened that Croesus came to rule.

I.

Candaules, tyrant of Lydia, of the Heraclidæ, had fallen passionately in love with his wife—that is, became erotically fixated on her (*erasthê tên heautou gynaika*); and being so in love, he believed her to be the most beautiful of women, and he could not help but praise her beauty to his most favored spearman, Gyges.[1] Based on believing that seeing is superior to hearing, Candaules urged Gyges to contrive (*poieó*) to see her naked. Why Candaules would think of privileging Gyges, of all men, Herodotus does not say. Regardless, the latter—both horrified at and fearful of the repercussions of acting in accordance with Candaules's demand—cried out aloud, "Oh master, what unhealthy words have you uttered, bidding me to gaze upon my mistress naked? When a woman removes her clothes, she sets aside her shame [*aidos*] as well. Long ago the most beautiful things were discovered by human beings from which one must learn, and among them is, 'let each look only upon his own'" (1.8.3). This principle, we know, Herodotus himself did not follow, as he looks upon the ways of

---

[1] Cf. Anne Carson Giacomelli, "*Odi et Amo Ergo Sum*," PhD dissertation University of Toronto, 1981, xvii: "The problem of eros, then, is the problem of being personally invaded. When the boundaries of the person are so invaded, the question of identity arises. The presence of want, eros, in the lover causes him to notice that he is not whole: his identity is adulterated, his boundaries breached, a part of him is gone."

life of various peoples other than his own.[2] Candaules would not take "no" for an answer, however, and so he set forth a plan. He commanded Gyges to hide in the couple's bedroom. Positioned to be unseen, invisible to Candaules's wife, he would witness her undress, which would allow him to see her unclothed, fully naked, in all of her glory, thereby able to bear witness to the beauty of her *eidos*, her form or shape—and see her he does. What was invisible to all other men save for Candaules, became visible to him. Apparently, two might go together better than one.

Gyges failed in this endeavor, though. Candaules's unnamed wife caught a glimpse of him fleeing the room and immediately judged that her husband had put him up to this; and while perhaps ashamed, she managed to remain silent.[3] Swiftly, she hatched a plan of her own, one of revenge against her husband, which she then foisted upon the spearman, just as her husband had done. Gyges was to slip into the royal bedroom once again, this time without being seen *at all*, both in coming *and* going, invisible to Candaules, and after Candaules had fallen asleep, he was to kill him. Should he not proceed in this manner, Candaules's wife would have *him* killed, instead. Aware, once again, of the necessity of the moment, Gyges agreed and, armed with the dagger she conveniently had the foresight to provide to him, he executed the plan and Candaules was no more: Gyges has been transformed from spectator to actor.[4] What Candaules's wife

---

[2] Cf. Seth Benardete, *Herodotean Inquiries* (The Hague: Martinus Nijhoff, 1969), 12: "Herodotus willingly violates the universal prohibition which Gyges himself has formulated. *The Inquiries* of Herodotus continually show him looking at alien things." Cf. also, 8–11.

[3] Cf. Sophocles, *Ajax*, 293.

[4] Cf. Andrew Laird, "Ringing the Changes on Gyges: Philosophy and the Formation of Fiction in Plato's *Republic*," *The Journal of Hellenic Studies* 121 (2001): 12–29, where the author asserts that "The stories in Herodotus and Plato obviously share certain characteristics. Both are concerned with the

could see, Candaules could not. Of course, Gyges had seen the former naked, but of the latter, Herodotus does not say; nor does he say anything about Gyges glimpsing Candaules undressing. Yet, he does straightforwardly declare that in Lydia it is shameful even for a man to be seen naked. What Herodotus does not record, though, is whether Candaules, prior to his death, had asked Gyges about the beauty of his wife, or whether Gyges's words mattered not at all. Seemingly, all that counted was the seeing and not a judgment about what was seen.

Irrespective of that, after taking Candaules's life, Gyges assumes rule and marries—oh, if only Herodotus had told us her name, as he has told us the names of various women throughout the work—the now free, former wife of Candaules.[5] Anger and concern about how all of this—that is, Candaules's death, Gyges (a former servant) coming to rule and marrying—has come to pass circulates throughout Lydia. However, an agreement is reached amongst the contentious parties that a messenger is to be sent to the oracle at Delphi to see whether Gyges is to be credited as ruler—especially given that he has taken Candaules's life—a decision the Pythia affirms, establishing the beginnings of Mermnadæ rule. After this, Gyges sends a large number of dedicatory offerings of beautiful gold and silver objects to Delphi (although the reader might ask if the decision to send these gifts had been communicated to the oracle in advance of the oracle's

---

successful usurpation of a monarchy by a man who uses stealth and special privileges to kill a king and take his wife" (13). This credits Gyges much too much, and does not credit his bride at all.

[5] On her name (Tudo, as related by Nicolaus of Damascus), cf. Georges Radet, *La Lydie et le monde grec au temps des Mermnades (687–546)* (Paris: Thorin & Fils, 1893), 76–79; 116.

declaration).⁶ However, the oracle decreed in addition that vengeance would descend upon the line of Gyges in the fifth generation—which hints at some element of wrongdoing on either Gyges's part or his wife's part—and the individual on whom it will fall turns out to be Croesus. We can read in chapter 8 of the Book of Genesis about the sins of the father being visited upon the son; here, the "sins" of a man are instead to be visited upon his great, great grandson.

Coeval with Gyges's ascent to ruling over the Lydians, Deioces ascends to ruling over the Medes. Like Candaules, Deioces had fallen in love (*éramai*)—not with a woman, though, but with tyranny;⁷ and, as we will see, whereas Gyges has been charged with seeing, Deioces, *qua* tyrant, will eventually seek not to be seen. Despite a deep longing to rule, though, he did whatever he could to acquire a reputation for being just, thereby currying favor with the Medes and, if we might put it this way, for being *seen* as just. With his reputation soon firmly in hand, he was appointed as a judge, and considered cases fairly and impartially, which, of course, generated for him an even more sterling reputation. All around, near and far, Medians sought out Deioces to adjudicate their own cases, for he was the man they trusted most to decide on matters of justice. But adjudicating on so many particular cases became unsustainable, much like the circumstance that befell Moses, and it scarcely satisfied his longing for tyranny. But rather than restricting himself just to fundamental matters of law, as Moses did, following his father-in-law's (Jethro's) advice,⁸ and with his longing unfulfilled, Deioces stepped away entirely, and

---

⁶ On the origin of coinage in Lydia and its relationship to tyranny, particularly with respect to Gyges, cf. Marc Shell, "The Ring of Gyges," *Mississippi Review* 17 (1989), 21–84.

⁷ Cf. Herodotus, 1.96.

⁸ Cf. The Book of Exodus 18:13–27.

the Medes lurched into lawlessness: no trustworthy power was to be found. The Medes conferred and concluded it would serve them well, so as not to be torn entirely asunder, to give themselves a *king* (1.98.1), a new beginning—so they sought one out, and given Deioces's initial successes, they did not have far to look. Deioces's masked concern for justice served him well, and thus he became the face of justice in Media.

He speedily sought the construction of royal homes worthy of his position, and bodyguards upon whom he could depend. His position as ruler cemented, he required of the Medes that they build him a palatial fortress, with every other building project in the land to be placed on hold. That fortress, a landmark of his passion and position, was surrounded by seven concentric walls[9]—perhaps mirroring the seven celestial objects thought to be circling the earth: in our own idiom, the sun, the moon, Mercury, Venus, Mars, Jupiter, and Saturn—each one painted a different color, with the last two painted silver and gold, the colors of wealth, and each outermost wall progressively higher than the previous one, such that one would have to surmount a great deal to get to the heart of things. Deioces created something akin to a world order—not a cosmos, but a *cosmion*[10]—a miniature order, one in which the lawgiver was not to be seen by those who were obligated to follow his laws and judgments.[11] Perhaps he thought his invisibility conferred some element of authority upon him; or perhaps he thought it conferred some element of divinity.

---

[9] Cf. Numa Denis Fustel de Coulanges, *La Cité Antique* (Paris: Durand, 1864), 37–38.

[10] Cf. Eric Voegelin, *The New Science of Politics: An Introduction* (Chicago: University of Chicago Press, 1952), 27–28; 52–54; 162.

[11] This inclination should be compared with Xerxes's stated interest later on in the *Histories* (7.8) to have the Persian empire achieve the same extent as Zeus's sky.

We should take note that nothing other than Deioces's own palace was to be built within those walls.[12] But that is not all. No one from outside of the palace was allowed simply to enter and to be in his presence, for Deioces insisted on being hidden from the view of others, magnifying his importance, lest they think, especially peers with whom he grew up, that they were at least his equals, on which basis they might possibly pose a threat to him. And inside of the palace no one was allowed to laugh or spit, for to do so would be to cast shame upon the royal presence. Once established as a *tyrant* (1.100.1), he took to judging disputes again, as in his former days, but now with a greater measure of severity. If there were a lawsuit that required a judgment by Deioces, the disputing claimants would write down their respective claims and arguments, and messengers would communicate these to the ruler's servants and staff. After Deioces had adjudicated the matter on his own, he would respond in kind. Yet, to make certain that all his edicts and decisions were carried forth and followed in every corner of the realm, he sent spies out both as onlookers and overhearers. In this way, while he himself was invisible to others, others were, conversely, in terms of their goings-on, visible to him. However, on those occasions when he heard back from one of his spies that someone had acted wantonly (*hubrizō*) and thus injuriously to others, that person would be brought before him, and through his judgment made to account for the injustice the person had wrought. In such a circumstance, remaining invisible was insufficient for the end in question: Deioces's physical presence as a human being was required for his

---

[12] Cf. Richard B. Onians, *The Origins of European Thought: About the Body, the Mind, the Soul, the World, Time, and Fate* (Cambridge: Cambridge University Press, 1954, second edition), where he notes that "*polis* itself, one might suggest, originally connoted 'ring-wall'," 440, n.1, and points the reader to Herodotus, 1.98, and Thucydides, 2.13 and 6.99.

judgment and the application of justice to take effect. Here, an unseen power would not suffice.

Deioces will rule Media for fifty-three years (and therefore his erotic leanings, unlike Candaules's, did not lead to his erasure), followed by Phraortes, Cyaxares, Astyages, and then, finally, Cyrus, born of Astyages's daughter, Mandane, and a Persian father, Cambyses—not the crazed Cambyses, but a prior one. As Croesus is of the fifth generation of Gyges's line of rule, Cyrus is of the fifth generation of Deioces's line of rule. Now the story Herodotus tells of Gyges, Candaules, and Candaules's and then Gyges's wife on the one hand, and the story he tells of Deioces on the other hand—two episodes that provide the scaffolding for all of Book 1—have remarkable parallels, of which this is one (but let us not forget the initiating *eros* of each).

To add to this, both accounts, almost stereoscopically, bring into play an interaction between *nomos*, on one side, and a divide between invisibility and visibility on the other. Gyges seeks to act only under the horizon of the *custom* that one should only look upon what is one's own. By looking upon Candaules's wife naked, stripped of the clothing and customs that hide her beauty and form, Gyges belies that custom and follows an antinomian course; and then there is the killing of Candaules! He would not have become tyrant of Lydia without being able to be invisible to Candaules.[13] Deioces, however, creates his own customs: he established the principle that the ruler cannot be seen. He understands that principle, a principle of invisibility, to be the source of his power. Of course, a question arises concerning Lydia: was it Gyges who had the power or his nameless wife?

---

[13] Cf. Herodotus, 1.14.

II.

At this juncture, though, let us turn, for reasons which will become apparent, to the reign of Astyages, which will allow us to observe the Medes and Lydians jointly.

One evening Astyages has a dream about his daughter, Mandane, making water to such an extent that it flooded his city and all of Asia. He turns to the Magi and their interpretation of the dream is not favorable. As a consequence, Astyages marries her off to a Persian—a decent enough fellow, from a decent enough household, but still, after all, someone beneath a Mede. After she is wed, he has another dream—Mandane's private parts spreading like a vine, overtaking all of Asia. He sends for his daughter from Persia and when she returns she is with child. Astyages seeks the guidance of the Magi yet again, and their interpretation is that the child will come to rule in his stead. Despite how many years, if true, this would take, Astyages is worried, and so once the child is born, he charges his faithful steward Harpagus with the task of extinguishing the baby's life. Harpagus's concerns are not dissimilar to those of Gyges—perhaps he will be made to suffer for extinguishing the life of a member of the royal family—so he enlists one of Astyages's herdsman to kill the baby. As luck would have it, the herdsman's wife—*Spako* (Median) or *Cyno* (Greek)—had just given birth to a child who died immediately thereafter, so she suggests that they substitute the newly-born child that has been handed to her husband for their own, and to bury their own as if it were the baby of another.[14]

The above Oedipean tale does not end well! Once the child comes of age, his natural leadership qualities shine through as he is assigned the role of king by the other boys in a game they were

---

[14] Cf. "The Story of the Hunchback," in *The Arabian Nights*, ed. Muhsin Mahdi, trans. Husain Haddawy (Norton: New York, 1990), 207–209.

playing; and in the midst of that game, this young boy punishes a nobleman's son for not following his orders. This quickly gets back to Astyages who, upon questioning the young boy, is eventually able to uncover the truth about his upbringing. To punish the disobedient Harpagus, Astyages invites him to dinner, where, in a Thyestean climax, he is served and unwittingly partakes of his already dead son. But soon thereafter Astyages is assured by the Magi interpreters that Mandane's son poses no threat, because he became king in the game the children were playing: that is what they had divined and what their interpretation truly meant. Now, we keep referring to this ten-year boy not by a name, but by a definite description, because, while we learn that upon being reunited with his mother in Persia, he is called Cyrus. Herodotus never tells us his Median name: in fact, Herodotus makes a show of the fact that he is withholding that name, as if he had no identity other than a Persian one.

Harpagus, reasonably enough, seeks revenge against Astyages for what had been visited upon his son, and he will attempt to use the now grown-up (grandson) Cyrus as his instrument (against his grandfather). As a prelude to this attempt, he sends gifts to Cyrus and circulates around several Medes the idea that they would be better off ruled by Cyrus rather than by Astyages—as if those were the only alternatives. With the groundwork prepared, Harpagus then sends a note with a most trusted servant to Cyrus, for his eyes only, which he hides inside of a dead hare, for Astyages was having the roads watched, lest someone inform Cyrus what he had done years ago. The note explained the circumstances of how the latter came to be raised by the unnamed herdsman and his wife Spako, and suggested to Cyrus a plan of how to proceed against Astyages and the Medes. Cyrus viewed the note favorably and took it to heart. The Persians had been living under the Medes' thumb, and Cyrus was able craftly to express to the Persians an idea of the freedom that could be theirs—not being subjected to others, while having others subjected to them—if they moved against the Medes and defeated them, which they did. Harpagus, filled with joy, sneeringly lorded that victory over the now captive Astyages. But the latter declared Harpagus the silliest of all men, because what Cyrus achieved, Harpagus could have, and Harpagus had simply replaced one master for another.

Afterwards Cyrus will move against the Lydians, defeating Croesus, helping to begin and shape the Persian empire. Absent Harpagus's note and encouragement, it is quite unlikely whether, on Herodotus's account,[15] Cyrus would have moved against the Median Astyages; and absent Croesus's arrogant misconstrual of a prophecy from the oracle at Delphi (that he took as encouragement to pursue an imperial endeavor), it is unclear whether Cyrus would have engaged the Lydians, leading to Croesus's defeat at the hands of the Persians. In any case, the line of rule begun by Gyges, and the line of rule begun by Deioces, both end in the fifth generation of the rule of each, at the hands of someone half-Median and half-Persian—in other words, a mule, albeit of a very different in kind from that of Socrates.[16]

Tellingly, Herodotus's story of the beginnings of the Ionian Revolt in Book 5—that is, of the onset of the Persian wars, more or less—makes use of a device similar to that used by Harpagus. Histiæus, tyrant of Miletus, had served Darius, ruler of Persia, well, and as a reward Darius offered him (and Cöes) a choice of lands. Histiæus picked Myrcinus, where he planned to construct a city with Thracian workers and materials. But Megabazus conveyed his worry to Darius that with so much wood for ship building, as well as silver there to support him, Histiæus, a Greek,

---

[15] Cf. Herodotus, 1.124–125.
[16] Cf. Herodotus, 1.95; and *Plato's Apology of Socrates*, 27e

might turn against Persia and should not be trusted. Darius, then, convinced that Histiæus might not be sufficiently loyal or motivated, sent a messenger to him with a note cunningly flattering him, along with an invitation to go with him to Sardis, which Histiæus accepted; and soon after arriving there, Histiæus accompanied Darius to Susa. Of course, Darius had already acutely demonstrated his rhetorical artistry as an interlocutor in Herodotus's revolutionary dialogue on the question of the best regime, wherein he successfully defended the propriety of rule by one. Moreover, he also proved himself (aided by a contrivance of Oibares, his groom) a resourceful trickster—as he was able to make use of his stallion's repeated "erotic" longing for a particular mare to be chosen as the ruler of Persia.

It quickly became clear to Histiæus, though, that he was being held captive in Susa, with little chance to leave. Yet, he thought that his cousin Aristagoras might be encouraged to revolt against the Persians; and indeed there would have been good reason to think this. Aristagoras, in part due to his hot temper, had failed in his campaign against Naxos, thereby incurring the fury of the Persian Artaphrenes (and he had also grievously angered the Persian Megabates), leaving him in fear for his life. Just as Aristagoras was in the midst of seeking counsel about leading an Ionian revolt against Darius and Persia to deal with the difficulties at hand, a messenger from Histiæus arrived. The latter had reasoned that if the Ionians pushed back against Persia, he might be sent back in the Aristagoras's service, and by escaping Susa he would regain his freedom. But just as was the case with Harpagus, Histiæus knew the roads were being watched, and any communication might be compromised—and thus hidden communication was vital—which could prove deadly to him. Faced with the need for a safe means of communicating with Aristagoras, he shaved a slave's head and tattooed a message upon it; then he waited for the slave's hair to grow back, following which the slave was sent on his way to Miletus. Upon his arrival, he was to inform Aristagoras that he should shave his head in order to discover the message he was bringing to him, the upshot of which was to urge him to revolt, which might result in Histiæus's freedom.[17]

Now, Aristagoras did turn against the Persians; however, Histiæus's appeal and advice seems to have carried little if any weight. And eventually Histiæus was set free by Darius because of events in Ionia, but soon after fleeing to Chios, the Milesians reject him, and he was soon captured by a Persian general named Harpagus,[18] coincidentally enough, and brought back to Artaphrenes in Sardis, who insisted that Histiæus be impaled and decapitated, after which his head was embalmed and brought back to Darius. Herodotus imparts that it is his judgment that had Histiæus been brought back alive to Darius, he would have been allowed to live. That was not to be, and so to honor him, Darius had his head buried with due care, because of the service that Histiæus had originally rendered to Persia.

Now, at the very end of Book 7, we encounter yet a third episode of writing that is covered over and hidden from view. The writer in this case was Demaratus, formerly one of the two kings of the biarchy of Lacedaemon, but at the time living in exile in Persia. Cleomenes, the other king of Lacedaemon, brought into question whether Demaratus was truly the son of Ariston, one of the two prior kings, and therefore a legitimate ruler. He cast sufficient doubt on the matter, however, that Demaratus was forced

---

[17] Cf. Herodotus, 5.23–24; and 5.35–36. The order in which Herodotus presents the events in question is intended to be somewhat disjointed, as we try to convey above.

[18] Cf. Herodotus, 6.28; and 6.30. The description and capture of Histiæus is the only time that Herodotus mentions this Harpagus.

to take a lesser magistrate position and then, under the threat of death, forced to leave, eventually winding up in Persia as a guest-friend of Darius.

As Book 7 begins, Darius was about to march into combat, and required as such by Persian law to name a successor lest he reach an untimely end. This would have had to have been one of his seven sons, three of whom were conceived with his first wife, and four with his current one, Atossa, daughter of Cyrus, and formerly the wife of the "crazed" Cambyses (and *de facto* the "false" Smerdis). Demaratus approaches Xerxes and counsels him to appeal to a Lacedaemonian principle of governance,[19] that the first son born to the king after he has become king is the legitimate heir to rule, counsel which Xerxes follows, becoming ruler of Persia following Darius's passing.[20]

Whether that advice was helpful is questionable, because shortly after informing us of this, Herodotus intimates that Xerxes would have succeeded Darius in any case because that is how Atossa wanted it, and "Atossa had all the power [*krátos*]."[21] Here, we should step back and take cognizance of Atossa's first appearance in Herodotus's work, in Book 3. Democedes of Croton, a physician who had been enslaved, is brought before Darius to heal his injured foot, which he manages to do, and for which he is handsomely rewarded. Soon thereafter, Atossa develops a growth on her breast, which then begins to spread, making it difficult to conceal. So, Democedes treats her successfully as well, but as a reward wants Persia to attack the Hellenes, which, while in bed in the evening, Atossa convinces Darius to do. Her power

---

[19] Herodotus does not tell the reader why Demaratus seemed to favor Xerxes.

[20] On Demaratus generally, see Deborah Boedeker, "The Two Faces of Demaratus," *Arethusa* 20 (1987), 185–210.

[21] Cf. Herodotus, 7.3.

seems to turn on the fact that she was always operating in the background, invisible in the face of day-to-day activities.[22]

Throughout Book 7, Xerxes will ask Demaratus for his judgment about various matters—going to war against the Hellenes, how to explain what to him seemed the bizarre and unexplainable conduct of the Lacedaemonians at Thermopylae, as well as whether free men or slaves make for better fighters (which is the question of subordination to law or subordination to despotism). Yet, Herodotus informs us at the very end of this book[23] that he is at this point presenting something out of chronological sequence; something that took place earlier. We glean that the Lacedaemonians were the first of the Hellenes to learn that the Persians planned to attack them, at which point they consulted the oracle at Delphi. The crucial point, though, is how they learned this, and that was by means of a hidden message that Demaratus sent to them.

Herodotus is not sure what Demaratus's motive was in doing so—whether it was due to concern for them or malignity towards them. Regardless, Herodotus is clear about the idea that Demaratus had hit upon about how to communicate with the Lacedaemonians. Concerned that any warning he sent might be discovered, he took a double-tablet, that is, a tablet made of wood, the top of which was coated in wax, upon which one would normally write. He stripped away the wax, wrote his message upon the wood, and then melted the wax back down and poured it back over the wood, where it hardened. Presumably, he would have told no one that there was anything hidden beneath the wax. This, Herodotus tells us, Demaratus sent to Lacedaemon. But how he sent it, Herodotus does not say; and on the matter to

---

[22] Cf. Herodotus, 1.91.1.
[23] Cf. Herodotus, 7.239.

whom he sent it, Herodotus is also silent. Of course, these features mark this instance as being very different from those of Harpagus and Histiæus.

Needless to say, the Lacedaemonians were perplexed upon receiving this double-tablet: it appeared to be blank. Herodotus informs us, however, that he heard tell that Gorgo, daughter of Cleomenes and wife of Leonidas, brought the truth to light—that the wax, instead of containing a message, covered over that message, which was then revealed when the wax was once again stripped away. Yet, Herodotus leaves us wanting to know how she figured it out, when no other Lacedaemonian could. They seemed incapable of looking beneath the surface.

But other questions arise, of course. Due to Demaratus's actions, the Lacedaemonians were forewarned. But why did they then consult the oracle at Delphi, and what exactly were they seeking to know about the impending attack?[24] In any case, despite having deposed Demaratus earlier, they seemed to trust him, nevertheless. Indeed, immediately after informing us that he had been deposed, Herodotus declares that the Lacedaemonians still viewed him as a distinguished man,[25] which underscores the significance of them pursuing guidance from Delphi. Perhaps his words were insufficient.

But setting those questions somewhat aside, earlier on we observed that the stories of Gyges and Deioces, and in particular the role of the visible and the invisible in each, structured the opening book of the *Histories*. What remains for us to consider is the extent to which the stories we have canvassed about the hidden writings of Harpagus, Histiæus, and Demaratus structure any part of Herodotus's work (which while they similarly treat of

---

[24] Cf. Herodotus, 7.220.
[25] Cf. Herodotus, 6.70.

things visible and invisible, do so in a quite different manner, insofar as they involve the realm of *logoi*). Here, we should first pay attention to where Herodotus locates them—in Books 1, 5, and 7, almost as if this kind of writing constitutes a through-line coursing through the work as a whole. But what also appears to matter is that such writing does not appear in Book 2, on Egypt, especially. There the nature of the movement and the flooding of the Nile River comes into view as antithetical to everything we know about rivers, and thus in a manner of speaking its nature is "invisible" to us. The Nile, though, belongs to the domain of external nature and not the human.[26] Also, in Egypt we find a divide between a principle of life and the corporeal that we do not find in Books 1, 5, and 7.[27]

Perhaps most important, however, is the possibility that the very notion of a hidden writing—either directed toward a specific person (witness the examples of Harpagus and Histiæus) or directed toward a whole people or to no one in particular (perhaps the example of Demaratus)—is an avatar for the kind of writing that Herodotus pursues *de haut en bas* in the *Histories* itself. That would make the structure of these three pieces of writing (which we never see directly) particularly interesting. Whatever the case may be, an appeal to things hidden or invisible is emblematic of Herodotus as the kind of storyteller both Aristotle and Walter Benjamin had in mind when referring to him as they did.[28]

Bibliography

---

[26] Cf. Herodotus, 2.19–27.

[27] Cf. Herodotus, 2.123.

[28] For many conversations about Herodotus over the course of all too many years, I am deeply indebted to Ronna Burger, Svetozar Minkov, Thomas Merrill, Charlotte Thomas, Charlie Sell, Gary Shiffman, Steven Grosby, and especially Marina Marren.

Arabian Nights, The. Edited by Muhsin Mahdi and translated by Husain Haddawy. Norton: New York, 1990.

Aristotle. *Generation of Animals. Loeb Classical Library 366.* Translated by Arthur L. Peck. Cambridge, MA: Harvard University Press, 1942.

Benardete, Seth. *Herodotean Inquiries.* The Hague: Martinus Nijhoff, 1969.

Benjamin, Walter. *Selected Writings, Volume 2: Part 2 1931–1934.* Edited by Michael W. Jennings, Howard Eiland, and Gary Smith. Harvard University Press, 2005.

Bible, The. The English Bible, King James Version: The Old Testament and The New Testament and The Apocrypha (Norton Critical Editions). First edition. Edited by Herbert Marks, Gerald Hammond, and Austin Busch. New York: W. W. Norton & Company, 2013.

Boedeker, Deborah. "The Two Faces of Demaratus," *Arethusa* 20 (1987): 185–210.

Giacomelli, Anne Carson. Odi et Amo Ergo Sum. Toronto: University of Toronto Press, 1981.

Coulanges, de Denis Fustel. *La Cité Antique.* Paris: Durand, 1864.

Herodotus. *The Landmark Herodotus: The Histories.* Edited by Robert B. Strassler. New York, NY: Pantheon Books Publishing, 2007.

Laird, Andrew. "Ringing the Changes on Gyges: Philosophy and the Formation of Fiction in Plato's *Republic.*" *The Journal of Hellenic Studies* 121 (2001): 12–29.

Onians, Richard B. *The Origins of European Thought: About the Body, the Mind, the Soul, the World, Time, and Fate.* Second edition. Cambridge: Cambridge University Press, 1954.

Radet, Georges. *La Lydie et le monde grec au temps des Mermnades (687-546).* Paris: Thorin & Fils, 1893.

Shell, Marc. "The Ring of Gyges." *Mississippi Review* 17 (1989): 21–84.

Sophocles. *Sophocles, Volume I. Ajax. Electra. Oedipus Tyrannus (Loeb Classical Library No. 20).* Translated by Hugh Lloyd-Jones. Cambridge: Harvard University Press, 1994.

Voegelin, Eric. *The New Science of Politics: An Introduction.* Chicago: University of Chicago Press, 1952.

Part II

THE OPENING OF THE ΨΥΧΗ IN ANCIENT GREEK THOUGHT

S. Montgomery Ewegen

…down from the mountain-top…and out of Crete, come to me here in your sacred precinct, to your grove of apple trees and your alters smoking with incense, where cold water flows babbling through the branches, the whole place shadowed with roses, sleep adrift down from the shimmering leaves, horses grazing in a meadow abloom with spring flowers, and where the breezes blow sweetly there, Cypris, taking in golden cups nectar delicately blended for our festivities, pour a libation. — Sappho, Fragment 2[1]

Introduction

Although the opening line of the *Phaedrus*[2] already gestures toward the temporal complexity of the soul—i.e., the manner in which it can both have a whither and a whence, a future and a history—it is not until Socrates and Phaedrus are ankle-deep in water and well on their way toward the resting place (καταγωγή) that the possibility of such complexity is expressly raised. By way of a refusal to pursue Phaedrus' question regarding the veracity of a certain myth (i.e., the myth of Boreas and Orithyia), Socrates poses another, more pressing question:

---

[1] Sappho, *Complete Poems and Fragments*, Stanley Lombardo, trans. (Indianapolis: Hackett, 2016), 56.
[2] "My dear Phaedrus—where have you been, and where are you going?" (227a). See Plato, *Phaedrus*, Christopher J. Rowe, trans. (Warminster: Aris and Phillips, 1986).

> For me, the question is whether I happen to be some sort of beast even more complex [πολύπλοκος] in form and more tumultuous than the hundred-headed Typhon, or whether I am something simpler and gentler, having a share by nature of the divine and the unTyphonic. (230a)

It is because he does not yet know himself, i.e., does not yet know the true nature of his soul, that Socrates claims to have no leisure to pursue the sorts of questions Phaedrus has raised and must instead dedicate his efforts on cultivating knowledge about himself, knowledge which, up to this point, has eluded him. And yet, despite the urgency of this question regarding the complexity of his soul, Socrates' posing of it is interrupted by their arrival at the meadow to which Phaedrus was leading them. Of this meadow, Socrates offers the following extended description:

> By Hera, it is a beautiful resting place [καταγωγή]. The plane-tree is tall and has wonderfully spreading branches; and there is the lovely shade of a tall willow shrub in beautiful bloom, diffusing throughout the place a most sweet perfume. And below the plane-tree a graceful spring flows with its cooling waters, as our feet bear witness. Judging from the statues and images, the spot seems sacred, a haunt of the Nymphs and the river god Achelous. And, if you permit me to go on, how adorable and delightful is the gentle breeze, re-echoing with the summery, high pitch of the cicadas' chorus. And most refined of all is the grassy slope, gentle enough for lying down and resting your head most beautifully. (230b–d)

Once situated within this resting place, Phaedrus commences his reading of Lysias' speech, the two having seemingly forgotten the urgent question regarding the complexity of soul.

And yet—and here is the guiding question of the present inquiry—what if Socrates' description of the resting place is not an *interruption* of the question of the complexity of soul, but rather an answer to it? What if it is meant as a description of the type of complexity characteristic of the human soul? In other words, what if this pastoral scene is itself an account that contributes to Socrates' pressing task of cultivating knowledge of the soul?[3]

In order to begin to hazard an answer to these questions, a turn to a different—and yet perhaps not so different—pastoral scene is instructive. In his 1943 lecture course on Heraclitus, Martin Heidegger offers a description of the Greek understanding of animality, one that resonates in certain essential ways with the description offered by Socrates above. A turn to this scene and the account of ψυχή implicit within it will help us better understand the manner in which Socrates' description of the resting place operates not merely as an ornate portrait of the beauty of nature, but rather as an account of what I will call "the simple complex" of the soul: a soul not to be thought of in terms of modern subjectivity, but rather as the opening up of, or the gathering together of, the world.

In order to forestall the impression that this turn to Heidegger's text is arbitrary, it is important to note that Heidegger himself was deeply interested in the *Phaedrus*, which he called "the most perfect of Plato's texts."[4] Between the 1920s and the 1950s, Heidegger offered various engagements with the *Phaedrus* (of varying length), including short treatments of it in

---

[3] Several commentators take Socrates' description of the resting place as ironic; see, for example, Paul Ryan, *Plato's* Phaedrus*: A Commentary for Greek Readers* (Norman: University of Oklahoma Press, 2012), 103; see also C. J. Rowe, *Plato: Phaedrus* (Warminster: Aris and Phillips, 1986), 141. Against such a view, see Hermias, *On Plato's* Phaedrus*: 227a—245e*, Dirk Baltzly and Michael Share, trans. (London: Bloomsbury, 2018).

[4] Heidegger, *Nietzsche: Volume 1*. (GA 6.1), Brigitte Schillbach, ed. (Stuttgart: Günther Neske/Klett-Cotta, 1996), 222.

the semesters immediately leading up to the Heraclitus lectures.[5] Moreover, as Katherine Davies has compellingly argued, some of Heidegger's own dialogical writing from the 1940s was strongly influenced by the *Phaedrus*.[6] Suffice to say, as Davies puts it, the "*Phaedrus* [...] provided Heidegger consistent nourishment over nearly thirty years of thinking," continually invigorating his own philosophical development.[7] The myths of the *Phaedrus* were of particular interest to Heidegger, owing to the manner in which myth remained exceptionally disclosive of the truth of being, even when it appeared in Plato.[8]

In what follows, I will leave it as an open question whether Heidegger's pastoral thinking from the 1943 lecture course on Heraclitus was directly influenced by the *Phaedrus*. Regardless of whether it was, I argue that Heidegger's pastoral thinking maintains essential connections to the *Phaedrus* and can help us better understand the latter. In other words, I show that Heidegger's and Socrates' pastoral descriptions "say the same" in a philosophical sense, both offering accounts of the manifold unfolding of being in its relation to the human ψυχή.

---

[5] Heidegger mentions the *Phaedrus* in his 1943 lecture course on Parmenides (GA 54), offered the semester before his lectures on Heraclitus's understanding of φύσις. He also deals specifically with *Phaedrus* 247c in his lectures on Hölderlin's *Ister* from 1942 (GA 53). See Heidegger, *Hölderlins Hymne "Der Ister,"* (GA 53) Walter Biemel, ed. (Frankfurt am Main: Vittorio Klostermann, 1984) as well as Heidegger, *Parmenides*, (GA 54) Manfred S. Frings, ed., André Schuwer and Richard Rojcewicz, trans. (Bloomington: Indiana University Press, 1992).

[6] On the influence of Plato more generally on Heidegger's dialogical writing, see Drew Hyland, "Heidegger's (Dramatic?) Dialogues," *Research in Phenomenology* 43, no. 3 (2015): 341–357.

[7] Katherine Davies, "Heidegger's Reading(s) of the *Phaedrus*," *Studia Phaenomenologica* 20 (2020): 191–221, 196 and 217.

[8] See, for example, GA 54, 189–190.

The bulk of Heidegger's 1943 lecture course on Heraclitus is oriented to the question of the meaning of the foundational Greek word φύσις. After developing an understanding of φύσις as the self-emerging of beings into the open of being, Heidegger turns to a consideration of another foundational word, namely, ζωή, which Heidegger argues is to be thought as conceptually synonymous with φύσις. Both φύσις and ζωή name the way in which a certain sort of being emerges into the open in such a way as to relate to that open. In a word, both φύσις and ζωή are words with which Heraclitus sought to articulate the clearing opening of being.[9]

During his analysis of ζωή, Heidegger offers the following account of a specific ζῷον, namely, a bird:

> [the bird is] the animal through whose swaying and hovering the free dimension of the open unfolds, and through whose singing the tidings, the call, and the enchantment unfold, so that its bird-essence whiles away and disperses in the open. To all of this also necessarily belong closure and the protecting of what is closed, for example, as in mourning. The bird, flying, singing, connects to and points to the open: it is entangled in this. In Greek, σειρά means tether. The Sirens are, 'in Greek,' the captivating ones in a manifold sense of the word.[10]

Heidegger's broader point is that the bird, as a living being, is to be understood as "the essence [or being] that emerges from out of itself and into emerging,"[11] that is, into φύσις understood as the emerging opening of being. To be alive—to "have" or to

---

[9] Heidegger, *Heraklit*. (GA 55), Manfred S. Frings, ed. (Frankfurt am Main: Vitoria Klostermann, 1979), 107 / 142.
[10] Ibid., 95–96.
[11] Ibid., 108.

be ζωή—is to be open to, or open in, or in some way open *as*, the open of being.

I have argued elsewhere that this description—what I am calling here Heidegger's "pastoral scene"—operates as an enunciation of the fourfold, Heidegger's occasional manner of speaking of the chiastic opening of the world into its proper dimensions. Although he does not use such language here, one can see a logic of the fourfold at play in his description of the bird who, soaring in the sky above, opens up the region of the earth below. Moreover, as it sings—a singing aligned by Heidegger to the song of the Sirens—the bird intimates the gods. Finally, insofar as the bird also bespeaks closure and mourning, it also intimates death and finitude, the proper provenance of mourning. Such a scene serves to situate the human within the complex and yet unified opening of the dimensionality of world; a simple complex of which the human is but one pole.

But what does all of this have to do with the soul? In his lectures on Heraclitus from the following semester, Heidegger offers a sustained account of ψυχή, thinking it almost entirely along the same lines that he had thought φύσις and ζωή during the previous semester. For Heidegger, ψυχή, as "the omnipresent, essential feature of the entire essence of what is alive,"[12] is the manner in which a living thing "emerges into the open, and by emergingly going out into the open enters into its characteristic relationship with the open, thereby bringing the open into that relationship."[13] Ψυχή is thus to be understood as the unfolding of an openness to (or as) the open, the open receiving of the open. To be alive, to be ensouled, is to be in the situation of finding oneself in the open in some way, of thereby relating to the open in some manner (a manner that depends, in each case, on

---

[12] Ibid., 55, 281.
[13] Ibid., 281.

the sort of living being in question): "The essence of the ψυχή [...] rests in the emerging self-opening into the open, an emerging that each time takes the open up and back into itself, and in this manner of taking upholds itself and abides in the open. Ψυχή [...] and ζωή [...] are thus the same."[14]

In light of this equivalence between ψυχή and ζωή (and, indeed, φύσις), one can return to the pastoral scene from Heidegger's 1943 lecture course, transcribing it now in such a way as to replace ζωή with ψυχή. Animality, thought in a Greek way, is determined from out of ψυχή; from out of the manner in which ψυχή, as the principle of life, disperses itself into the open and abides in it. To think all of this in terms of the elements of the fourfold, one can say that the ψυχή is the manner in which earth and sky, as well as human and gods are opened up and sustained in their opening. It is the way in which they are all held together as apart so as to let a world stand as open. Soul is the chiastic unfolding and sustaining of the fourfold of being. What this means, of course, is that the soul is *complex*—that is, it "is" a complex of interrelated parts, and the unfolding of those parts in their interrelation. As such a complex, soul is the weaving (*plectere*) together (*com*) of various elements of world so as to encircle or encompass (*complexus*) them. Soul, as this encircling complex, unfolds as the opening of being.

It is crucial to note that this is not something that the soul, understood as subject or *ego*, is *doing*; it is not the action of a subject upon objects that it finds in the world. Rather, the soul is nothing other than the opening of this world itself. Soul unfolds as the receptive gathering together of world, the opening *to* the opening *of* world. As Heidegger writes,

---

[14] Ibid., 281.

> The soul—i.e., that which animates—is the essence of the living thing insofar as "ensoulment" means precisely this: that through it a being arrives and abides in such a manner of being that, as emerging, it unfolds into the open and, thus unfolding, gathers the open and what is encountered in the open [i.e., beings] to itself.[15]

So understood, soul is the onefold / fourfold—the simple complex—of world. It is the site of the unitary unfolding of being in its chiastic dimensionality.

With all of this in mind, we return to the *Phaedrus*, only to see that we never really left it in the first place.

As previously mentioned, it is just after posing the question of the complexity of soul that Socrates seemingly interrupts that question in order to offer his description of the pastoral scene. In a certain rather obvious sense, Socrates' description clearly gestures toward the complexity of the soul, insofar as it points to the various δύναμαι and πάθη of which the soul is capable (i.e., the manner in which it can *see* the spreading branches of the tree, *smell* the perfume of the willow shrub, *touch* the cool water of the stream, *hear* the song of the cicadas, etc.).[16] However, there is a much more fundamental way in which this description gestures toward the complexity of the soul. To paraphrase Socrates' description, now inflected in a Heideggerian way, we can say that the plane tree opens up the horizon of the sky, its extreme height[17] first giving a sense of depth to the resting place. Within that depth, cutting through the earth, is a spring in which Socrates and Phaedrus stand. Its waters (blessed to the god Achelous) are coming into the light of day from out of the concealed dark

---

[15] Ibid., 301.
[16] See Eugene Walter, *Placeways: A Theory of the Human Environment* (Chapel Hill: University of North Carolina Press, 1988), 147.
[17] See 299a.

below. Amidst the fragrant odor of the willow shrub and the gentle breeze, statues of gods stand forth, statues that make present the immortal ones.[18] Within this scene, then, earth, sky, and immortals all unfold into their proper dimensions.

What, then, of mortals? Here it is not the bird (as it was for Heidegger), but rather the cicadas singing from the trees above, who bespeak mortality. Much later, Socrates will tell a story about these cicadas, a story which is first and last a story of death. It is a story of humans *singing* until death and becoming cicadas (259c)—a singing likened by Socrates to the song of the Sirens (259b). It is this song—the song of mortality—that the cicadas sing while Socrates and Phaedrus stand on the earth beneath the sky amongst the showing forth of the gods.[19]

I suggest, then, that we are given a certain account of soul here, an account of its complex operations—or, rather, an account of its operation as a complex. On this account, the soul is the site of the unfolding of the dimensions of world, i.e., the unfolding of *being*: soul is where being opens itself—it is the self-emerging opening to being that holds being open and allows beings to show themselves in their being. Earth, sky, gods, and mortals open up within this soul, a soul that bears and sustains the presencing of beings within (and as) the open of being.[20]

---

[18] Indeed, Socrates offers an invocation of the goddess Hera at the threshold of his description.

[19] Heidegger, in his 1932 lecture course on the *Phaedrus*, draws a relation between the cicadas and the divine. See Heidegger's, *Seminare: Platon—Aristoteles—Augustinus*. (GA 83), Mark Michalski, ed. (Frankfurt am Main: Vitoria Klostermann, 2012), 83, 373.

[20] See *Cratylus* 400b, where Socrates suggests within his etymological play that the word ψυχή refers to the soul's capacity "to carry and hold nature [φύσιν ὀχεῖ καὶ ἔχει φυσέχην]." In Plato, *Opera: Volume 1. Euthyphro, Apologia Socratis, Crito, Phaedo, Cratylus, Sophista, Politicus, Theaetetus*, Elizabeth A. Duke, Winfred F. Hicken, William S.M. Nicoll, David B. Robinson, and J. Christopher G. Strachan, eds. (Oxford: Clarendon Press, 1995). On my

In order to better grasp this operation of soul—or soul *as* this operation—we turn to Socrates' palinode. Within this account, Socrates offers an image meant to serve as a likeness of the soul: namely, the image of the horse-drawn chariot. In the case of the human soul, a pair of horses—one well-ordered and the other truculent and intractable—draw the chariot forward in clumsy imitation of the more elegant movements of the divine souls. An arduous ascent is undertaken to the summit of the heavens where the souls gaze upon, or in many cases merely glimpse, what is outside of the heavens. Socrates then purports to speak the truth of this place beyond the heavens: "This is the place [τὸν τόπον] of being, the being that truly is—colorless, shapeless, and untouchable, visible to νοῦς alone, the soul's pilot [ψυχῆς κυβερνήτῃ], and the source of true knowledge" (247c). Although the human soul, like that of the gods, looks upon this place, it does so incompletely or in a confused manner, seeing some aspects but not others. As a result, all such souls leave this place unsated; and yet, no such soul leaves entirely hungry, for "only a soul that has seen the truth can enter a human form" (249b).

Thus, to be human—to have the soul characteristic of being human—is to have beheld, already in advance (albeit in an incomplete manner), the place, the τόπος, of being: "by our very nature every human soul has already viewed the things that are, or else she wouldn't have come into this life form" (249e). In other words, the human (in order *to be* human) must always already have been opened to being so as to be able to grasp beings within that open. To be human, a soul must have gazed upon the place of being. The human soul is thus the theatre of being; the theatre in which being shows itself. Only because soul unfolds as

---

interpretation of this passage, see S. Montgomery Ewegen, *Plato's Cratylus: The Comedy of Language* (Bloomington: Indiana University Press, 2014), 129.

this theater of being can the human encounter beings within a world.

In light of this, it is important to return to Socrates' claim above that νοῦς is, as he puts it, "the soul's pilot [ψυχῆς κυβερνήτῃ]" (247c). The initial sense of this phrase is that νοῦς, as the only faculty of the soul capable of apprehending true being, is that which correctly navigates the soul by orienting it away from opinion and deception and toward the truth. Although this is true in a sense, everything depends here on understanding νοῦς less as an ability (in the sense of an active principle) and more as the process or potentiality of *receiving*. As Stephen Menn argues, νοῦς operates within Plato not as the mind or rational soul (as it is often translated) but rather as something *with which* the mind or rational soul can participate[21] (a function evident in the fact that the most common use of the word νοῦς in Plato is νοῦν ἔχειν, i.e., "to *have* νοῦς"). As Menn writes, "*Noun echein* [...] is to possess reason, to know, to be intelligent: so νοῦς here is reason in the sense of rationality, that by possessing which something thinks rightly or is in accordance with reason."[22] In other words, νοῦς is something that one can (or cannot) *have*; or, better still, it is something in which one *participates* to varying degrees (i.e., the human less than the gods, the philosopher more than most humans, etc.). As Menn goes on to develop, νοῦς is to be understood as the orderliness of things (cf. *Laws* 967b) to which the human soul can be exposed (cf. *Timaeus* 51e). It is the "king of heaven and earth" (*Philebus* 28c) to whose rule the soul can be subject.[23]

---

[21] Stephen Menn, *Plato on God as Nous* (Carbondale: Southern Illinois University Press, 1995), 14.

[22] Ibid., 15.

[23] Ibid., 18: "The νοῦς that God *is* is just the νοῦς that these souls *have* when they act according to reason."

As Menn also argues, although νοῦς is not the same as the soul (but rather something in which soul can participate), νοῦς nonetheless *needs* soul in order to manifest itself within the world. As he writes, "Plato is saying not that the virtue [i.e., of νοῦς] cannot *exist* without soul but that it cannot *come-to-be* without soul, that is, that although the virtue [i.e., of νοῦς] exists by itself, no temporal thing *participates* in it except a soul, or something that has a soul."[24] In other words, soul is the site, the τόπος, of the unfolding of νοῦς within the world. And yet, as said above, νοῦς is to be understood as the principle of the orderliness of the κόσμος, the "king of heaven and earth." Soul is thus the site of the unfolding of the orderliness that directs the cosmos and the correct apprehension of it.[25] Within the myth of the *Phaedrus*, such orderliness is nothing other than true being.[26] The soul, to the extent that it participates in νοῦς, is thus nothing other than the place of the shining forth of true being.

To bring this back to Socrates' claim that νοῦς is the pilot of the soul, one could now say that the soul, only to the extent that it participates in (or receives) νοῦς, allows itself to be guided by true being. So understood, it is not, strictly speaking, νοῦς that does the steering, but rather true being itself.[27] Said otherwise, νοῦς is nothing other than the radiance of true being that steers

---

[24] Ibid., 19.

[25] Ibid., 24: "[…] a single supreme νοῦς with the power to coordinate the actions of the many rational souls, and so to impose a single master plan on the universe."

[26] See 248d, where the more of being a soul has beheld, the more orderly it is.

[27] See David White, *Rhetoric and Reality in Plato's Phaedrus* (New York: SUNY Press, 1993), 109: "If mind pilot's the soul, it must do so on the basis of what mind discerns when viewing the region beyond the heavens, i.e., the truth."

the soul.[28] In making a space for the radiance of true being through νοῦς, the soul allows itself to be steered.[29]

To better understand what such steering entails, one can look to Heidegger's analysis (from the 1944 lecture course) of Heraclitus' Fragment 64, "All is steered by lightning [τὰ δὲ πάντα οἰακίζει Κεραυνός]."[30] As Heidegger interprets, "Fire, as lightning, 'steers,' surveys, and shines over the whole of beings in advance and permeates this whole pre-luminously in such a way that, in the blink of an eye, the whole joins itself, kindles itself, and excises itself each time into its conjoinedness."[31] Through its essential character of emergence, being lets beings unfold into their conjoinedness, into their relation to one another (as being together apart), each into its own dimension. A bit later, and in light of Fragment 41—"Wisdom is One: to know the notion by which all is steered through all [ἓν τὸ σοφόν, ἐπίστασθαι

---

[28] Heidegger himself, in his 1932 Lectures on the *Phaedrus*, seems to suggest this reading:

> Νοῦς μόνος – κυβερνήτης (ἰθύνειν) – οὐσία ὄντως οὖσα, the "be-ingly beingly being." Here is the γένος τῆς τοῦ ἀληθοῦς ἐπιστήμης. Ἀ—λήθεια: beyond any *masking* by arches, no immersion (247e) in a particular something that veils and conceals it. This vision, but a meal, the vision of a feast. (GA 83, 127).

Although the meaning of this terse passage is hardly clear, I read it as drawing an equivalence between νοῦς, κυβερνήτης, and being in its truth (as Ἀλήθεια). It is this true being—pure unconcealment—that the soul feasts upon, and which thereby steers it by orienting it toward beings.

[29] To cast this is more concrete terms, one could say that when the helmsman of a ship truly apprehends the stars and thereby navigates correctly, it is really the stars themselves, and not the helmsman, who is steering the ship. The helmsman only steers to the extent that he gives himself over to (or participates in) the true showing of the stars. Likewise, when the soul is guided correctly, it is guided by the pure radiance of being (i.e., νοῦς).

[30] My translation.

[31] GA 55, 162.

γνώμην, ὁτέη κυβερνᾷ πάντα διὰ πάντων]"[32]—Heidegger offers the following further elucidation:

> To steer means to forgather everything together in advance onto a pathway, and thereby, in forgathering, to point out the way and hold it gathered open in advance. In steering, presence unfolds in advance of all else: namely, that presence within which, on that steered pathway, what is encountered can presence and absence.[33]

Phrased otherwise, being, in unfolding in advance of all beings, lets those beings show and conceal themselves, steering them into their proper places and into relation to all other things.

Applying all of this to Socrates' description of pure being, we can say that being emerges in such a way as to open up a world and gather it together, thereby allowing beings to come to presence. As such pure emergence, being orients the soul toward beings, steering the soul in this way. And yet, soul itself, in a very real sense, is this τόπος of being: that is, soul is the place, the *there*, where being opens up so as to let beings show themselves—soul is the *da* of *Sein*. As this *there*, soul is the resting place, the καταγωγή, of beings, the simple complex of world in which all things may come to presence.[34]

One wonders if Socrates intimates as much when he says that soul *cares* (ἐπιμελεῖται) for all things soulless, traversing the entirety of the heavens (246b).[35] Or, to inflect all of this in a

---

[32] My translation.

[33] GA 55, 263.

[34] Walter marks the resonance between καταγωγή and ψυχαγωγία. See Walter, *Placeways: A Theory of the Human Environment*, 147.

[35] ψυχὴ πᾶσα παντὸς ἐπιμελεῖται τοῦ ἀψύχου. See Charles Griswold, *Self-Knowledge in Plato's Phaedrus* (New Haven: Yale University Press, 1996), 92.

Heideggerian way: *the ground of Dasein is care.*[36] Heidegger himself seemingly interprets this passage thusly in his 1932 course on the *Phaedrus*. In his effort to understand the immortality of the soul and the manner in which the soul stays with itself (245c), Heidegger writes that

> Being-with-itself, while still profoundly veiled, is visible as the highest and most genuine way of being, pure Da-sein itself: presencing and the ground of the possibility of all presence. Thus the οὐσία τῆς ψυχῆς as ἀθανασία is the genuine ἕν and the genuine being, οὐσία pure and simple."[37]

The being of the soul, understood as deathless, is being itself.[38] It is pure being, pure presencing, on account of which beings are able to show themselves as such. Said otherwise, soul is the onefold fourfold, the simple complex, of the unfolding of being.

As Jean-François Mattéi has argued, Heidegger's use of the fourfold is "the purest form" of a broader chiastic structure at play

---

[36] See GA 83, 119.

[37] "Das Bei-sich-selbst-Sein wird, wenn auch noch tief verhüllt, sichtbar als die höchste und eigentliche Art des Seins, das reine Da-sein selbst: Gegenwärtigkeit und Grund der Möglichkeit aller Anwesenheit. So ist die οὐσία τῆς ψυχῆς als ἀθανασία das eigentliche ἕν und das eigentliche Sein, οὐσία schlechtin...." (GA 83, 356).

[38] As Francisco Gonzalez notes, Heidegger provides a purely ontological interpretation of the palinode: "What he finds expressed in Socrates' account of the soul and of its relation to things without soul is an interpretation of being itself and relation to beings. This is disconcerting because, at least on the surface, Socrates appears to describe the soul as *a* being that exists in relation to being understood as distinct from itself. The soul is that which flies up to being, that which is nourished by being; it is not itself being" (Gonzalez, "'I Have to Live in Eros': Heidegger's 1932 Seminar on Plato's *Phaedrus*," *Epoché* 19, no. 2 (2015): 217–240), 224. This concern is somewhat allayed for Gonzalez through Heidegger's differentiation of the οὐςια and the ἰδέα of the soul (227).

within his path of thinking.³⁹ Evocative of the Greek letter χ, the fourfold is a manner of thinking being that frees the latter from its metaphysical interpretations and allows it to unfold in its full dimensionality. As Mattéi puts it, "[T]he chiasmus bears witness to the unavoidable necessity forcing Heidegger to take four paths toward the emergence of the origin."⁴⁰

As Mattéi further argues, one can already find such chiastic thinking in Plato,⁴¹ such as in the structure of the cosmos as described in the *Timaeus* (which is expressly said to look like the letter χ) (36b–c), but even more clearly in the binding together of heaven and earth / gods and humans through friendship mentioned by Socrates in the *Gorgias* (507e).⁴² Further, as Mattéi writes, "if one considers the totality of Plato's eschatological myths in order to propose the law of their composition, one will have to acknowledge the existence of a structure of chiasmus."⁴³ Such a structure is visible in the "demonic place" in the myth of Er in the *Republic* (615c); in the meadow in the *Gorgias* (524a); in the crossroads in the concluding myth of the *Phaedo* (107d); and, of course, in the palinode in the *Phaedrus* where Socrates speaks of the meadow (λειμῶνος) of the plain of truth (τὸ ἀληθείας ἰδεῖν πεδίον) (248b). Regarding such τόποι, Proclus (whom Mattéi cites) writes

---

³⁹ Jean-Francois Mattéi, "The Heideggerian Chiasmus," in *Heidegger: From Metaphysics to Thought*, Michael Gendre, trans. (New York: SUNY Press, 1995), 39–150, 44.

⁴⁰ Ibid., 52.

⁴¹ Ibid., 99.

⁴² Consider, also, the following from Mattéi, "It is less from Hölderlin's fourfold of the poems than from Plato's *koinonia* of the *Gorgias* that Heidegger's *Geviert* derives its profound genealogy" (*Heidegger From Metaphysics to Thought*, 124).

⁴³ Ibid., 101.

[these] three terms, 'demonic location,' 'crossroads,' and 'meadow,' designate the same location in the cosmos. The demonic location is in the middle of sky and earth, such that the crossroads and meadow are there, too [....] Consequently, demonic location, meadow, and crossroads are nothing but the middle (*to meson*) of the entire sky according to Plato.[44]

Interpreting this passage, Mattéi observes that "the chiasmus in indeed the *center* of the world: its four branches bind together the microcosm (the soul) and the macrocosm (the universe) in order to ensure the correspondence of the totality."[45]

Although this center is presented within each eschatological myth as a place to which a soul journeys, there is some textual grounds within the Neoplatonic tradition for identifying the center as the soul itself.[46] Speaking specifically of the journey to the τόπος of true being in the *Phaedrus*, Porphyry suggests that the knowledge attained by the soul through its journey already in fact belongs to the soul, though it is only able to grasp it on account of coming to participate in νοῦς.[47] In other words, the place to which the soul journeys is itself, i.e., the (divine) knowledge already within, but theretofore invisible to, itself. Ahbel-Rappe has recently argued precisely this, suggesting that the palinode describes the soul's journey of self-knowledge as it moves to ever higher levels of divine knowledge *within* itself; a journey that thus "ultimately goes nowhere."[48] As she writes regarding this journey that never leaves home,

---

[44] Ibid., 101. See also Proclus, 133, 1–10, 76–77.

[45] Mattéi, *Heidegger From Metaphysics to Thought*, 101–102.

[46] See especially Marsilio Ficino, *Platonic Theology: Volume 1*, Michael Allen, trans. (Cambridge: Harvard University Press, 1482/2001), 45–57.

[47] See Sara Ahbel-Rappe, *Socratic Ignorance and Platonic Knowledge in the Dialogues of Plato* (New York: SUNY Press, 2018), 119.

[48] Ibid., 123.

There is a broadening from the confinement of the self, which is no longer conceived as the individual, but rather as sharing the same nature as the form. To lose one's separate self, to be carried away or ravished, to be seized by a god and lifted into the *hyperouranian topos*—this is the madness described in the *Phaedrus*. Hermias calls it a form of *ekstasis*—of self—transcendence.[49]

That such ἐκστάσις is at play in the *Phaedrus* is suggested by Phaedrus' comment, immediately following Socrates' description of the pastoral scene, that Socrates is acting "most out of place [ἀτοπώτατός]" and "like a stranger [ξεναγουμένῳ]" (230b). Bracketing here whatever resemblances there might be between this ἐκστάσις, Hermias' ἐκστάσις, and that articulated by Heidegger in *Being and Time*, we note only the consequence that if the soul's journey to the τόπος of pure being is carried out within the soul itself, then the soul itself, in some very really sense, *is* that very τόπος, or at least *crosses* with it in some intimate manner.[50]

One can perhaps see all of this more clearly in Proclus' understanding of the soul. The relationship between the world soul and individual souls in Proclus is complicated and extraordinarily nuanced, but for the present argument it suffices to note that alt-

---

[49] Ibid., 128–129. In general, it seems to me that Hermias interprets Socrates' description of the καταγωγή as an analogy of the soul. See sections 24–25 in Hermias, *On Plato's Phaedrus*, 104–105.

[50] That a similar ἐκστάσις is at play in the *Phaedrus* is suggested by Phaedrus' comment, immediately following Socrates' description of the pastoral scene, that Socrates is acting "most of place," and "like a stranger" (230b).

hough souls (and human souls in particular) are temporal and divided, they nonetheless maintain contact with both the Intellect and the pure, undivided One.[51] As Finamore and Kutash write,

> every soul is incorporeal, indestructible, and imperishable. This includes human souls, which exist in the natural world in a corporeal body and so are more liable to become overwhelmed by the material world, but can still return to commune with the Intelligible.[52]

Thus, despite the various differences between the types of soul in Proclus' hierarchy, there remain certain essential affinities among them, most notably the manner in which all souls remain linked, even if at a great distance, to the One. Regarding this linkage, Finamore and Kutash write that "the individual soul works in tandem with the cosmos as a whole […]. In this way, the individual soul, a microcosm itself, has a key role to play in the cosmos."[53] One might say that the human soul *crosses* with world soul, that the two are joined together chiastically in their difference from, and connection to, the One. The soul, which Proclus says in his commentary on the *Timaeus* has a chiastic structure,[54] is the site, the center, of this crossing.[55] This idea is perhaps stated most strongly by the Renaissance thinker Marsilio

---

[51] "The soul acts within nature in time, but it also has links to the Intellect and the One." See Pieter D'Hoine and Marije Martijn, *All from One: A Guide to Proclus* (Oxford: Oxford University Press, 2017), 123.

[52] Ibid., 132.

[53] "Proclus on the *Psychê*: World Soul and the Individual Soul" in *All from One: A Guide to Proclus*, 122–138, 135.

[54] Proclus, *Commentary on Plato's Timaeus. Volume IV*, Dirk Baltzly, trans. (Cambridge: Cambridge University Press, 2009), 220 and 243.

[55] Another way to say this is that the soul is an intermediary between the One and nature. See D'Hoine, *All from One*, 122. See also 110: "The function of the soul is that of a mediator between the intelligible and the sensible which governs the realm of generation and guides, by means of its reason—principles, the production of natural beings."

Ficino who, in speaking of the soul as "the universal mean" of all things, writes the following:

> Since it [i.e., the soul] is the true bond [*connexio*] of everything in the universe [...] it can with justice [...] be called nature's center [*centrum naturae*], the mean [*medium*] of everything in the universe, the succession or chain of the world, the countenance [*vultus*] of all things, and the knot and bond [*copula*] of the world.[56]

As mentioned above, one finds this center, this *copula*, thematized in Socrates' eschatological myths from the *Phaedo*, the *Republic*, the *Gorgias*, and the *Phaedrus*. As I hope to have shown, such a chiastic structure is also visible in Socrates' description of the resting place where he and Phaedrus sit on the earth beneath the towering plane tree. That meadow (which serves as the *middle* that holds together earth and sky, gods and mortals) is a meadow that is nothing other than the τόπος, the *there*, the *Da*, of the happening of being.[57] As I've argued, this meadow is offered by Socrates as an account of the complexity of the human ψυχή—that is, of the human ψυχή as a simple complex. The meadow is the place of the crossing of the human with all beings, a place that vividly brings to light the intermingling of the human ψυχή

---

[56] Ficino, *Platonic Theology*, 243. Given all of this, one would perhaps be tempted now to avoid using the word "soul" at all, and to revert instead to the Greek ψυχή, where the *chi* would invoke the chiastic structure being discussed here.

[57] On the soul as "the unified—unifying middle" between beings and being, see GA 83, 360; see also Gonzalez, "I Have to Live in Eros," 227.

and world, the human being and being.[58] In this way, ψυχή *is* the καταγωγή, the open pasture and resting place, of being.[59]

Bibliography

Ahbel-Rappe, Sara. Socratic Ignorance and Platonic Knowledge in the Dialogues of Plato. New York: SUNY Press, 2018.

Aristotle. De Anima. Edited by William D. Ross. Oxford: Clarendon Press, 1979.

Davies, Katherine. "Heidegger's Reading(s) of the Phaedrus." Studia Phaenomenologica 20 (2020): 191–221.

D'Hoine, Pieter, and Martijn, Marije. All from One: A Guide to Proclus. Oxford: Oxford University Press, 2017.

Ewegen, S. Montgomery. Plato's Cratylus: The Comedy of Language. Bloomington: Indiana University Press, 2014.

---

[58]"For in this way, all Forms are in human souls […] in order that all things may be known through them" (Proclus, *Commentary on Plato's Timaeus*, 221). This calls to mind Aristotle's claim that "soul is, in a certain way, all things" (*De anima*, 431b21). On this latter passage, see the following comment by Eugene Fink in Heidegger, *Heraclitus Seminar*, 144: "As Dasein, a human is distinguished from the rest of what is, but at the same time he has the ontological understanding of all of what is. Aristotle says: ἡ ψυχὴ τὰ ὄντα πώς ἐστι πάντα. The soul is in a certain sense all things (περὶ ψυχῆς, Γ 8, 431 b 21). That is the manner in which a human comes nigh to σοφόν, to λόγος, to the articulated joining of the κόσμος. Because he himself belongs in the clearing, he has a limited lighting capacity. As the one who can kindle fire, he is nigh to the sun like and the *sophon*-like."

[59] In his *Vom Wesen der Wahrheit*, Heidegger offers a translation and then interpretation of *Phaedrus* 249b that seems to affirm the reading I have offered here. First, the translation: "For the soul could not assume this form (namely, the form of the human, his fate; that is, it could not comprise the essence of the human) if it did not always already carry along with itself a vision of unconcealment." See Heidegger, *Vom Wesen der Wahrheit. Zu Platons Höhlengleichnis und Theätet*. (GA 34.), Hermann Mörchen, ed. (Frankfurt am Main: Vitoria Klostermann, 1988), 114. Then, the interpretation: "If the soul did not always already understand what being means, the human would not be able to exist as the being that relates to beings and also to itself" (Heidegger, GA 34, 114).

Ficino, Marsilio. Platonic Theology: Volume 1. Translated by Michael Allen. Cambridge: Harvard University Press, 1482/2001.
———. All Things Natural: Ficino on Plato's Timaeus. Translated by Arthur Farndell. London: Shepheard-Walwyn, 1496/2010.
Gonzalez, Francisco. "'I Have to Live in Eros': Heidegger's 1932 Seminar on Plato's Phaedrus." Epoché 19, no. 2 (2015): 217–240.
Griswold, Charles. Self-Knowledge in Plato's Phaedrus. New Haven: Yale University Press, 1996.
Heidegger, Martin. Heraklit. (GA 55). Edited by Manfred S. Frings. Frankfurt am Main: Vitoria Klostermann, 1979.
———. Hölderlins Hymne "Der Ister." (GA 53). Edited by Walter Biemel. Frankfurt am Main: Vittorio Klostermann, 1984.
———. Vom Wesen der Wahrheit. Zu Platons Höhlengleichnis und Theätet. (GA 34.) Edited by Hermann Mörchen. Frankfurt am Main: Vitoria Klostermann, 1988.
———. Parmenides. (GA 54) Edited by Manfred S. Frings and translated by André Schuwer and Richard Rojcewicz. Bloomington: Indiana University Press, 1992.
———. Nietzsche: Volume 1. (GA 6.1). Edited by Brigitte Schillbach. Stuttgart: Günther Neske/Klett-Cotta, 1996.
———. Vorträge und Aufsätze. (GA 7). Edited by Friedrich-Wilhelm von Herrmann. Frankfurt am Main: Vitoria Klostermann, 2000.
———. Seminare: Platon—Aristoteles—Augustinus. (GA 83). Edited by Mark Michalski. Frankfurt am Main: Vitoria Klostermann, 2012.
———. Heraclitus: The Inception of Occidental Thinking and Logic: Heraclitus' Doctrine of the Logos. Translated by Julia Goesser Assaiante and S. Montgomery Ewegen. London: Bloomsbury, 2018.
Heidegger, Martin and Fink, Eugene. Heraclitus Seminar 1966/67. (GA 15). Translated by Charles Seibert. University of Alabama Press, 1979. Reprint: Evanston: Northwestern University Press, 1993.
Hermias, On Plato's Phaedrus: 227a-245e. Translated by Dirk Baltzly and Michael Share. London: Bloomsbury, 2018.
Hyland, Drew. "Heidegger's (Dramatic?) Dialogues." Research in Phenomenology 43, no. 3 (2015): 341–357.
Mattéi, Jean-Francois. Heidegger: From Metaphysics to Thought. Translated by Michael Gendre. New York: SUNY Press, 1995.
Menn, Stephen, Plato on God as Nous. Carbondale: Southern Illinois University Press, 1995.
Plato. Plato: Phaedrus. Translated by Christopher J. Rowe. Warminster: Aris and Phillips, 1986.

———. Opera: Volume 1. Euthyphro, Apologia Socratis, Crito, Phaedo, Cratylus, Sophista, Politicus, Theaetetus. Edited by Elizabeth A. Duke, Winfred F. Hicken, William S.M. Nicoll, David B. Robinson, and J. Christopher G. Strachan. Oxford: Clarendon Press, 1995.

Proclus. Commentary on Plato's Timaeus. Volume IV. Translated by Dirk Baltzly. Cambridge: Cambridge University Press, 2009.

Ryan, Paul. Plato's Phaedrus: A Commentary for Greek Readers. Norman: University of Oklahoma Press, 2012.

Sappho. Complete Poems and Fragments. Translated by Stanley Lombardo. Indianapolis: Hackett, 2016.

Walter, Eugene. Placeways: A Theory of the Human Environment. Chapel Hill: University of North Carolina Press, 1988.

White, David, Rhetoric and Reality in Plato's Phaedrus. New York: SUNY Press, 1993.

THE TELEOLOGY OF DESIRE: NUTRITION IN *DE ANIMA* B.4

Michael M. Shaw

Introduction

De Anima B.4 contains an unusual instance of the middle-voiced verb, ὀρέγεσθαι, to describe a striving of the nutritive soul (τὸ θρεπτικόν). At 415b1, Aristotle states that all things strive after (ὀρέγεσθαι) the eternal and divine. This verb appears frequently in the corpus, but generally to describe human striving after the good.[1] Here, it describes the activity of the nutritive soul in pursuit of its ends. This capacity designates the entire soul of plants and a necessary component of all human and non-human animal souls. Not only is this instance of ὀρέγεσθαι curious in that it expresses the striving of non-animal life, but it also appears just one Bekker page after Aristotle explicitly excludes the faculty of desire (τὸ ὀρεκτικόν) from plant life at 414a32–414b2. Aristotle's exclusion of the faculties of desire, sensation, and local motion from the plant soul has led contemporary scholars to discount this strange instance of ὀρέγεσθαι as describing any kind of meaningful desire or process of the nutritive capacity. Because plants unquestionably lack the ὀρεκτικόν, they should be as incapable of striving or desiring as they are of sensation.

What, then, is the meaning of this nutritive, or *threptic*, striving as described in *De Anima* B.4? Does it indicate a significant aspect of Aristotle's understanding of life and soul, or should it be given little weight in interpretation?

---

[1] LSJ, s.v. See *Nicomachean Ethics*, A.1 1095a15 and *Politics*, Γ.6 1278b21 and E.2 1302a28–9 for clear instances.

The Teleology of Desire

This paper argues that no mechanism exists to motivate teleological activity in Aristotelian thought in the absence of desire. This is clear in the case of human action, animal behavior, and even in the cosmology of the divine.[2] Nutrition and generation also characterize things that are and come-to-be by nature, but desire-like striving is less evident in the activities in those cases. Interpreters rarely consider the possibility based on Aristotle's faculty psychology, which characterizes animal and human life by the ὀρεκτικόν while denying it to plants. Yet, extant text contains traces of a different kind of desire, a striving for an end that seems to indicate a basic property of life. Rather than describing this with the noun ὄρεξίς or its cognate, ὀρεκτικόν, Aristotle chooses the middle-voiced verb, ὀρέγεσθαι, to name the power of this desire-like-striving that exceeds animals capable of locomotion and sensation.

In *De Anima* B Aristotle maintains a hierarchy of ends with respect to the nutritive capacity in such a way that the ultimate τέλος, together with the activity directed towards that τέλος, motivates all nutritive functions, including the continuous

---

[2] "It moves by being loved (κινεῖ δὴ ὡς ἐρώμενον)" (*Metaphysics*, Λ.7 1072b3); "All human beings by nature desire (ὀρέγονται) to know" (*Metaphysics*, A.1 980a22); "We say (φαμεν)...that what desires (ὀρέγεσθαι) the form is the matter" (*Physics*, A.9 192a18–22); "For we say in all things nature always strives after the better (ἐπεὶ γὰρ ἐν ἅπασιν ἀεὶ τοῦ βελτίονος ὀρέγεσθαὶ φαμεν τὴν φύσιν)" (*On Generation and Corruption*, B.10, 336b27); "For all things strive after that... (πάντα γὰρ ἐκείνου ὀρέγεται)" (*De Anima*, B.4, 415b1). See Joseph Owens, "The Teleology of Nature in Aristotle," for an excellent treatment of Aristotelian teleology. Owens attributes the motivation of all teleology to the cosmic desire for the Prime Mover (145–7). See his "The Teleology of Nature in Aristotle," in *Aristotle: The Collected Papers of Joseph Owens*, John R. Catan, ed. (Albany: State University of New York Press, 1981), 136–147. For Aristotle's works, see Aristotle, *The Complete Works of Aristotle: The Revised Oxford Translation*, 2 volumes, Jonathan Barnes, ed. (Princeton: Princeton University Press, Bollingen Series LXXI-2, 1984).

preservation of the individual and the perpetual generation of offspring.³ *De Anima* B.4 attributes the processes of nutrition such as self-maintenance and the digestion of food to the power of heat in conjunction with food. However, he explicitly identifies such heat as only a joint cause (συναίτιον) at 416ᵃ14 and food as a helping cause ("ἡ δὲ τροφὴ παρασκευάζει ἐνεργεῖν") at 416b19. What, then, he wonders, prevents earth and fire from dispersing into opposite directions according to their natural upward and downward motions? Something holds the body together (τὸ σύνεχον) and causes proportional growth according to the shape and limits of the substance. This must be the soul that causes growth and nutrition: the θρεπτικόν (416a6–9). As joint and helping causes, food and fire cannot be the primary sources of this work. So, what is the main cause of nutrition and generation? The only answer available through the text of *De Anima* B.4 is the *threptic* striving described by ὀρέγεσθαι. I view this as a motivating power, and moving cause, of nutrition, growth, and generation in Aristotle's natural teleology.

The paper begins by developing the interrelationship of the psychic δυνάμεις, maintaining that the processes described in Aristotle's analysis of the θρεπτικόν belong to all perishable οὐσία. The second section focuses on Aristotle's conception of nutritive striving and the difficulties inherent in attributing such a desire to the nutritive soul. Section Three examines the relationship between nutrition and generation, developing Aristotle's argument that in fact the former occurs for the sake of the latter.

---

[3] This project is developed from my 2006 Doctoral Dissertation, *Oregesthai and Natural Teleology: The Role of Desire in Aristotle's Ontology*, especially Chapter Four, "Ontological Striving and the Nutritive soul in *De Anima* B.3–4." For a recent treatment of *De Anima* B.4 that emphasizes the *telos* of generation as the motivation of nutrition, see Coates and Lennox, "Aristotle on the Unity of the Nutritive and Reproductive Functions," *Phronesis* 65, no. 4 (2020): 414–466.

The Teleology of Desire

The conclusion reflects upon the implications of this interpretation for Aristotle's overall ontology.

The Nested Soul

The Presocratic philosophers recognize a connection between plant and animal life that exceeds the interpretations of the post-Aristotelian tradition. Empedocles, likely following the Pythagorean understanding, emphasizes that the cycle of reincarnation includes plants. "For ere now I have been a boy, a girl; a bush, a fowl, and a fish travelling in the sea" (Empedocles, B117). This Empedoclean conception of the unity of all life proposes similarities between plants and animals that may involve attributing processes that characterize animal life to plants as well. Traces of this view are preserved in Pseudo-Aristotle's *On Plants*: "Now Anaxagoras and Empedocles say that [plants] are influenced by desire; they also assert that they have sensation and sadness and pleasure" (Pseudo-Aristotle, *On Plants*, 815a24–26). On this point, Aristotle is thought to differentiate himself from these predecessors. *De Anima* distinguishes animal life from plants based on the presence and operation of the locomotive, sensing, and desiring powers of the soul. Animals have them and plants do not. While the text is clear on the presence and absence of the ὀρεκτικόν in animals and plants, it does not insist that plants lack a motivational power for striving after their ends. If fact, *De Anima* B.4 insists that they do have such a power and describes it in language characteristic of human and animal striving, or desire.

Aristotle's basic methodology in *De Anima* B finds a consistent interpretation in the commentaries. First, he provides a general account of ψυχή that describes the essential character of all souls but does not address specific capacities of any individual soul.[4] This single definition for such disparate beings as plants, fish, horses, and human beings provides a truly generic understanding of the most common features of every soul. Following the general account, Aristotle investigates the exact features of particular psychic capacities as the second component to his analysis. This provides a specific account of soul that supplements and sublates what the most general account offers by examining features of soul that belong to some living beings but not to others.

The first and fourth chapters of *De Anima* develop this project with very different accounts of the soul. *De Anima* B.1 almost reluctantly defines the soul in its most general sense, corresponding to a definition of *figure*. "If indeed it is necessary to say something common about all soul, it must be the first actuality of a natural body with organs" (*De Anima*, B.1 412b4–6).[5] At 414b20–28, Aristotle explains the limitations of this definition by developing the analogy between soul and figure. Just as there

---

[4] On Aristotle's two-part account in *De Anima*, see Apostle, *De Anima*, 95, in *Aristotle's On the Soul (De Anima)*, Hippocrates G. Apostle, translation with commentaries and glossary (Grinnell: The Peripatetic Press, 1981); Aquinas, *De Anima*, 118, in St. Thomas Aquinas, *A Commentary on Aristotle's De Anima*, Robert Pasnau, trans. (New Haven: Yale University Press, 1999); and Simplicius, 112–113, in *On Aristotle's On The Soul 1.1-2.4*, James O. Urmson translation with notes by Peter Lautner (Ithaca: Cornell University Press, 1995).

On the most general account that holds for every soul, see Themistius, *On Aristotle's On The Soul*, Robert B. Todd, trans. (Ithaca: Cornell University Press, 1996), 56 and David Ross in *Aristotle: De Anima*, with introduction and commentary by Sir David Ross, ed. (Oxford: Oxford University Press, 1999), 211. Themistius characterizes the first part as stating, "what the soul is in its genus" (59). See *De Anima*,1412a4–6 on the general account of soul, and1 414b19–415a1 on the comparison between soul and figure. The first account of soul is compared to a general account of "figure" and the second is compared to that of a circle or square.

[5] Translations of Aristotle's *De Anima* are my own.

are only triangles, squares, etc., so are there only plant souls, animal souls, and human souls. The most generic concept does not describe an ontological reality; only specific instances of the genus achieve actual existence in Aristotle's worldview. To supplement this general account, Aristotle offers a second definition of soul that describes each of the actually existing souls in their unique specificity: the nutritive soul, the sensitive soul, the desiring soul, the locomotive soul, and the thinking soul.

This second account is also universal, but unlike the first, the second refers to something that also actually exists as a substance. The first definition, that "the soul is an actuality of the first sort of a natural body having life potentially in it" (*De Anima*, B.1 412a26–27), describes the common and essential features of all souls without detailing specific features of any existing thing. This definition of soul thus resembles a definition of "color," "shape," or "figure." It identifies only common features without including any specific differences. The second account will offer a second common definition of soul. However, instead of concentrating on the common features of all soul, it describes only the plant soul, τὸ θρεπτικόν. Yet this is also a common account of soul, as it describes the basic life functions belonging to all perishable living things without exception.

At 414b28–31, Aristotle develops the similarity between the cases of figure and soul, giving a very clear account of what Gareth B. Matthews calls *nesting*.[6] "The cases of figure and soul are exactly parallel; for the particulars subsumed under the common name in both cases—figures and living beings—constitute a single series, each successive term of which potentially contains the predecessor, e.g. the square the triangle, the sensory power

---

[6] Gareth B. Matthews, "De Anima 2.2–4 and the Meaning of Life," in *Essays on Aristotle's* De Anima, Martha C. Nussbaum and Amélie O. Rorty, eds. (New York: Oxford UP, 1992), 185–193, 188.

the self-nutritive" (*De Anima*, B.3 414b28–31). Just as the triangle is contained potentially within the square, and the square within the cube, so is the nutritive soul contained potentially within the sensitive soul, and the sensitive soul within the thinking soul.[7] In this way, an account of a square must include that of a triangle and an account of the sensitive soul must include that of the nutritive soul. Because of this, Aristotle will proceed successively by describing first the nutritive soul and then each of the more complex souls that include all the previously described capacities within their being. This nested relationship requires that whatever is determined regarding the nutritive soul holds to a significant extent for all perishable living things. It is in this sense that the discussion of the θρεπτικόν provides a *second kind of universal account* of the soul. In short, any psychic characteristics that belong to all perishable beings must be properties of only the nutritive soul.[8]

The truths concerning the θρεπτικόν in plants do not describe the θρεπτικόν in human beings and other animals in an identical manner, yet the processes are sublated and remain. The powers of sensation, desire, locomotion, and thought all add components to life that go well beyond anything that can be accounted for by mere nutrition and growth. The infusion of the power of nutrition with any of these other powers also changes its manner of being.[9] However, the higher life forms also undergo

---

[7] Hicks explains, "[i]n every case the lower faculty can exist apart from the higher, but the higher presupposes those below it." See *Aristotle: De Anima*, introduction and notes by Robert D. Hicks, trans. (New York: Arno Press, 1976), 335. See also Aquinas, *De Anima*, 157.

[8] See R. A. H. King, *Aristotle on Life and Death* (London: Gerald Duckworth & Co. Ltd., 2001), 3 and 40–48, and Themistius, 68.

[9] Simplicius explains, "[b]ut in the case of figures the triangle is present in the quadrilateral and the nutritive is in the sensitive. But not in the same way even in these. For the triangle is not actually present in the quadrilateral

growth and nutrition, and these activities owe their origin to the nutritive soul. The analysis of the θρεπτικόν alone describes only the life of plants; yet it also describes the most common features of all mortal creatures, and we have no separate account of the power of nutrition in animals and in human beings.

While the nested soul proves helpful for the question of generation, it significantly problematizes the ensuing discussion of nutritive striving. "Only the nutritive capacity [τὸ θρεπτικόν] belongs to plants, to other things [belong] both this and the capacity of sense-perception [τὸ αἰσθητικόν]. And if [they have] the capacity of sense-perception, then also the capacity of desire [τὸ ὀρεκτικόν], for ὄρεξις is the genus of which ἐπιθυμία, θυμὸς, and βούλησις are the species" (*De Anima*, B.3 414a32–414b3). Aristotle explains that based on this understanding of the nested soul, the ὀρεκτικόν never exists without the θρεπτικόν, but that a plant soul consists of the θρεπτικόν existing without the ὀρεκτικόν. Because desire is produced by the ὀρεκτικόν,[10] and plants unquestionably lack this potentiality of soul, they should be as incapable of striving or desiring as they are of sensation. However, Aristotle never directly states that plants lack desire in every possible sense. He only argues that plants lack the ὀρεκτικόν and all desire produced by it (ἐπιθυμία, θυμὸς, and

---

as it was on its own, nor is the nutritive present in the sensitive as on its own. For it is altogether inseparably in plants, but in animals the element of use appears more obvious and is in correspondence with sensation. For the soul of these others that have sensation is a whole through the whole itself, so that its nutritive element is, as it were, fused with the sensitive" (*On the Soul*, 145). In animals, then, the nutritive soul is fused with the sensitive soul; it does not achieve separate existence as a unique capacity in animals as it does in plants.

[10]At *De Anima* B.3 414b1–2, Aristotle describes ὄρεξις as a generic sort of desire that incorporates ἐπιθυμία, θυμὸς, and βούλησις. B.3 414a29–414b1 clarifies that all animals possess the ὀρεκτικόν and experience ὄρεξις; plants, however, have only the θρεπτικόν and so necessarily lack the ὀρεκτικόν and all forms of ὄρεξις.

βούλησις). Rather than being an omission of an obvious point, this may indicate an essential relationship between a non-intentional (non-animal) striving to Aristotle's conception of the nutritive soul.

De Anima's second account of ψυχή defines potentialities, or δυνάμεις, according to their capacities, powers, or functions. Aristotle insists that this project requires knowledge of the activities produced by each capacity, as well as the objects or ends of those activities. "[A]ctivities [αἱ ἐνέργειαι] and actions are prior in account to the potentialities [τῶν δυνάμεων]. And if this is so, still before these the things to which [these activities] correspond [τὰ ἀντικείμενα] must be investigated" (*De Anima*, B.4 415a18–21). He thus proposes a precise order of investigation, with the ultimate goal being an account of each psychic δύναμις. To achieve this account and develop an understanding of each capacity, the philosopher must investigate both the activities of those capacities as well as the objects towards which those activities are directed.[11] For example, the sensitive capacity causes the activity of sensation directed toward the object of the sensible. This strategy is thoroughly teleological because a capacity can only be understood in relation to its end. An appropriate understanding of the nutritive capacity, too, requires knowledge not only of this capacity's powers, but also of the activities caused by those powers and the ends of those activities.

---

[11] See Themistius *On the Soul* 68 on Aristotle's use of τὰ ἀντικείμενα as relating capacities for and objects of activities. See Aquinas, *De Anima*, 161–162 and Apostle, *On the Soul*, 107 on the priority of actuality to potentiality and why the objects of activities are prior in knowledge to the activities themselves.

Generation and Striving After the Divine

Aristotle's approach requires identifying the end of a psychic power in order to understand that capacity and its activities. Making an error with respect to the end of nutrition will result in subsequent mistakes regarding nutritive activities as well as the capacity itself. Some scholars, such as Martha Nussbaum, prohibit either inquiring into any end of nutrition beyond self-maintenance or attributing the cause of nutritive processes to any sort of "mysterious strivings."[12] This reading denies both the striving itself as well as its end of perpetual generation to have any relevance to Aristotle's nutritive soul. However, Aristotle appears to maintain both things as central to his conception of this δύναμις. As he develops the τέλος of nutrition, the motivating factor of the θρεπτικόν is shown to be the desire for the eternal and divine.

---

[12] See Nussbaum, "Aristotle on Teleological Explanation," in *Aristotle's De Motu Animalium: Text with Translation, Commentary, and Interpretive Essays*, commentary by Martha C. Nussbaum, trans. and ed. (Princeton: Princeton University Press, 1985), 85.

"Teleological accounts show the relevance of an organ or a process to this self—nourishing activity, and contribute to an analysis of it" (85). She argues that the goal of self—maintenance provides an *absolute limit* to teleological accounts of the nutritive soul. "What we cannot do is (1) to ask what the function of self—maintaining itself is (that we take as given, and as "most natural"), or (2) to ask what the function of a certain type of animal is, in some larger scheme of things" (81). Nussbaum thus prohibits both inquiring into the purpose of self—maintenance and developing any conception of a "cosmic teleology of design" (81). She rejects "mysterious strivings in matter to realize form" as a prime example of "mysterious, non—empirical processes" (74), a view attributed to Edward Zeller. I follow Zeller, *Aristotle and the Earlier Peripatetics*, 2 volumes, Benjamin F. C. Costelloe, M.A. and John H. Muirhead, M.A., trans. (New York: Longmans, Green, and Co, 1897), 415 and 458–9, over Nussbaum.

The definition of any capacity of soul requires understanding both the activities and objects of that capacity. Aristotle thus distinguishes various objects of a given activity: both food and self-preservation describe the objects of the nutritive capacity (τὸ θρεπτικόν). These objects toward which an activity is directed serve as ends and goals of that activity.[13] At 415a29, Aristotle identifies sharing in the eternal and the divine (τοῦ ἀεὶ καὶ τοῦ θείου μετέχωσιν) as the ultimate end of the nutritive soul, whose capacities include generation and self-preservation. He cryptically remarks that all things strive after and desire (ὀρέγεται) this goal, postulating this striving as an activity that both causes generation and belongs to the θρεπτικόν itself. At 416b2–25, Aristotle identifies generation as the highest τέλος of the nutritive soul and suggests that nutrition occurs for the sake of generation. This opens the possibility that *all* nutritive activities find an original motivation in the desire for the divine.

Because whatever holds for the θρεπτικόν will hold for the souls of *all* perishable living beings, Aristotle endeavors to give a comprehensive account of the soul with an elaborate discussion of this capacity. "Consequently, we must speak first concerning food and generation; for the nutritive soul belongs also to the others and it is both the first and most common capacity of soul, being that in virtue of which life belongs to all things (ὥστε πρῶτον περὶ τροφῆς καὶ γεννήσεως λεκτέον; ἡ γὰρ θρεπτικὴ ψυχὴ καὶ τοῖς ἄλλοις ὑπάρχει καὶ πρώτη καὶ κοινοτάτη δύναμίς ἐστι ψυχῆς καθ' ἣν ὑπράρχει τὸ ζῆν ἅπασιν)" (*De Anima*, B.4 415a22–25). This passage emphasizes that the analysis of the θρεπτικόν will provide the primary and common (πρώτη

---

[13] On the distinction between active and passive powers in this context, see Aquinas, *De Anima*, 161 and Mary Louise Gill, "Aristotle on Self-Motion," in *Self-Motion: From Aristotle to Newton*, Mary Louise Gill and James G. Lennox, eds. (Princeton: Princeton University Press, 1994), 15–34, 17–24.

καὶ κοινοτάτη) account of the soul. Aristotle clarifies that the nutritive capacity is *responsible for generation*. Correspondingly, it is the basic principle of life for all perishable substances. As such, this most common capacity and the source of life will afford a second universal definition of soul. Unlike the first, which develops common features but fails to refer to any actually existing substance, this common account describes the actually existing soul that motivates generation and nutrition in all living things. This comprises the totality of plant souls and serves as a necessary component of animal souls.

As the investigation of the θρεπτικόν begins, the question of generation becomes fundamental to Aristotle's account of the nutritive soul, even surpassing nutrition and growth.[14] 415a22 identifies food and generation (περί τροφῆς καὶ γεννήσεως) as the objects and ends of nutritive activity.[15] The work, function, and action (ἔργα) of the nutritive capacity involves the activities of generating and using food.[16] These most universal life functions belonging to every perishable living being have their source in the nutritive soul.

---

[14] Nussbaum views self-maintenance as the primary function of this capacity (*Aristotle on Teleological Explanation* 76–77). Brentano also supports this view, understanding nutrition as that, "toward which the activities of all vegetative powers are directed" (*Psychology*, 51). Coates and Lennox argue that that nutrition and reproduction are different expressions of the same end ("Aristotle on Unity," 37–42). Aquinas (*De Anima*, 165) and Themistius (68–69) agree regarding the primacy of generation. Interpreters who favor nutrition generally deny the relevance of *threptic* striving, while those who favor generation affirm its import.

[15] See Themistius, 68 and Aquinas, *De Anima* 165–166 on the relationship between these objects and their corresponding activities.

[16] At *Metaphysics Θ 1–3*, 41, Heidegger understands "ἔργον" as "activities at work and in work."

The works of this are generating and using food; for this is the most natural of the works belonging to living things,[17] as many as are complete and not mutilated or are generated spontaneously, to produce another thing like itself, *an animal an animal, a plant a plant*, in order that they may partake of the eternal and the divine as far as it is possible; for *all plants and animals strive after* that, and for the sake of that they do whatever they do according to nature.

ἧς ἐστὶν ἔργα γεννῆσαι καὶ τροφῇ χρῆσθαι; φυσικώτατον γὰρ τῶν ἔργον τοῖς ζῶσιν, ὅσα τέλεια καὶ μὴ πηρώματα ἢ τὴν γένεσιν αὐτομάτην ἔχει, τὸ ποιῆσαι ἕτερον οἷον αὐτό, *ζῷον μὲν ζῷον, φυτὸν δὲ φυτὸν*, ἵνα τοῦ ἀεὶ καὶ τοῦ θείου μετέχωσιν ᾗ δύνανται; *πάντα γὰρ ἐκείνου ὀρέγεται*, καὶ ἐκείνου ἕνεκα πράττει ὅσα πράττει κατὰ φύσιν (De Anima, B.4, 415a25–415b2, emphasis mine).

This passage deserves careful attention. Ὀρέγεται is a present indicative active first person singular verb with the neuter plural, πάντα, as its subject. Here, πάντα, all things, does not mean all things without exception. The neuter nouns ζῷον and φυτὸν, plant and animal, are the clear antecedents of πάντα, which therefore means "all plants and animals." This is because the nutritive soul belongs to all plants and animals. The common feature of every living thing, the θρεπτικόν, strives or desires in the sense of the verb ὀρέγεται, which commonly describes human and animal pursuit of the good. In those cases, such *orectic* striving is understood as desire. In this case, a *threptic* striving is expressed by ὀρέγεται.

---

[17] Τοῖς ζῶσιν is translated as "living things" because it is immediately clarified to include both animals and plants. Here, Aristotle uses ζῷον in both a generic (415a27) and specific (415a28) sense.

The nutritive soul, universal in all perishable life, is explicitly identified as the seat of nourishment and generation,[18] which are called the most natural (φυσικώτατον) of all life processes. As the activities of this capacity, γεννῆσαι καὶ τροφῇ χρῆσθαι (generating and using food) correspond with τροφῆς καὶ γεννήσεως (food and generation) as the objects of those activities.[19] Aristotle uses φυσικώτατον, a singular superlative adjective, to describe these activities as the most natural of all. This is strange because there are two activities in question, generation and using food, suggesting that Aristotle does not describe the most natural *activities*, but rather the most natural *activity*. Themistius and Aquinas agree that the activity in question refers to generation rather than nutrition.[20] This interpretation is supported by Aristotle's reasoning as he proceeds to discuss only reproduction in reference to this point at 415a28.

While the passage begins by identifying both generation and nourishment as the two activities caused by the θρεπτικόν, Ar-

---

[18] Simplicius explains that Aristotle includes growth in nourishment (*On The Soul*, 148).

[19] Aquinas understands food as the object and generation as the act of the nutritive soul (*De Anima*, 164–165). Simplicius develops a distinction between nutrition and generation as different activities with distinct objects at *On The Soul*, 147. Hicks cites *On The Generation of Animals*, B.4 740b34 on how nutrition and generation are identical in origin: self-preservation being for the sake of facilitating continued propagation (339–340).

[20] The two most natural characteristics of the nutritive soul are: (1) it is the most common (κοινοτάτη) psychic faculty, belonging to all perishable living things; and (2) it is the first (πρώτη) psychic faculty, as the primary source of life for all such substances. Aquinas finds generation to be the most natural, "because it applies in this respect even to other beings that lack souls" (*De Anima*, 166). Themistius argues that generation is the ultimate end of all psychic capacities (68–69). Ross, *De Anima*, 225 finds that φυσικώτατον refers specifically to generation.

istotle immediately focuses on generation alone as the most natural of all activities. Aristotle thus provides the first indication of what will become increasingly clear as the chapter progresses: that nourishment actually occurs *for the sake of generation*. A living being capable of reproduction finds its most natural and most divine activity in the generation of another living being such as itself. Both plants and animals continuously produce a new member of the same species. Through the species, perishable creatures achieve eternity in continuous reproduction throughout time.[21]

Aristotle identifies the fact that all things strive after the eternal and the divine as the cause (ἐκείνου ἕνεκα) of this eternally continuous reproduction. "Strive after" translates ὀρέγεται,[22] so that this passage suggests a desire for the eternal and the divine within the nutritive soul itself. Aristotle therefore asserts that the work and function of the *nutritive soul* is motivated by *the desire for the divine*. The soul that lacks the faculty of desire and all types of desire produced by it paradoxically desires the divine and for this reason engages in reproduction, generation after generation, for eternity.

Aristotle's method begins by investigating the objects and activities of each psychic capacity and using this analysis to develop an understanding of the capacity itself. The activities of using food and reproduction are motivated precisely by *threptic* striving. This "most common capacity (κοινοτάτη δύναμις) of soul" by which "life belongs to all things (ὑπάρχει τὸ ζῆν ἅπασιν)" (*De Anima*, B.4 415a24–25) is motivated by an active

---

[21] Compare with *On Generation and Corruption*, B.10–11 (and ὀρέγεσθαὶ in reference to nature at 336b27), *Politics*, A.2 1252a27—32 (and ἐφίεσθαι in reference to plants at 1252a29), and Plato's *Symposium* 207d–208b.

[22] The present indicative middle third person singular, used with a neuter plural subject.

The Teleology of Desire

power or internal force that strives after, or desires, the good. This good is the reproduction of another member of the species and the preservation of itself in existence for the sake of that latter end. This basic force of life permeates and motivates all ensouled beings, all perishable substances, in Aristotle's universe. It motivates growth and nutrition, as well as generation.

As the source of life for all things, this striving must be a necessary activity that always belongs to the θρεπτικόν: not something that plants or other living things can control, but something that describes an essential aspect of their being.[23] Aristotle does not indicate conscious awareness or voluntary action with respect to nutritive striving, which is precisely the kind of striving belonging to the ὀρεκτικόν, and cannot be operative in plants. Instead, *threptic* striving describes something fundamental to all living things, including plants.

---

[23] Alexander explains, "this divine life is in fact [the good] for which every natural being yearns" (*De Anima*, 49) and is careful to include plants in his discussion. Themistius comments, "everything that acts in accordance with nature desires this [end], and performs actions for the sake of it" (69); see also Themistius, 72. Simplicius affirms striving and seeking as belonging to plants, stating, "one should not take seeking an end to be always cognitive, but also to be a grasp of the superior by essential power, if even matter may be said to aim at the divine" (*On The Soul*, 148). Aquinas pushes the meaning further: "[t]ake any given thing, at the time it is going from potentiality to actuality. This thing, while it is in potentiality, is directed toward its actuality and naturally desires that" (*De Anima*, 167). Contemporary commentators generally ignore this passage. Ross translates ὀρέγεται as "aim at" and avoids dealing with the question of ontological desire at all (*De Anima*, 225 and 228). Hicks does not mention desire, striving, aiming, or ὀρέγεσθαι in conjunction with this passage (339–341). Apostle does not deal with this passage in terms of desire in his commentary (*On the Soul*, 108 footnote 6), and he places desire in scare quotes in his translation (*On the Soul*, 24). Coates and Lennox translate "ὀρέγεται" as "striving," but do not address it in their analysis ("Aristotle on Unity," 29–30).

Aristotle confirms that it is precisely as a goal and final cause that the divine motivates this most natural of activities: "and *for the sake of that* [ἐκείνου ἕνεκα] they do whatever they do *according to nature* [κατὰ φύσιν]." The striving, or necessary desire, described by ὀρέγεται is caused by the goal of sharing or participating in (μετέχωσιν) the divine (τοῦ θείου) to the greatest possible extent. No perishable living thing can fulfill its desire for the divine by achieving eternal existence for itself. Instead, these beings participate in eternity not through individual immortality, but by contributing to the perpetual existence of their species: "and what lives on is not itself but of the same sort as itself, not numerically one, but one in species [εἴδει]" (*De Anima*, B.4 415b6–7).

All perishable creatures fulfill their desire for the end of immortality through reproduction. Such striving must belong to plants as well as animals, for the investigation into what constitutes the totality of plant souls leads to Aristotle's conclusions on this matter. As such, this striving, which describes the reaching out of the nutritive soul towards its end, must occur (at least in the case of plants) without the ὀρεκτικόν. The passage considers the functions, work, and activity of generating and using food, so that the desire belonging to the θρεπτικόν must be either an object, activity, or capacity of this soul. It cannot be an object of the nutritive soul because it strives after the object of immortality. It is never named as a nutritive capacity, which makes it an unlikely candidate to join nourishment, growth, and generation as powers of this soul. *Threptic* striving in this context must therefore be an activity of the nutritive soul through which the capacity of generation realizes its end of eternal being.

The Teleology of Nutrition

From 415b28–416b31, Aristotle elaborates on the power of nourishment. He admonishes Empedocles for asserting that natural growth is motivated by the tendencies of the material elements. On Empedocles' view, the roots of plants move downwards because they are made primarily of earth, while the prevalence of fire in the stems and leaves causes these components to move upwards. Against this view, Aristotle questions the behavior of the four material elements as components of living bodies compared to their natural activity when not part of such living beings: "what is *that which holds together* fire and earth from being carried away in contrary [directions] [τί τὸ συνέχον εἰς τἀναντία φερόμενα τὸ πῦρ καὶ τὴν γῆν]? For they will be torn apart, if there is not something to prevent this; if there is [some such thing], it is the soul, and the cause of growth and maintenance [τοῦτ' ἔστιν ἡ ψυχή, καὶ τὸ αἴτιον τοῦ αὐξάνεσθαι καὶ τρέφεσθαι]" (*De Anima*, B.4 416a6–9, emphasis mine). According to Aristotle's conception of the four elements, earth and water naturally move towards the center of the universe (down), while fire and air naturally move away from the center of the universe (up).[24] When they form component parts of living bodies, they fail to exhibit their natural motion.

Aristotle pointedly questions why this occurs. Contrary to the view of Empedocles, earth does not motivate downward growth nor fire upward growth. Instead, these elements are held

---

[24] See *On Generation and Corruption*, B.2–3 and *Meteorology*, A.2 and Δ.1 for Aristotle's account of the four material elements. See also R.J. Hankinson, "Science" in *The Cambridge Companion to Aristotle* 140–158; Helen Lang, *The Order of Nature in Aristotle's Physics*, 180–218, 256–262, and 265–275; and Friedrich Solmsen, *Aristotle's System of the Physical World: A Comparison with his Predecessors*, 253–286, 336–352, and 368–378.

together as the unity of a living body, forcing them to move contrary to their own natural tendencies. As such, there must be a counteracting force that acts upon the elements to keep them from being carried off according to their natural motion. This other force is the soul—as Aristotle affirms at 416a8—and it acts as a cause of unity that holds the four elements together in a living body against their natural tendencies to dissipate.[25] Further, Aristotle relates that the soul causes growth and the self-maintenance of nourishment insofar as it forces the four elements to move contrary to their natural motions.[26] As such, the counteracting force caused by the soul is not a traditional Aristotelian external force, but an *internal* and natural force, or rather an active *power*.

The chapter proceeds to consider the degree to which fire is the cause of both nutrition and growth in all living beings, thereby introducing an alternative candidate to nutritive striving as the cause of growth and nutrition. Ultimately, Aristotle concludes that it cannot be the cause of these processes simply and by itself (ἁπλῶς), although it is certainly in a way (πῶς) a joint

---

[25] Themistius emphasizes this point: "[t]his [cohesive force] would not be one of the elements; it would be the soul. In that case, it is the soul that is the cause of growing and of being nourished, not the elements" (70). Aquinas highlights the importance that the "elements exist in a mixture" when combined in a living body with respect to overcoming their natural tendencies (*De Anima*, 172–173).

[26] Gill cites *Physics*, Θ.2 253a11–13 and Θ.6 259b8–16 as attributing the cause of nutrition and growth to external factors ("Aristotle on Self-Motion," 23). She does find that the soul as active δύναμις and final cause provides another source of the motion beyond these external environmental factors. However, her expressed purpose is to "determine how a first mover operates in contexts that do not involve desires" (16).

The Teleology of Desire

cause (συναίτιον) with the soul of these activities.[27] The difficulty is that the growth of fire is limitless; as long as fire has access to fuel, it will consume all of it indiscriminately and grow increasingly larger without end. Contrarily, when ensouled bodies consume food, they grow towards a strict limit and proportion determined by their essence. Therefore, fire by itself cannot account for the growth of living things; something else must determine the limits and proportions of organic growth, which Aristotle attributes to soul.

If the material properties of fire do not provide the most fundamental cause of these natural motions responsible for organizing and uniting each living being, by what force does the soul *counteract* the natural motions of the four elements, prevent its body from being scattered, and unite the material components of its body into an organized being according to the limits and proportions of its essence? Aristotle provides no alternative to fire in this passage, although he definitively dismisses fire from consideration as the primary cause in question. Perhaps he does not need to suggest an alternative here because he has already provided one at 415b1: the *threptic* striving of the nutritive soul for its final cause.[28]

As developed above, the nutritive striving of 415b1 refers explicitly to the cause of generation rather than of growth and nutrition. To solidify the interpretation that *threptic* desire motivates all activities of the nutritive soul, it must be demonstrated that growth and nutrition themselves ultimately occur for the sake of generation. If generation is the final cause of nutrition

---

[27] See *De Anima*, B.4 416a9–18. This "joint cause" indicates the relevance of external environmental factors to nutrition and growth, but also reveals that external factors do not account for the entirety of these processes.

[28] Themistius attributes growth and nutrition to the desire of the nutritive psychic capacity (72).

and growth, then the motivating force behind generation would also be the motivation of these other two processes. If generation occurs because of the desire to participate in the divine, and nutrition and growth occur for the sake of generation, then nutrition and growth will find their most originary cause in the desire to participate in the eternal and divine.

The remainder of B.4 offers a detailed analysis of nourishment (τροφή) itself. The close link between nutrition and generation is immediately highlighted at the outset of the inquiry. "Since then the same potentiality of soul is nutritive and generative [θρεπτικὴ καὶ γεννητική], it is necessary first to determine [the facts] about nourishment; for it will be distinguished in relation to other potentialities by this work [τῷ ἔργῳ]" (*De Anima*, B.4 416a19–21). As clarified at 415a25, τῷ ἔργῳ shows that Aristotle here considers *work and function* in the sense of the nutritive soul's activity. Regarding nutrition, this work uses food.

Aristotle turns to a careful examination of this relationship between the intake and appropriation of food and being an ensouled body. Here, he draws a distinction between the body that grows through nourishment and the soul that is maintained through nourishment.

> Being nourishment and Being growth are different (ἔστι δ' ἕτερον τροφῇ καὶ αὐξητικῷ εἶναι); for insofar as the ensouled thing is some quantity, it is growing, but insofar as it is a this and substance, it is being nourished (for it maintains its substance [σώζει γὰρ τὴν οὐσίαν], and it is up to this point as long as it is being nourished [τρέφηται]), and is capable of producing the generation, not of the thing being nourished, but of something like the thing being nourished [καὶ γενέσεως ποιητικόν, οὐ τοῦ τρεφομένου, ἀλλ' οἷον τὸ τρεφόμενον]; for the substance of this already exists [ἤδη γὰρ ἔστιν αὐτοῦ ἡ οὐσία], and nothing generates itself from

itself, but preserves itself from itself [γεννᾷ δ' οὐθὲν αὐτὸ ἑαυτό, ἀλλὰ σώζει]. (*De Anima*, B.4 416b11–17)

The θρεπτικόν causes both nourishment and growth. The body is a quantity that uses food to increase its quantity by growing. The soul does not grow, but is rather nourished as a substance is being nourished (τρέφηται) in order to maintain and preserve (σώζει) itself. In this way, two of the primary functions of the nutritive soul are explained: one describes the relationship of the θρεπτικόν to the body and the other describes its relationship to itself as soul, so that it may be said to maintain itself. The ensouled body, insofar as it is a quantity, grows spatially by increasing its quantity. Insofar as the ensouled body is a substance, nutrition allows the soul to maintain itself as an actual οὐσία.

With this distinction established, Aristotle engages the question of generation, focusing on the relationship between maintenance and reproduction. He now provides a more coherent argument that the psychic capacity of nutrition actually occurs for the sake of generation as its final cause. First, the final cause of growth is linked to the final cause of self-maintenance because these two activities designate different results of the same process; the former describes the result of using food on the body and the latter describes the result of using food on the soul. Biological growth and preservation are thus motivated by the same end. Aristotle distinguishes between the function of the nutritive soul, τροφῇ χρῆσθαι (using food at 415a25), as the effect of growth on the body and the effect of nourishment or preservation (τρέφηται, σώζει) on the soul.

Through nourishment, then, the soul maintains its substance and preserves itself in existence. Aristotle continues, "and [it] is capable of producing the generation, not of that which is nourished, but of something like that which is nourished [καὶ γενέσεως ποιητικόν, οὐ τοῦ τρεφομένου, ἀλλ' οἷον τὸ τρεφόμενον]." The discussion of generation does not initiate a new thought but rather emerges out of the discussion of preservation. Ποιητικόν refers specifically to the *capacity* to produce, while the genitive noun γενέσεως describes *what* is produced. The clause explains that through the preservation of its substance made possible by nourishment, the soul sustains the capacity to produce a generated offspring like itself. Nothing can generate itself, so to fulfill the final cause of sharing in the eternal and divine—the final cause that motivates all activities of the nutritive soul through *threptic* striving—the soul maintains itself for the sake of being able to generate another being like itself. In this way, Aristotle argues that the preservation of substance accomplished by the nutritive soul through nourishment occurs for the sake of generation. Growth is the effect of using food on the body, whereas maintenance is the effect of using food on the soul. Consequently, as the *effect* of the nourishment that occurs for the sake of generation, growth also occurs *for the sake of* generation.

The single goal of sharing in the eternal and divine, the τέλος that inspires the *threptic* striving demanded by the verb ὀρέγεται, motivates every activity of the nutritive capacity without exception. Aristotle argues that insofar as the soul maintains a being's existence, that individual is able to fulfill the function of generation. Since nothing can generate itself, a living being preserves itself in order to generate an offspring like itself. Thus preservation, growth, and nutrition all occur *for the sake of generation*.

Conclusion

The conclusion of B.4 validates this reading. Aristotle directly confirms that nutrition and maintenance do indeed occur for the sake of generation. After defining the nutritive potentiality as the capacity for maintenance at 416b17–9, he reveals what his analysis has so strongly suggested: that the final cause of maintenance is generation. "Since then it is just to call all things after their end [τοῦ τέλους], and the end [τέλος] is to generate a thing such as itself, the first soul will be that which can generate [γεννητική] a thing such as itself" (*De Anima*, B.4 416b23–25). Aristotle identifies the τέλος of the first soul as generation. The θρεπτικόν is the first soul because it is the essential component of life shared by *all* perishable living things. This nutritive soul is the capacity for self-maintenance, growth, and generation. Aristotle's unambiguous assertion that generation is the τέλος of this soul subordinates growth and maintenance to this guiding purpose.[29]

The preservation of the living being—accomplished both through growth and self-maintenance—results from the *threptic* desire of the nutritive soul. Because generation is motivated by the desire for the eternal, and preservation occurs for the sake of generation, *all* nutritive activities owe their source to this desire.[30] As such, any interruption in nutritive desire would mean the cessation of preservation, leading to the death of the animate creature. This desire therefore can be viewed as *the very force of life itself*, which is appropriate if we recall that at 415a24–25 Aristotle

---

[29] The subordination of growth and maintenance to generation is confirmed by Themistius, 72; Aquinas, *De Anima* 183; Apostle, *On the Soul*, 11; Hicks, 347; and Ross, 227.

[30] Themistius' maintains a nutritive desire as motivating all the activities of the θρεπτικόν. "Certainly, this [nutritive] capacity desires what is divine, and imitates it, as best it can, by preserving its substrate and so establishing a link in the process of coming into existence" (72). He explains, "the end is to reproduce something like itself, so that we would be more justified in calling such a soul capable of reproducing its like than capable of preserving what exists; for that is its end, and that for the sake of which there is preservation" (72). See also Simplicius, *On the Soul*, 155 on the relationship between preservation and generation, and Aquinas, *De Anima*, 181–182 on the relationship between nutrition, growth, and preservation.

relates that the nutritive soul, "is both the first and most common potentiality of soul, being *that in virtue of which life belongs to all things*" (emphasis mine). This "force" is not an external force, as the term is commonly used in Aristotle. Instead, it is the activity of an internal power—that is, an active power or internal force—that describes the necessary and most natural activity of terrestrial organisms in Aristotle's universe: a striving and desire for eternity.

In *De Anima* B, Aristotle offers two definitions of the soul: a first universal account that describes all soul generally but none specifically, and a second that is developed with the analogy of a figure. Just as figures are nested as squares inside of cubes, so are the capacities of soul nested as the θρεπτικόν within the αἰσθετικόν. This nested conception allows for a second universal account of soul, as the description of the θρεπτικόν, which describes the totality of soul in plants, also describes a universal aspect of every soul because of nesting. The θρεπτικόν exists without the ὀρεκτικόν, so that all *orectic* desire is excluded from plant souls at 414a32–414b2.

However, Aristotle begins his second account of particular kinds of soul in chapter 4. Here, he designates a motivating power that stimulates all activities of the θρεπτικόν in pursuing the objects of generation and food. Nutrition and the use of food are for the sake of generation, and generation is caused by the power of a *threptic* striving through the verb, "ὀρέγεσθαι." Because this most common capacity belongs to every soul, this power describes a universal cause of nutrition and generation: the basic principles of life. Aristotle investigates how soul holds the body together, rejecting food and heat as only joint (συναίτιον at 416a14) and preparatory (παρασκευάζει at 416b19), thus demanding a more fundamental cause of both reproduction and preservation (holding the soul together). Only the *threptic* striving of the nutritive soul itself, described by ὀρέγεσθαι in the necessary absence of all animal desire, can provide such a cause from the text of *De Anima* B.4 itself. In short, *threptic* striving is the cause of all growth and self-maintenance. Both occur for the sake of generation, so that the same source motivates both activities. As this source, *threptic* striving describes the power of life itself in Aristotle's ontology. Grounded in the text of *De Anima* B.4, this striving motivates the nutritive activities of nutrition, maintenance, growth, and generation.

The continuous character of nutritive desire provides a reason for Aristotle to dissociate it from the ὀρεκτικόν, for this faculty produces various desires that can be satisfied or otherwise temporarily eliminated. A satiated animal will not desire food, anything that can move according to place can also not move, and one can decline to act upon any rationally desired end. However, immediate death would result from the failure of nutritive striving. According to this reading, the ὀρεκτικόν has the potential to produce or not produce the desires of which it is the source. *Threptic* striving—a desire that cannot be associated with this faculty—lacks this capacity *not* to be produced. As such, *threptic striving proves to be the most essential activity belonging to any living thing.*

An important distinction emerges between the ὀρεκτικόν, the generic ὄρεξις, and the specific desires of ἐπιθυμία, θυμός, and βούλησις. Together, these nouns characterize the desire caused by the ὀρεκτικόν. The verb ὀρέγεσθαι, however, describes a different kind of striving, indicating a distinction between it and the nouns forms. The ὀρεκτικόν is not the source of all desire, but only animal desire capable of being pursued or avoided. Necessary *threptic* desire, a striving that can never be rejected, provides the motivation for all activities characterizing the most common features of mortal life. Aristotle's unambiguous use of the indicative "ὀρέγεται" with the unmistakable subject of "all plants and animals" provides the definitive explanation of the activities of the θρεπτικόν.

Bibliography

Alexander of Aphrodisias. *The De Anima of Alexander of Aphrodisias: A Translation and Commentary*. Translation and commentary by Athanasios P. Fotinis. Washington, D.C.: University Press of America, 1979.

Aristotle. *Aristotle: De Anima*. Edited, with introduction and commentary by Sir David Ross. Oxford: Oxford University Press, 1999.

———. *Aristotle: De Anima*. Translation, introduction and notes by Robert D. Hicks. New York: Arno Press, 1976.

———. *Aristotle's De Motu Animalium: Text with Translation, Commentary, and Interpretive Essays*. Edited, translated, and with commentary by Martha C. Nussbaum. Princeton: Princeton University Press, 1985.

———. *Aristotle's On the Soul (De Anima)*. Translation with Commentaries and Glossary by Hippocrates G. Apostle. Grinnell: The Peripatetic Press, 1981.

———. *The Complete Works of Aristotle: The Revised Oxford Translation*. Edited by Jonathan Barnes. 2 vols. Princeton: Princeton University Press, Bollingen Series LXXI–2, 1984.

Aquinas, St. Thomas. *A Commentary on Aristotle's De Anima*. Translated by Robert Pasnau. New Haven: Yale University Press, 1999.

Brentano, Franz. *The Psychology of Aristotle: In Particular his Doctrine of the Active Intellect with an Appendix Concerning the Activity of Aristotle's God*. Edited and translated by Rolf George. Berkeley: University of California Press, 1977.

Coates, Cameron F. and Lennox, James G. "Aristotle on the Unity of the Nutritive and Reproductive Functions." *Phronesis* 65, no. 4 (2020): 414–466.

Gill, Mary Louise. "Aristotle on Self-Motion." In *Self-Motion: From Aristotle to Newton*. Edited by Mary Louise Gill and James G. Lennox, 15–34. Princeton: Princeton University Press, 1994.

Gotthelf, Allan. "Aristotle's Conception of Final Causality." In *Philosophical Issues in Aristotle's Biology*. Edited by Allan Gotthelf and James G. Lennox, 204–242. New York: Cambridge University Press, 1987.

Daniel W. Graham. *The Texts of Early Greek Philosophy: The Complete Fragments and Selected Testimonies of the Major Presocratics*, Parts 1 and 2. Cambridge: Cambridge University Press, 2010.

Hankinson, Robert J. "Science," in *The Cambridge Companion to Aristotle*, ed. Jonathan Barnes. New York: Cambridge University Press, 1996.

Heidegger, Martin. *Aristotle's Metaphysics Θ 1–3: On the Essence and Actuality of Force*. Translated by Walter Brogan and Peter Warnek. Bloomington: Indiana University Press, 1995.

King, R. A. H. *Aristotle on Life and Death*. London: Gerald Duckworth & Co. Ltd., 2001.

Lang, Helen S. *The Order of Nature in Aristotle's Physics*. Cambridge: Cambridge University Press, 1998.

Liddell, Henry George and Scott, Robert. *Greek-English Lexicon with a Revised Supplement*. Oxford: Clarendon Press, 1996.

Matthews, Gareth B. "De Anima 2.2–4 and the Meaning of Life." In *Essays on Aristotle's* De Anima. Edited by Martha C. Nussbaum and Amélie O. Rorty, 185–193. New York: Oxford UP, 1992.

Owens, Joseph. "The Teleology of Nature in Aristotle." In *Aristotle: The Collected Papers of Joseph Owens*. Edited by John R. Catan, 136–147. Albany: State University of New York Press, 1981.

Plato. *Lysis, Symposium, Gorgias*. With an English translation by Walter R. M. Lamb. Cambridge: Harvard University Press, 1996.

Shaw, Michael M. *Oregesthai and Natural Teleology: The Role of Desire in Aristotle's Ontology*. Ann Arbor: UMI Dissertation Services, 2006. UMI Number: 3207390.

Simplicius. *On Aristotle's On the Soul 1.1-2.4*. Translated by James O. Urmson with notes by Peter Lautner. Ithaca: Cornell University Press, 1995.

Solmsen, Friedrich. *Aristotle's System of the Physical World: A Comparison with his Predecessors*. Ithaca: Cornell University Press, 1960.

Themistius. *On Aristotle's* On the Soul. Translated by Robert B. Todd. Ithaca: Cornell University Press, 1996.

Zeller, Eduard. *Aristotle and the Earlier Peripatetics*. Translated by Benjamin F. C. Costelloe, M.A. and John H. Muirhead, M.A. 2 Vols. New York: Longmans, Green, and Co, 1897.

THE PLACE OF FORMS

Daniel P. Maher

Introduction

This paper relates Aristotle's thesis that the soul is substance in the sense of form to his characterization of knowledge as reception of form. My title comes from *De Anima*:

> And indeed, they speak well who say that the soul is a place of forms, except that it is not the whole soul but the intellective soul, and not the forms in actuality but in potency. (3.4.429a27–29)[1]

Not originating the thesis, he praises it as modified. Mind or *nous*, he has just stated, has no bodily organ through which it operates, unlike the sense powers. Forms are determining actualities of the beings constituting the world. The soul becomes the place of forms by knowing the beings, which means receiving the forms of those beings. *Aisthêsis*, he says, "is that which is receptive of the sensible forms without the matter" (2.12.424a17–18). *Noein*, or intellectual knowing, is something like this (3.3.427b6–14), and so mind is *apathes*, unaffected, and yet receptive of the intelligible because mind is in potency to be such as what it knows but not to be this thing (*dunamei toiouton alla mê touto*) (3.4.429a13–18).

---

[1] For the Greek text I have relied on A. Jannone, and I use Mark Shiffman's English translation, *Aristotle: De Anima* (Newburyport, MA: Focus Publishing, 2011). Other translations of Aristotle (with some modifications) come from *The Complete Works of Aristotle*, 2 vols., ed. Jonathan Barnes (Princeton: Princeton University Press, 1984). Unidentified textual citations refer to *De Anima*.

The tension between being impassive and yet receptive reflects the difference between being changed or altered by another and becoming aware of another. To know is "to have the form of another as other—not to have another form."[2] The form we know belongs to something other, and to know it involves having it *as* determining that other. Although sense perception somehow involves the sense organ, perceptual awareness either is not an alteration or is an unusual kind of alteration (2.5.417b2–16). Whatever *reception of form* means, the forms known are not in the knower as qualities are in a body. We can express this by saying forms are present *to* the soul or are together *with* the soul.

In putting the matter this way—*present to*, rather than *in*—I aim to avoid interpreting Aristotle along Cartesian lines according to which entities called *ideas* are somehow in the soul. Even before Descartes there was a tendency to internalize knowing. Aquinas speaks of an impressed species or intelligible species through which we know real things.[3] "Whatever is known must be in some way, at least in the one knowing."[4] This is sometimes called intentional or cognitional being to distinguish it from existential or real being.[5] I mention these alternative views in order to provide a contrast for my approach here.

---

[2] Thomas Prufer, unpublished notes on Frege's "The Thought."

[3] Thomas Aquinas, *On the Unity of the Intellect against the Averroists*, Beatrice H. Zelder, trans. (Milwaukee: Marquette University Press, 1968), 52 (#66).

[4] "Quicquid cognoscitur, aliquo modo oportet esse, ad minus in ipso cognoscente." Thomas Aquinas, *Commentary on the Sentences*, I, dist. 38, q. 1, a. 4, solution, cited in Joseph Owens, "Quiddity and Real Distinction in St. Thomas Aquinas," *Mediaeval Studies* 27 (1965): 1–22, 3n7. My translation.

[5] Aquinas distinguishes between *forma* and *species*, using the latter primarily to refer to a likeness of the form. And he attributes *esse naturale* to a form found in matter, while a *species* is said to have *esse intentionale* or *esse*

Aristotle says, "actual knowledge is the same as the thing."[6] And I want to try to take that literally or almost literally, doing away with internal intermediaries between us and what we know. I rely on the work of Robert Sokolowski, who wrote a paper many years ago entitled "Exorcising Concepts."[7] We need a kind of exorcism to rid us of devilish concepts, understood as mental entities that we know or through which we know beings. We do better to think of this word according to its Latin root, *conceptum*, which is a past participle. A concept is the being or the thing *conceived*. It's not another being but is a part of the world as apprehended. Sokolowski's more recent work, *The Phenomenology of the Human Person*, drawing on Husserl, argues at length against mental representations. Sokolowski presents illuminating readings of Aristotle in that book, and I make arguments different from but still consistent with his book, which has informed my reading of Aristotle.

I say *almost literally* because there remains a distinction between a being in itself and the same being as known. For Aristotle, just as it would not make sense to call anything visible if there were light but no eyes with the power of sight anywhere in existence, so beings are not intelligible in themselves but only in relation to the intellect that can know them.[8] He regards knowledge

---

spirituale. See *Commentary on Aristotle's De Anima*, Kenelm Foster and Sylvester Humphries, trans. (New Haven: Yale University Press, 1951), #552–53.

[6] *De Anima*, 3.5.430a19–20. The text is repeated at 3.7.431a1–2.

[7] *Pictures, Quotations, and Distinctions* (Notre Dame and London: University of Notre Dame Press, 1992), 173–85.

[8] "It is not the same thing to be fire and to be an element" (*Metaphysics*, 10.1.1052b11–12). Fire is an element not in itself but only in relation to a compound made from it. Similarly, actual being is true and is *noēton* not in isolation but in relation to the knowing soul. Similarly, again, nothing is food in itself; things become food in relation to a living being that can metabolize them.

not merely as a relation between knower and known, but as their identity. Nevertheless, Aristotle distinguishes between being in the sense of the categories and being in the sense of true.[9] We must respect the identity and the distinction. In several writings, Kurt Pritzl has explored this identity, emphasizing the primacy of intellect's reception of substantial form as articulated in *De Anima* 3.4–8.[10] Herein, I follow Pritzl and presuppose he is substantially correct. My particular concern here is to explore Aristotle's account of the reception of form in relation to his account of soul as itself a substantial form. In other words, Aristotle defines soul as form (2.1) before he explains the soul's activity of grasping such a form (3.4–8). In a sense, the deed precedes the speech. I return to this in the last section of the paper. Now I sketch my understanding of soul as the place of forms.

According to Aristotle, we know the world by cognitively becoming or taking on the forms of the beings in the world. The forms, then, are in the world, and the metaphor has the soul expanding outward to the forms rather than copying them internally. The realities we know establish the soul's range.

> Knowledge also, and perception…as a matter of fact are measured rather than measure other things. But it is with us as if some one else measured us and we came to know how big we are by seeing that he applied the cubit-measure a certain number of times to us. (*Metaphysics*, 10.1.1053a31–35)

---

[9] See esp. *Metaphysics*, 6.2, 6.4, and 9.10.

[10] See Kurt J. Pritzl, "The Unity of Knower and Known in Aristotle's *De Anima*," PhD dissertation (University of Toronto, 1982); "The Cognition of Indivisibles and the Argument of *De Anima* 3.4–8," *Proceedings and Addresses of the American Philosophical Association* 58, no. 140 (1984): 140–50; "The Place of Intellect in Aristotle," *Proceedings of the American Catholic Philosophical Association* 80 (2007): 57–75.

As actualities in matter the forms the soul can receive are potentially intelligible (3.4.430a6–7). We have paired potentialities here. The intellect potentially knows, and the actual being is potentially known.[11] Actualization comes through the agent intellect, which, Aristotle says, is like light (3.5.430a15). I propose reading this very simply as expressing that what we need in order to make the potentially intelligible actually intelligible is always active between us and things.[12] Their intelligibility is available to us as colors are available when light actualizes the medium between us and colored things, rendering it transparent (2.7.419a7–20). We see the object's color through the medium, but we don't activate the medium. If the agent intellect is like light, we don't exert ourselves in making it operate. There must nevertheless be an active principle because intelligible things don't make themselves actually understood; they don't make everything know them. The active principle renders the medium between us and knowable things intelligibly transparent and permits the intelligibility of forms in the beings to be active with respect to our receptive intellect. The medium between us and things becomes intellectually transparent, without likenesses of the forms, the *eidê*, traveling from things to us through sensible qualities. An

---

[11] Form's determinacy founds potency in two ways. Soul is the first actuality of a body, carrying with it additional potencies, including the power to know. Any substantial form's determinacy gives it its specific potencies and (in relation to the human soul) the power to be known.

[12] The status of the agent intellect has been famously controversial for centuries. For two opposed and interesting readings, see Victor Caston's "Aristotle's Two Intellects: A Modest Proposal," *Phronesis* 44, no. 3 (1999): 199–227, and Jonathan Buttaci's "Aristotle's Intellects: Now and Then," *Proceedings of the American Catholic Philosophical Association* 87 (2014): 127–43. Whether the agent intellect is a part of the soul or separate is not an issue in this paper.

eidos is the "invisible look" of a thing.[13] The look of a thing is in the thing and not in us. It is the appearance of the being, which is available to us because we are cognitive beings. The agent intellect is like a light that is always on; it makes the potentially intelligible looks actually present to us.

After this initial sketch of my reading, the paper has two remaining sections. In the next, I offer some support for my reading, by considering sense perception, pictures, and intellectual cognition. In the third section, I relate this reading to Aristotle's two definitions of soul in *De Anima*.

Supporting Considerations
Sense Perception

Aristotle identifies *nous* as the place of forms, but immaterial reception occurs also in sensation, which must be distinguished from ordinary alteration in material bodies. The hand, for example, is material and is subject to receiving the form of heat from a cup of coffee in a material way. This is normal alteration, where the actuality in the cup changes the hand and causes it to grow warm. Before that happens, the hand (or the organ of sense within it) receives the form of heat in an immaterial way. We *become* aware that heat is in the cup. This is not (ordinary) alteration but is, rather, "preservation of what has being as a potency by what has being in *entelecheia* and is like it (like it in the way potency stands with respect to *entelecheia*)" (2.5.417b2–5). In material change, we have destruction of a contrary, but in this case, we have a potency brought to its proper nature (see 2.5.417b9–16).

---

[13] Jacob Klein, "Speech, Its Strength and Its Weaknesses," in *Lectures and Essays*, edited by Robert B. Williamson and Elliott Zuckerman (Annapolis: St. John's College Press, 1985): 361–74, 371.

Aristotle's saying that the sense power is *like* (*homoios*) the actuality in the warm object is the sort of text that leads to thinking there are likenesses of actual things in the soul.[14] I resist that reading for two reasons. First, it makes sensation too much like ordinary alteration, where a form comes to be *in* the sense power. Second, the defining mark of sensation is that, independently of heat occurring in the hand, we become *aware* heat is in the cup. We don't have a feeling and infer the cup is warm; we have warmth as other.

Receiving form without matter (e.g., 2.12.424a17–20) means both that we do not receive the matter of the sensed object *and* that the form of heat in the sense power is not there materially. As Themistius puts it, "Sharpness cannot cut, but a knife can."[15] This reveals one limitation of the wax and signet ring analogy. Although wax receives the figure of the ring without the ring's matter, the wax receives that figure in the wax's matter, which is unlike sensation. Nevertheless, the image suggests another way to understand the phrase *place of forms*. The wax conforms to the ring's figure by constituting the ring's place. Place is the innermost motionless boundary of a surrounding or containing body (*Physics*, 4.4.212a20–21). The wax grips the ring and conforms itself to the form of the ring, temporarily constituting the ring's place. Similarly, the soul is the potency for acclimating entirely to the determinacy of form; it assumes concavity in response to form's convexity. The soul binds itself to the formal

---

[14] For debate on the issue, see the essays by Burnyeat, Nussbaum and Putnam (writing together), and Cohen in *Essays on Aristotle's De Anima*, Martha C. Nussbaum and Amélie Oksenberg Rorty, eds. (Oxford: Clarendon Press, 1992).

[15] *Themistii in libros Aristotelis De Anima paraphrasis*, 78.2–3, which is cited in and translated by Pritzl, "Unity of Knower and Known," 19.

contours of what it knows rather than contains those forms like a cabinet would.

Pictures

My appeal to pictures is taken directly from Sokolowski, who develops this theme from Husserl.[16] According to this understanding, we constitute a painting or a photograph as a picture when we take it as presenting something other. In itself, a painting is canvas and paint, and for a dog, this is all the painting can be. But for us it can present something distinct from itself as a material object. It becomes actually a picture when we look at it. As Aristotle says, when we look at images, we see "that this is that" (*hoti houtos ekeinos*, *Poet.* 4.1448b17, my translation). Two-dimensional lines, shapes, and colors (this) present a three-dimensional being (that). We see the original in the image. George Washington, say, is present to us through his portrait.

A picture of Washington differs from a sign of him; footprints in the snow are a sign of an animal but not a picture. When we see the portrait as a picture, we don't turn away from it to our memory or our understanding of him. The picture gives us Washington as pictured, the same Washington who crossed the Delaware and who is spoken of in the history books. It can present him because it is like him, but mere likeness does not make something a picture. Two Toyota Camrys are similar, but neither is a picture of the other. Not just anything can be taken as a picture, but even something very unlike an original can be a picture. A cartoon-quality drawing of a rabbit pictures a rabbit even though black lines on white paper are nothing at all like a real rabbit and would not interest a dog. Our intelligence actualizes

---

[16] See Robert Sokolowski, "Picturing," in *Pictures, Quotations, and Distinctions*, 3–26.

the potential found in the physical canvas or paper, rendering it a picture. There is not another image within us, an image of the image on the wall. There is no reason to move the seeing inside us, which internal seeing would itself be unexplained. We should just admit that the item on the wall can present Washington as pictured.

To frame this in Aristotle's language, the agent intellect makes the picture actual for us in a way no comparable power does for a dog. Similarly, grasping the intelligibility of a material substance requires us to transform its potential intelligibility into actual understanding. When the form becomes actually *present* to our intelligence, we know the being and not an idea of it, much as we know Washington through the picture without having an internal copy.

Aristotle's well-known thesis that the soul never thinks without an image—technically, a *phantasma* (3.7.431a16–17)—may lead us to conceive imagination as functioning like a storehouse of images on which the agent intellect shines and from which it extracts intelligible content. I think this is inaccurate, but I cannot here develop an interpretation of Aristotle's mysterious account of imagination and unfold a complete argument.[17] In place of that, I note that Sokolowski has argued convincingly for the difference between imagination and picturing, according to which imagination functions more like a reenactment of a prior awareness (or the rehearsal of a potential awareness) than it does like looking at an internal image.[18] Furthermore, the sense

---

[17] The importance and the challenge of understanding Aristotle's view of imagination is appreciated by many authors. See Seth Benardete, "Aristotle: *De Anima* III.3–5" and, e.g., essays by Malcolm Schofield and Dorothea Frede in *Essays on Aristotle's De Anima*, ed. Nussbaum and Rorty.

[18] See *Pictures, Quotations, and Distinctions*, 16—21, and *Phenomenology of the Human Person*, 140–47. In the latter text, Sokolowski develops how we move from perceptual awareness of things to grasping them through names

experience we need in order to grasp a form—for example, the form of a horse—is not a high-quality, internal image of the animal. We need to experience the horse in the diversity of its vital motions, as a living organism that is identical though it is young and then old; stationary and then walking or running; healthy and then sick; awake and then asleep; sometimes eating, sometimes hearing; and so on. Imagination does not store pictures of those activities in the idiosyncratic ways we happen to encounter them, but it re-presents our experience of the horse's activities, both actual and potential. Horse-form is not embedded in the percepts we have; the horse is the identity that gives rise to our experience and could give rise to many percepts we do not have. Accordingly, to grasp the intelligibility of the horse, we need not so much an image of it as we need the horse present in our experience, whether directly or through imagination. With that sketch I turn to intellectual cognition.

Intellectual Cognition

Aristotle says, "Considered as a whole, then, intellect in its being-at-work is the things it thinks" (3.7.431b16–17). More generally:

> The parts of the soul capable of perceiving and knowing are, in potential, these knowable and perceptible things. But they must either be the things themselves or the forms. To be sure, they are not the things themselves: the stone is not in the soul but rather the form. (3.8.431b26–432a1)

I read this as the soul's being where the stone is; the soul is the stone's place. Intellect is not confined to an organ of the body, and so there is little reason to think the understood form is inside

---

and then exploring them through speech. See especially chapters 4, 10, 13, and 14. Importantly, he argues that this process is shaped decisively by the fact that we do not develop language from within but we are surrounded by speakers who articulate the world for us before we are able to do so ourselves.

us, somewhere behind the eyes. I actualize a picture by looking at it, and similarly I do not need a copy of the stone in me, in imagination or memory.[19] The form in the stone is potentially intelligible (3.8.431b22), and that form becomes actually understood but not by being copied.

For actual beings, then, the place of forms is the world, and for those beings as known, their place is the soul cognitively embracing them. Technically, forms actualizing matter have no place because only bodies have place (*Physics*, 4.1.209a26–27). The soul is in place accidentally (*Physics*, 4.5.212b11–12) because the living being is in a place. So, forms as actualities have (accidental) physical places in the world, and as known, their place is the soul that knows them. Instead of conceiving the soul as increasingly filled by what it knows, I think of soul as reaching toward what it knows, an image reflected in Aristotle's comparison of the soul to the hand: "Thus the soul is just like the hand; for the hand is a tool of tools, and intellect is a form of forms, and perception a form of perceptibles" (3.8.432a1–3). Eva Brann says, "Human thinking is wonderfully prehensile."[20] The hand conforms to what it holds, not unlike wax, and, in its contact with the tool, actualizes the tool's potential instrumentality (see *Parts of Animals*, 4.10.687b2–7). The mind's potential for knowing is paired with potential intelligibility in beings as the hand's potential is paired with the tool's potential utility.

---

[19] In a footnote to his translation of *De Anima* 3.8 Mark Shiffman expresses the sort of view I am criticizing: "When we are surrounded by potentially knowable things, or (more relevantly to this chapter) when we have formed images in which knowable things are enabled to lie embedded and dormant in our memories, the intellect exists as a pure principle of form, enabling the intelligible forms latent in them to become fully what they potentially are" (91n25).

[20] "Thinking, Reading, Writing, Listening," *St. John's Review* 53, no. 2 (2012): 135.

In book three, Aristotle gives only an obscure account of the objects we know, the *onta* that become *noêta*. In chapter four, he speaks of our knowing sensible composites and the essences of sensible composites (3.4.429b10–17) and mathematical beings and the essences of mathematical beings (3.4.429b18–21). He mentions but does not discuss beings identical with their essences, usually called separate substances (3.4.429b11–12).[21] In chapter six, he contrasts the cognition of things indivisible in number or in form with the cognition of synthetic units produced by thinking in making judgments, conceiving privations, and grasping genera. These synthetic productions lack the inerrantly truthful character of the reception of form. If the intellect receives an indivisible form, its cognition is always true, and the opposite of receiving that form is ignorance (see *Metaphysics*, 9.10). With predications, where something is said of something, unity is produced by mind (3.6.430b5–6), but the possibilities are truth and falsity (3.6.430a26–b4). In these cases, we are talking about discursive thinking (*dianoeisthai* rather than *nous*), and this involves speech (3.3.427b11–14).

There are many complexities here, but I focus on the obscure passage at the end of *De Anima* 3.6, which I have just paraphrased in part.

> An assertion (*phasis*) says something about something (like an affirmation [*kataphasis*]), and every assertion is either true or false. But it is not so for every act of intellect: that which thinks what something is with respect to the essence of what it is (*ti esti kata to ti ên einai*) does not think something about something; and it is true. But just as the seeing of what is

---

[21] See also 3.7.431b18–19: "Whether or not it is possible for it to think something among separated things while itself not being separate from a magnitude remains to be considered later." This promise does not appear to be fulfilled in *De Anima*. In this summary, I am closely following Pritzl's, "Cognition of Indivisibles," 140–48.

proper to sight is true, while whether the white thing is a man or not is not always true, so too does it hold for as many things as are without matter. (3.6.430b26–31)

Aristotle distinguishes apprehending the *ti esti* in the proper sense—the form or essence of the particular—from other senses of the *ti esti*, the universal species or genus, for example.[22] I underline Aristotle's delicate assertion of an intellectual parallel both to the sense powers' inerrancy with proper objects and to their fallibility in apprehending incidental sensibles. Pritzl's analysis of these issues is complex; I restate it in an outline to support my thesis that the cognitive soul achieves intellectual contact with particular beings constituting the world.

Aristotle distinguishes different senses of the *ti esti* formula. One sense is form or essence (*to ti ên einai*), but others include matter (the composite and the genus). On Pritzl's reading, the primary indivisibles received by intellect are determinate substantial forms or essences of particulars encountered in sense perception. He cites this text from *Metaphysics*:

> The statement that all knowledge is universal…is in a sense true, although in a sense it is not. For knowledge, like knowing, is spoken of in two ways—as potential and as actual. The potentiality, being as matter, universal and indefinite, deals with the universal and indefinite; but the actuality, being definite, deals with a definite object—being a "this," it deals with a "this." But *per accidens* sight sees universal color, because this individual color which it sees is color; and this individual *a* which the grammarian investigates is an *a*. For if the principles must be universal, what is derived from them must also be universal, as in demonstrations; and if this is so, there will be nothing capable of separate existence—i.e., no substance.

---

[22] See Pritzl, "Cognition of Indivisibles," 144–48.

But evidently in a sense knowledge is universal, and in a sense it is not.[23] (*Metaphysics*, 13.10.1087a10–25)

First, essences are properly indivisible according to form, but the genus is not a *this* and is divisible in species.[24] Second, those essences are not inherently universal, but they are the basis of universality when we think them in relation to multiple particulars.[25] Similarly, the genus is thought in relation to at least two species that constitute it as a genus. This means genera are understood similarly to privations. A privation is thought by understanding the form whose absence constitutes it, and a point is thought by understanding the intersection of two lines. Because there is composition and division in the constitution of these objects of thought, we do not have the same guarantee of truth. In the context where he has just asserted the soul's truthful grasp of particular form, possibilities for falsehood in grasping the universal, the species, and the genus remain. And this calls to mind Aristotle's earlier aside: the soul spends the "majority of its time" in error (3.3.427a29–b2).

These complications lead away from my main concerns, and so I refocus on the soul and its reception of form. When we con-

---

[23] Compare: "For that which is potentially possessed of knowledge becomes possessed of knowledge not by being moved itself but by reason of the presence of something else; for when it meets with the particular object, it knows in a manner the universal through the particular" (*Physics*, 7.3.247b4–7).

[24] See *Metaphysics*, 5.6.1017a1–6.

[25] Pritzl ("Cognition of Indivisibles," 150n27) does not spell out the argument, but he cites these passages: *Metaphysics*, 5.26.1023b29–31, 7.13.1038b10–16, 3.6.1003a9; *Cat.* 5.3b13–18. Pritzl often connects this sense of the grasping of the essence with the famous passage in *Metaphysics*, 9.10.1051b24, where Aristotle speaks of touching (*thigein*) the object of knowledge.

ceive soul as receiving form and distinguish that from the discursive reasoning that composes and divides, we tend to understand the former as preceding the latter. We think we apprehend form first, and then we can speak and reason about it. Aristotle's text reinforces this by emphasizing our reliance on *phantasmata* through which we abstract forms or essences of things we speak about. The text supports this approach. Nevertheless, I argue now in the final portion of my paper, Aristotle has also given us ample evidence that this is misleading.

Knowing Soul
The Arc of *De Anima*

We do well not only to pore over Aristotle's terse and troublesome account in *De Anima* book three, but also to pay attention to his practice. That practice suggests that conceiving the agent intellect as abstracting intelligible content from sense percepts is altogether too silent.

By the time Aristotle tells us in book three about the cognitive reception of form, he has already done a good deal to help us understand soul. That is, we've been receiving that form for some time. He did not begin by helping us gather many percepts of living things and inspect them closely. Rather, he began in book one with the word *soul* and what others say about it. At the beginning of book two, he presented soul as *ousia* in the sense of form (2.1.412a19–20), as the first *entelecheia* (2.1.412b5), and as the essence (2.1.412b11). In other words, he told us there that soul is the sort of form that (he will later tell us) the contemplative intellect receives in cognition. True, the formulation of a definition is a more complex achievement than the simple reception of a form (*Metaphysics*, 9.10.1051b30–33). It is the work of *dianoia* rather than *nous*.[26] Nevertheless, Aristotle leads us to discern what soul is through a discursive process.

The first definition formulates soul universally (2.1.412b9–10). It identifies soul in relation to body while leaving completely implicit whatever the life of the organism may be. The second definition—"the soul is that primarily by which we live, perceive, and think" (2.2.414a11–12)—comes closer to formulating the nature of a specific kind of soul, but it achieves that only partially. It particularizes some but not all activities that belong to a human being. Soul is the single principle of all such powers, and understanding soul would require understanding their unity. Moreover, Aristotle explores the several powers through their operations, which are known through their objects (2.4.415a14–23). We need a complete list of the powers and their objects. This is lacking. He does distinguish proper, common, and incidental sensibles (2.5), but, as mentioned above, he gives only the barest account of objects of intellectual cognition. If he were to follow through on his principle, we could not even understand this sketch of a definition of the human soul without knowing all beings, for the soul, he says, is somehow all things (3.8.431b21; 3.4.429a18). Intellect is unknowable until it knows. It becomes fully itself in *entelecheia* when it has received the intelligibles (3.4.429b26–430a3). It seems we can know fully the defining power of the human soul—intellect—only when we encounter the one who knows fully. To know the soul, we must know all things. More cautiously put, we are not done knowing the soul before knowing all things.

---

[26] The definition unfolds the simple essence in a *logos*, whose parts are related like the relation of form and matter, and the definition formulates it as a universal (*Metaphysics*, 7.10.1035b31–1036a2). See Pritzl, "Place of Intellect," 57–75, 61–68.

This recalls the beginning of *De Anima*, where he says one type of knowledge is more noble and honorable than another if it is more precise or concerned with more wonderful things. Knowledge of soul belongs "in the first ranks" for both reasons:

> Knowledge of it seems, indeed, to contribute enormously toward all uncovering of truth, but especially truth about nature—for soul is in some way a governing principle of living things (*archê tôn zôôn*). We seek to discern and to understand both its nature and its *ousia*, and then also whatever comes along with it. (1.1.402a4–8)

Inquiry into soul expands beyond the study of nature.[27]

I have laid out tension between the prospect of knowing soul through intuitive abstraction from sense perception and knowing soul through a potentially limitless discursive inquiry. The latter approach also depends on sense perception and experience. For, a few lines later, Aristotle adds:

> Now it seems not only to be the case that understanding what a thing is helps us to see the causes of the attributes belonging to substances,…but also the attributes in turn contribute a great deal toward understanding what it is. For when we are able to give an account of all or most of the attributes in accord with our *phantasia*, then we will also be able to speak most excellently about the substance. (1.1.402b16–25)

Phantasia (imagination) must be combined with a dialogic movement between substance and attribute, that is, between the core and the surface, with the intermediate level of powers in between. This coheres with Aristotle's description in *Metaphysics*.

---

[27] See *Parts of Animals*, 1.1.641a32–b4.

Inquiring into *Ousia*

At the end of his aporetic examination of sensible substance in *Metaphysics* book seven, Aristotle makes a fresh beginning in chapter seventeen and reintroduces the notion that substance is a principle and cause. Principles are not first for us. A principle is a principle *of* something else (*Physics*, 1.2.185a4–5). Substance as principle is an answer to a question, but the question is elusive. We cannot meaningfully ask "Why is a man a man?" The same answer would be given for anything: because each is itself (*Metaphysics*, 7.17.1041a14–20). Causal inquiry requires otherness, not simple identity; the otherness permitting us to inquire why a man is a man arises from the plurality of parts. Sometimes unity is so evident that we overlook what is not expressly stated, namely, "that these are this" (*hoti tade tode*), that is, that these material parts are this one being (*Metaphysics*, 7.17.1041a 32–b2). We perceive *that* the living being moves as one whole, but we need a cause to explain why the several parts (eye, foot, flesh, bones, etc.) are one being and not a heap (*Metaphysics*, 7.17.1041b5–6).

Substance as form explains why "these are this," but we have no direct access to form. We approach it through the several parts and the motions and accidents evident in them. *Soul* names the principle causing unity. In *De Anima*, the problem of the unity of the living being is expressed through the implicit question of how multiple potencies can be rooted in a single actuality.[28]

---

[28] This problem is implicit in, e.g., the ordering of soul's powers: nutritive, sensitive, and intellectual. See 2.3.414b33–415a13. The soul has these and other powers but is itself essentially an actuality. The soul's unity is overlooked or denied by those who speak of soul as a plurality. Jennifer Whiting, for example, calls soul a "set of capacities." See Whiting's "Living Bodies" in *Essays on Aristotle's De Anima*, edited by Nussbaum and Rorty, 87.

De Anima opens with the soul. It does not begin with the whole being and question its unity. It begins further along in the inquiry with the name for the cause of unity. A name is like a picture in that it presents something to us, although it achieves this without resemblance. The picture presents Washington through a particular image, but the name introduces the whole being as a subject for articulation and discursive reasoning. *Soul* names a principle of being, not a concept. Nevertheless, we have and use the name before we know fully what it names. *De Anima* enacts a discursive process through which we begin to discern what *soul* names. Aristotle begins with competing understandings of soul, and in book two, chapter one, he delivers a generic definition. In chapter two he sketches a specific definition of human soul partially identifying the powers united in this soul. In book three, chapter six, he focuses on grasping the particular soul in its essential determinateness. In this discussion, he questions whether intellect itself is intelligible (3.4.429b26). But this is the question of self-knowledge. Can I know this defining power of my soul? The arc of the whole book is clear: He begins with what people say; he identifies the genus of living beings to which we belong (implicitly raising the issue of mortality); he locates our species as thinking; and then he shows how I must try to know the particular, that is, me. *De Anima* leads us to ask: *What am I? What unifies the activities and powers I find in myself?*

De Anima does not precisely answer this question. It displays what we would have to know to answer the question. We can see three levels of thinking operative here. The first level is the natural recognition that a human being is something one. This level prompts us to search for the cause of the unity we experience. The second level pursues this question through biology or another scientific exploration of human nature by considering all our operations. This doesn't fully happen in *De Anima* or *Metaphysics*; perhaps the *Ethics* and *Politics* contribute significantly to this. (Interestingly, those texts unify the human being through a *telos* and not through the ontological *archê* of soul.) In *De Anima*, we find Aristotle operating at a third level, the philosophical level, where he shows us what would have to occur for us to grasp the principle of unity and identity in a being, in *our being*. In other words, *De Anima* is not so much the science of soul as it is the phenomenological account of how we might come to know the soul.

If we seek soul as the cause of unity in a complex substance, we should admit the possibility that the unifying form we aim to discern might not be there. What seems to be one might not actually be one. When we are dealing with anything sufficiently complicated, we necessarily imagine the unity before we understand it. By using a name, such as *soul*, we anticipate having the essence before we have it fully. As we learn more and more about some being, we gradually fill in the content of the essence we seek. None of this guarantees an actual, unifying form or that we will know it adequately. For example, to search for the cause of an event that has come about by chance is to search within an apparent unity for something that ultimately falls apart into two. The principle of unity is never first for us; it is always less evident than the multiplicity in which it is embedded, as the plot or soul of tragedy is accessible only through its component parts (*Poetics*, 6).

My conclusion then is not negative, but it is chastening, as is Aristotle's text. "To reach any trustworthy conviction about soul is one of the most difficult of all tasks in every way" (1.1.402a10–11; cf. *Metaphysics*, 7.1.1028b2–4).

Selected Bibliography

Aquinas, Thomas. *Commentary on Aristotle's De Anima*. Translated by Kenelm Foster and Sylvester Humphries. New Haven: Yale University Press, 1951.

———. *On the Unity of the Intellect against the Averroists*. Translated by Beatrice H. Zelder. Milwaukee: Marquette University Press, 1968.

Aristotle. *Aristotle: De Anima*. Edited by Robert D. Hicks. Cambridge: Cambridge University Press, 1907.

———. *De Arte Poetica*, 2nd edition. Edited by I. Bywater. Oxford: Clarendon Press, 1911.

———. *Metaphysics*, 2 volumes. Revised text with introduction and commentary by W. D. Ross. Oxford: Clarendon Press, 1924.

———. *The Complete Works of Aristotle*, 2 volumes. Edited by Jonathan Barnes. Princeton: Princeton University Press, 1984.

———. *Aristote: De l'âme*, 3rd Edition. Translated with notes by Edmond Barbotin and Antonio Jannone. Paris: Les Belles Lettres, 1989.

———. *Aristotle: De Anima*. Translated by Mark Shiffman. Newburyport: Focus Publishing, 2011.

———. *Aristotle: De Anima (On the Soul)*. Translated by David Bolotin. Macon: Mercer University Press, 2018.

Benardete, Seth. "Aristotle: *De Anima* III.3–5." *Review of Metaphysics* 28 (1975): 611–22.

Brann, Eva. "Thinking, Reading, Writing, Listening." *St. John's Review* 53, no. 2 (2012): 133–49.

Buttaci, Jonathan. "Aristotle's Intellects: Now and Then." *Proceedings of the American Catholic Philosophical Association* 87 (2014): 127–43.

Caston, Victor. "Aristotle's Two Intellects: A Modest Proposal." *Phronesis* 44, no. 3 (1999): 199–227.

Klein, Jacob. "Speech, Its Strength and Its Weaknesses." In *Lectures and Essays*. Edited by Robert B. Williamson and Elliott Zuckerman, 361–74. Annapolis: St. John's College Press, 1985.

Nussbaum, Martha C., and Amélie Oksenberg Rorty, eds. *Essays on Aristotle's De Anima*. Oxford: Clarendon Press, 1992.

Owens, Joseph. "Quiddity and Real Distinction in St. Thomas Aquinas." *Mediaeval Studies* 27 (1965): 1–22

Pritzl, Kurt, J. "Aristotle's Door." In *Truth: Studies of a Robust Presence*. Edited by Kurt J. Pritzl, 15–39. Washington, DC: The Catholic University of America Press, 2009.

———. "The Cognition of Indivisibles and the Argument of *De Anima* 3.4–8." *Proceedings and Addresses of the American Philosophical Association* 58, no. 140 (1984): 140–50.
———. "The Unity of Knower and Known in Aristotle's *De Anima*." PhD diss., University of Toronto, 1982.
———. "The Place of Intellect in Aristotle." *Proceedings of the American Catholic Philosophical Association* 80 (2007): 57–75.
Sokolowski, Robert. *Phenomenology of the Human Person*. New York: Cambridge University Press, 2008.
———. *Pictures, Quotations, and Distinctions: Fourteen Essays in Phenomenology*. Notre Dame and London: University of Notre Dame Press, 1992.

ARISTOTLE'S PSYCHOLOGY AS FUNDAMENTAL ONTOLOGY

Kevin Marren

Introduction

Aristotle speaks of Psyche or the soul in many ways: as οὐσία, πρώτη ἐντελέχεια, and εἶδος. However, the meaning of each designation can only be understood through his primary ontological thesis about the soul: [...] ἡ ψυχὴ τὰ ὄντα πώς ἐστι πάντα.[1] But how can a substance be everything? As though to clarify, Aristotle makes a comparison between the way that Psyche is all of the beings and the way that knowing and sensing *are* the knowable and the sensible.[2] Yet this clarifies nothing, unless we already understand how the *being* in potential of knowledge and sense *become* and then *are* the *being* actual of the knowable and the sensible. And if the intellectual soul, as Aristotle says, *is* that which it thinks when thinking,[3] nevertheless, this raises a difficult question concerning the meaning of the 'ἐστι' stated in the relation, i.e., of the mediating verb that stands between the hand and its tool, sense and the sensible, and thinking and that which is thought.[4] This question is not answered by saying, as Aquinas does, that "[o]bviously [!] the soul

---

[1] "The soul is somehow all of the beings." All quotations of Greek come from the side-by-side edition: Aristotle. *On the Soul. Parva Naturalia. On Breath*, *t*rans. W. S. Hett, Loeb Classical Library 288 (Cambridge, MA: Harvard University Press, 1957), 432b2–3. All translations of the Greek are my own.

[2] Ibid.

[3] 429b30.

[4] The three items in the list allude to the famous analogy at 432a1. An extensive analysis of this analogy has been cut from the present paper.

is not simply identical with the things it knows; for not stone itself, but its formal likeness *exists* in the soul."[5] For one may still wonder what it means for a stone or a form to *be* at all.

This essay claims that when Aristotle says Psyche is somehow all of the beings, he means that the unity of Being is fundamentally psychological. This fundamental psychological interpretation of Being implies a peculiar ontological connection between living beings and their surroundings. The way of this connection may be indicated in the juxtaposition of several ideas from *De Anima*. First, Psyche *is* the potentiality of the αἰσθητόν and the ἐπιστητὸν, not the πράγματα themselves that are sensed and known.[6] We understand this insofar as Aristotle draws a direct linkage between the faculties as δυνάμεις and the δυνάμεις in the πράγματα themselves (…δυνάμει εἰς τὰ δυνάμει…).[7] Second, faculties are determinative of the Being of beings with respect to form. That is, while a faculty grasps just the thing, Psyche as regards the faculty *is* the very Being of the thing as potentiality.[8] Third, Psyche is proximally distinguished by life

---

[5] Aquinas, *Commentary on Aristotle's De* Anima, trans Foster and Humphries (New Haven: Yale University Press, 1951), III.VIII.13.

[6] 430a.

[7] 432a.

[8] On this point, Daniel Maher's excellent essay in this volume is the duck to this essay's rabbit. Our interpretations draw on so many points in common, that it is surprising how different are our conclusions. But a subtle difference in interpretive framework can lead to pronounced consequences. On page three of his essay, Maher says, "I take the claim 'actual knowledge is the same as the thing' … *almost literally* because there remains a distinction between a being in itself and the same being as known." For my part, I do not know exactly what it means to take such a claim literally or figuratively. However, I hold that there is no distinction between the "being in itself" and the "being as known"; but rather, that as the soul *is* all of the beings, so knowing *is* the knowables. The "is" states the way that entities have their *Being*, not a relation between one entity and an *other* (see Maher's use of "otherness"). If there is a distinction here for Aristotle it is not a distinction between entities (as between

(...διωρίσθαι τὸ ἔμψυχον τοῦ ἀψύχου τῷ ζῆν),[9] which for the most part is recognized by having some potency (e.g., for growth). Taking these lines together, the "ἐστι" that mediates between Psyche and beings in Aristotle's claim (that the soul is somehow all of the beings) indicates a provocative ontological thesis. Meaning accrues to the "ἐστι"—as to Being in general—through the powers by which life orients itself to the beings. Thus, we say that an entity "is" insofar as its very Being conforms to such a vital power. Of the sensible, the knowable, the tool—Aristotle is telling us that Psyche is the Being of each as it is displayed in an organism's potential for a certain way of life.

---

knowledge and the thing itself), but only one between beings and Being, i.e., an ontological distinction.

A long commentary is due regarding Aristotle's analysis of thinking and the thinking faculty beginning at 429a10. However, for now, several highlights are necessary, from which the reader might glean what is at stake overall.

Both the faculty of sense and thinking are to the sensible and thinkable *the same* in form and potentiality (429a15–18). Forceful over-translations of the Greek—as well as over-interpretations—have obscured this point. It is possible for Aristotle to claim that forms and potentialities are *the same* because they are not entities for Aristotle, but ways of Being.

Thinking discriminates between the things and the Being of things; i.e., taken with what's said above, that which thinking is in potentiality and when thinking actually, *is* the form or the Being of a thing with respect to an ontological domain (429b10).

Therefore, thinking *is* (from above *the same as*) that potentiality that is formally the Being of a thing, and which is therefore separate as Being is distinct from beings, but not separate as two entities would be in respect to each other.

But as much as sensing *is* also *the same* potentiality as the sensible, and thinking *is* all potentialities formally, what distinguishes thinking from sensing is that the latter is directed at a thing "as though in a straight line," while thinking is directed at a thing such that it "turns back" to itself (429a20).

[9] 413a10.

To illustrate the above, we may consider Aristotle's own example of the most rudimentary way in which all living beings insinuate potentiality into their surroundings—as is displayed by nourishment in the case of plants:

> All plants seem to be alive because they display [φαίνεται...ἔχοντα] in themselves a potency and source through which growing and decaying take opposite places [λαμβάνουσι κατὰ τοὺς ἐναντίους τόπους]. For not only up rather than down, but in both and all directions alike, [plants] always nourish themselves and live towards their end, to the extent that they are able to take nourishment.[10]

This rough translation is meant to help suggest how the first differences in place (up and down) correspond to the potential of the plant for growth and decay. The ontological place of food is defined by the plant's insinuation of the potential for making a mass of soil into itself. The plant relates to this potentiality in taking-place between the up and the down, which are—for a plant—not indifferent directions, but which are coordinated with the soil and the sunlight from and in the presence of which the growth and decay of plants must be seen to arise. The sense is clearly that the potency of life is *in* the place, not merely that plants grow in different directions. The latter is a mere truism; the former says that the consistency of the place of growth itself, as well as the beings that occur therein, are due to a way of life.

---

[10] 413a15–20. The Greek in full:
[T]ὰ φυόμενα πάντα δοκεῖ ζῆν· φαίνεται γὰρ ἐν αὐτοῖς ἔχοντα δύναμιν καὶ ἀρχὴν τοιαύτην, δι' ἧς αὔξησίν τε καὶ φθίσιν λαμβάνουσι κατὰ τοὺς ἐναντίους τόπους· οὐ γὰρ ἄνω μὲν αὔξεται, κάτω δ' οὔ, ἀλλ' ὁμοίως ἐπ' ἄμφω καὶ πάντῃ, ὅσα ἀεὶ τρέφεταί τε καὶ ζῇ διὰ τέλους, ἕως ἂν δύνηται λαμβάνειν τροφήν.

The plant-soul lays out the up and down, and the *totality* of directions, as the place of its growth, of its assimilation, and its (aversion to) decay.

If, taking a clue from the example, we address ourselves to the question raised implicitly in Aristotle's ontological thesis (Πῶς?), we can say that Psyche is the self-relation between beings and Being as *mediated* by life. *Immediately*, however, Psyche and Being coincide just inasmuch as there is no difference between the Being of beings and what life itself makes possible. Taken together, these claims also suggest a negative proposition: namely, Being would remain in pure immediacy and indiscernible if not for living beings. For in life's essential taking place and stretching out,[11] there is an originary making possible, an insinuation of an organism's potentiality for life into the Being of beings, which lays out concretely the ontological regions to which belong things as fundamental as food, soil, breathable air, etc. That is, the ontological dimensions that characterize beings have a psychological form commensurate with the capacities of living

---

[11] "Stretching out" is meant to convey the original sense of *orexis*. Especially in light of this essay's Heideggerian inspiration, we might consider an instructive essay by Francisco Gonzales, "Movement Versus Activity: Heidegger's 1922/23 Seminar on Aristotle's Ontology of Life" in *The British Journal for the History of Philosophy* 27, no. 3 (2019): 615–634. Gonzales writes,

> One of Heidegger's key moves already alluded to [in the 1922/23 seminar] is to give priority to *orexis* in the ontology of life and to make *nous* only a moment of *orexis*: the sight inherent to desire, as it were [...]. Yet Heidegger immediately clarifies that *orexis* purely by itself cannot be seen as constituting the being of life: it too is only a moment. The key is to grasp *orexis* and *nous* in their unity, where this unity is what makes it possible for *nous* to be eventually abstracted from *orexis* and given priority over it: a process that, Heidegger grants, already begins with Aristotle. The unity is expressed most radically when we read: '*nous* (in the broad sense of a thinking, *noêsis*) is *orexis*'. 7

beings, which are displayed as *ways of life* and realized as an environment. Thus, we must put Being on display in view of the ways a living being takes place and makes beings possible.

The Way in which Psyche is οὐσία

If Psyche is *in any way* all of the beings, she cannot be one among beings; for in the sense that she would be all of them, she would have to be abstractly indeterminate,[12] which is just the same in concept as nothing. John Manoussakis makes this point well. "In order for the soul to be all of beings, it itself has to be none. For if the soul [were] one [of the] beings, it could not be other than itself [i.e., any other being] and certainly not all the beings [...]."[13] This has the further consequence that no definition of soul can be given by specific differentiation. Thus, one must needs be perplexed when Aristotle gives what Stephen Menn (and unaccountably many others) calls a "first step" towards a "definition"[14] of the soul. [...] τὴν ψυχὴν οὐσίαν εἶναι ὡς εἶδος σώματος φυσικοῦ δυνάμει ζωὴν ἔχοντος. Or as Menn translates, "The soul is the substance-as-form of a natural body potentially having life (412a19–21)."[15] Of course, this is more a saying in the sense of a λόγος (rather than a definition or delimiting, i.e., an χωρισμός), and so the saying 'substance as form' may indicate a logical predicate, rather than a real property of the soul. In fact, if a definition is that which tells us what species a substance is, then to say that the soul *is a substance* can never be a

---

[12] This claim, of course, echoes the Doctrine of Being in Hegel's *Science of Logic*.

[13] John P. Manoussakis, *God after Metaphysics: A Theological Aesthetic* (Bloomington: Indiana University Press, 2007), 129.

[14] Stephen Menn, "Aristotle's Definition of Soul and the Programme of the De Anima," *Oxford Studies in Ancient Philosophy* 22 (2002): 83–139, 104.

[15] Ibid.

definition, since everything that can be thoroughly defined by some property would have its definition related to a substance. That is, "οὐσία" is not some defining "what" of an entity, but the kind of Being that certain entities have. The question, then, must arise in what precise sense Psyche is the substance of a living being, i.e., as the kind of Being that living beings have. However, this sense hinges on what is meant by the "εἶναι" in the above quote, which cannot be settled without further discussing the respective meanings of δυνάμις, ἐντελέχεια, and εἶδος. Therefore, the long answer to the question is the concern of the following sections of this paper.

Yet, if Psyche is no entity, one may also wonder how she is to be studied. As Manoussakis says, "By not being a [being, the soul] cannot be known or sensed—it is neither intelligible nor perceptible."[16] Manoussakis is correct that the soul is neither a sensible or intelligible thing as such—there is no region of beings corresponding to knowledge of the soul. However, to say that Psyche cannot be known is a self-refuting claim, which can neither coincide with Aristotle's ontological thesis, nor with what can be marked as true. Rather, we might notice what Socrates says in Plato's *Phaedo*—our typical ways of speaking about beings make us "soul-blind" and ignorant of what is a more philosophical sense of the truth about the soul.[17] But proceeding otherwise than the mythmaker Socrates, a program of study may be suggested in three related points. First, Psyche is the living being,

---

[16] Manoussakis, 129.

[17] Plato, *Euthyphro. Apology. Crito. Phaedo.* Translated by Christopher Emlyn-Jones, William Preddy, Loeb Classical Library 36 (Cambridge, MA: Harvard University Press, 2017), 99d–e.

Blindness as a theme in the dialogues has been treated extensively by Marren. For example, Marina Marren, *Plato and Aristophanes: Comedy, Politics, and the Pursuit of a Just Life* (Evanston: Northwestern University Press 2021), 7.

clearly more intimately than she is all of the beings. Further, the meaning of this intimacy is determined as a matter of organization (τοιοῦτον δὲ ὃ ἂν ᾖ ὀργανικόν).[18] Second, she can be made the logical subject of certain well-formed judgments such that we may speak truly or falsely about her—i.e., she is the subject of a logical inquiry (… οὐσία γὰρ ἡ κατὰ τὸν λόγον).[19] Third, Psyche is somehow coincident with the Being of beings and indeterminate when left in immediacy. However, she is not otherwise than the totality of beings, but *is* them. Now taking all of these points together, a way of study suggests itself. For Psyche is determinable in the form of a substantial living body such that she may be displayed in the way its organization makes an understanding of beings possible.

Psyche is πρώτη ἐντελέχεια

Life and the vital capacities of organisms stand between Being and beings, and we can recognize the soul only in view of this mediation. Thus, having said how substance lies at the center of our and Aristotle's inquiry, we should turn to consider the matter concerning δύναμις (potentiality) and ἐντελέχεια (actuality). Aristotle of course says that Psyche is a πρώτη ἐντελέχεια (412a30). But again the question arises: what is the meaning of the "is" that joins Psyche and ἐντελέχεια in this statement? Perhaps it means that she is the self-regulating end of vital activity—the actuality that is essential to maintaining life. Or perhaps as some interpreters take Aristotle to mean, the soul could be a "second potentiality"—that is, the set of abiding potentialities that define an organism, e.g., as growth seems to define all life or as reason seems to define the human kind.[20] Frey

---

[18] 412b.

[19] 412b.

[20] Of recent notables, this view belongs to Burnyeat. See M. F. Burnyeat, "De Anima II.5," in *Phronesis* 47, no. 1 (2002): 28–90.

claims there are but two interpretations of Psyche in Aristotle: the conception that says she is a set of capacities,[21] and the conception of her as the source and end of vital activities. However, this seems like a false dichotomy. For the alternatives are not mutually exclusive if Psyche is, rather than an entity herself, the kind of Being belonging to an entity that is defined both by its capacities and its vital activities. And second, the alternatives are unintelligible if we conceive of the potentiality and entelechy of a living being as properties.

It is also sometimes said that Psyche *has* capacities herself, which would imply that there are activities of the soul as well. Indeed, Aristotle occasionally speaks of a δύναμις τῆς ψυχῆς,[22] a capacity of soul. Such phrases threaten to mislead someone who is accustomed to everyday thinking—i.e., ousialogical thinking wherein we take the soul as having some stock of defining properties. However, Aristotle is clear that Psyche herself does not *have* capacities, holding that only the living being *has* such.[23]

---

[21] The prevalence of this interpretation is catalogued best in an excellent article of Aristotle scholarship which convincingly speaks against the mainstream identification of "first actuality" and "second potentiality." See Rebekah Johnston's, "Aristotle's De Anima: On Why the Soul is Not a Set of Capacities," *British Journal for the History of Philosophy* 19, no. 2 (2011): 185–200.

[22] *De Anima* 416a20, 433b.

[23] Aristotle, *De Anima* 408b12–18. "Not the soul, but the human being...." Aristotle's suggestion here is that one avoid attributing to Psyche any of the activities or capacities of the living being. Many have misunderstood this point, perhaps on the evidence presented at 433b, concerning "potentialities of the soul" or on the well-known "definition" of happiness as an activity of the soul in the *Nicomachean Ethics*. Concerning capacities, see, for example Charles Goetz and Stuart Taliaferro, *A Brief History of the Soul* (West Sussex: Wiley-Blackwell, 2011), 29. The usual interpretation is that the soul has, e.g., desire as a potentiality or capacity. This raises a series of questions: Does the animal desire also? Does it desire *with the soul*? or *through it*? How does the capacity of the soul relate to the capacity of the animal? The only coherent answer is that the potentiality of the soul is that which the living being has as

Consider, that if a capacity were to belong to Psyche, as a capacity belongs to some living being, then Psyche herself would sometimes enact certain things like growing and decaying or feeling anger. That is, if capacities were attributable to Psyche, then she would have a life of her own. But this is an incorrect way of thinking. Besides the fact that the soul does not move (except perhaps in a non-originary sense) if the soul had capacities, it would mean that two living beings were located in the same place.[24]

Psyche is in some way the source of life, which draws together the potentiality and actuality of living beings. On this point, take the activities that Aristotle explicitly assigns to the human being, while he denies the same to psyche. These are pitying, learning, and discursive thinking (ἐλεεῖν ἢ μανθάνειν ἢ διανοεῖσθαι). Such might be called activities of life, as they correspond to the concrete experiences of a living human being. Aristotle is quite clear: the motions that characterize these activities never take place in the soul; rather, he states, they sometimes begin from this here (ἀπὸ τωνδί), and other times come to (μέχρι) the soul. But, the 'to and fro' here is ambiguous. Perception comes from such and such (Aristotle is not decisive in locating the place from which it starts) and goes to the soul. But, clearly perception does not move the soul to any of the activities of life, but just the human being moves. And in moving, Aristotle seems to say, the human being either comes to the soul or brings the motion to it. Aristotle goes on to say that recollection (ἀνάμνησις) issues from the soul, and goes to the movements of the "sensors" (αἰσθητηρίοις); but it does not itself move the

---

its own potential, and which the soul *is* as a living being's mediation between Being and beings.

[24] Aquinas deals with this topic tangentially in his *Commentary on the Posterior Analytics*, Fabian R. Larcher, trans. (New York: Magi Books), Lecture 3, 91a12–b11.

sense organs, instead it goes to the movements that are already *there* (presumably having a cause in nature), and it is somehow *in* these movements, not as a separate movement, but rather as the actuality of a potentiality as such. That is, the soul is the actuality of a body with the potential to move naturally to and fro. What is the sense, though, of the "to and fro" that displays the soul in the vital movements of life? What is the sense in which we locate the soul at the site of the living being? For these movements are not merely from here to there, but they seem to move in the midst of possibilities, which correspond to a living being's capacities and surround it everywhere. All of the activity belongs to the living being. Yet, if we are to avoid the double attribution whereby we predicate the same action twice—once to the soul and once to the living being—then it is unclear what, if anything, the soul contributes to the motions, e.g., in the form of direction or force or anything of this kind. And yet, all of the motions here considered seem to take place between the potential in the living being for a certain way of life and the potential in something else to fulfill it.

What Aristotle means to put on display, therefore, is the kind of Being that living motion has—not the source of motion as motion, i.e., as caused generally, since in each case, the source of motion as such can be made plain without knowing the cause in terms of its kind of Being. For instance, the body, or just the thing with respect to which the body is affected, is the cause of a motion. But the Being of the motion, which gives living motion its place and direction "to and fro," and which makes it, e.g., desiring rather than just a flux and relocation of the matter, is not an entity. What makes the *being* affected, or effecting beings, in each case *possible*—what brings the possibility of living becoming to bear on Being—is the soul.

By way of summary, it is best said that to be a "capacity of Psyche" indicates that the living being's potentiality provides for the psychological dimension of Being in which something like sensing or nutrition can take place. The potentiality, in other words, belongs to the living being, but the potentiality has a psycho-ontological significance as itself providing for the kind of vital discernment that makes the Being of beings possible—that is, by mediating between Being and beings through different ways of life. There is no more difficulty then in attributing the name of a capacity to Psyche than there is a difficulty in saying that there are different kinds of Being. Provided we understand that "capacity of soul" means that a certain potential of the living being lays out a region of beings, we do not run afoul of either Aristotle's claim that Psyche is all beings nor of his interdiction of attributing a capacity to Psyche herself. In any case, more recent thinkers provide a basis for thinking about how ways of life as potentialities for Being can correspond to kinds of Being. One who has read Heidegger is familiar with several such kinds of Being or "ontological categories"[25] e.g., tool-being, Dasein's kind of Being, etc.

Psyche as "the Place of Forms"

Aristotle provides a critical reinterpretation of the notion that Psyche is a place of forms, stating this is primarily in the sense of intellect. This notion of place is fascinating, and the sense of place deserves further comment. To say what 'place' means depends on understanding the claim that a living being is Being's mediate self-relation such that the inner structure of this relation is laid out in an organism's potentiality for certain ways of life. Of

---

[25] Heidegger, *Sein und Zeit*, (Max Niemeyer Verlag, Tübingen: 1927/1967), 88, 135.

course, the meaning of "organism" calls for a deeper investigation into the meaning of organization than can be undertaken in the present essay. However, it can here be shown how the kind of Being that accrues to an organism involves displaying different dimensions of Being—that is to say, how there is some original making possible of beings that is accomplished through the living being, and upon which the very Being of beings depends for its psychological meaning. In this case, what it means for a "form" to exist "in the soul" is nothing other than what it means for the (form of a) thing to exist.

Aristotle states, τὸ δὲ ζῆν τοῖς ζῶσι τὸ εἶναί ἐστιν. The living being is alive as existing.[26] In this line, the sense of the "ζῆν" is thoroughly entangled with the "εἶναί ἐστιν," which again invokes precisely that sense of 'εἶναί' that was questioned in the section on substance. Aristotle means by it both that the living being's essence is its "to be," and that its "to be" is a way of life.[27] As such, life is ontological—in the peculiar arrangement of a living being's organism there lies an articulation (λόγος) which displays Psyche herself, i.e., as the psychological form of different ways of life.[28] Reading Aristotle this way, Being is made psycho-

---

[26] *De Anima*, 415b14. Heidegger comes rather close to modeling his characterization of Dasein on this line: Das »Wesen« dieses Seienden liegt in seinem Zu-sein. Das Was-sein (essentia) dieses Seienden muß, sofern überhaupt davon gesprochen werden kann, aus seinem Sein (existentia) begriffen werden (*SZ*, 45).

In other words, just as Heidegger claims that the essence of Dasein lies in its to be, so Aristotle claims that the being alive of the living being lies in its to be.

[27] *De Anima* 412b26. There is a tension here between our interpretation and the ousialogical tenor of the cited passages. We make no denial, however, that Psyche is the substantial being of an organism; however, on our interpretation, this substance is defined most by its kind of Being, i.e., by the kind of Being that characterizes the vital potentiality in an organized body.

[28] *De Anima* 412b10.

logical through the living being in accordance with the way that such a living being fundamentally *is*. For Aristotle is not telling us about Psyche as though she were a being; he is not presenting a stock of predicates when he calls her a first entelechy or a form. He is telling us how to read the "εἶναί ἐστιν" of the above quotation, or the "εἶναί" of "τὸ τί ἦν εἶναι" (the "what it is *to be*") of living beings.[29] In more contemporary terms, he is telling us that the essence of living beings is fundamentally ontological, as it informs the "is" and the meaning of the "to be" by which the living being takes place in its surroundings.[30] And he is telling us that ontology is fundamentally psychological, since the meaning of "to be" is displayed by living beings and as ways of life.

It must be admitted that living beings do not occur in empty space like points in a Cartesian coordinate system, but rather as at the center of dimensions of vital possibilities. The shape and measure of life's possibilities corresponds to the living being's potentiality for Being. Aristotle himself does not have a systematic theory of world or environment, no way to speak to the oneness or interconnectedness of a living being's possibilities with beings. Even where Aristotle speaks of the universe as a whole, or speaks

---

[29] Ibid., 412b14.

[30] We must note that ζωή in our understanding is not the "bare life" of which someone like Agamben speaks. See Giorgio Agamben, *Homo Sacer: Sovereign Power and Bare Life,* Heller-Roazen trans. (California: Stanford University Press, 1995/1998). "Bare life," in Agamben's sense, is something like the biological life of plants and animals understood in a privational sense. He speaks of ζωή as opposed to "ways of life." Βίος corresponds to the various ways of life, to the biographical life of human beings in politics, history, etc. (13).

Our way of speaking of life, in a sense, is closer to what Agamben calls "sacred life." He describes sacred life as a "zone of indistinction in which *zoē* and *bios* constitute each other in including and excluding each other" (56).

of "the all," he always returns the discussion to beings as a plurality.[31] How, though, shall we understand this plurality? What kind of togetherness do beings have, in virtue of life or otherwise, that makes them both more than one but also a unity (an all) together? To explain this, one would look in vain for anything like the Timaen κόσμος (the solitary "visible animal," the ζῶον ὁρατὸν, embracing other living beings)[32] in Aristotle's *De Caelo*, for instance.[33] And yet there seems to have been some expectation of a cosmological theory by Aristotle's early interpreters. According to Kukkonen, both Simplicius and Alexander Aphrodisias attempt to derive from, or rather impose upon, Aristotle's physics a "cosmic theory." Understandably, Kukkonen treats the absence of such a theory as a central flaw and oversight in the Philosopher's thought—a point to which we must agree, though with some qualification.[34] For in the *De Anima*, the organism itself can be taken as a microcosmic reflection of the togetherness of beings. Such a view is already implied in everything above. The various capacities of a living being when they are taken together lay out the overlapping dimensions of existence to which everything that can be encountered or be at all belongs. And "the soul is somehow all of the beings" says just this.

Despite the absence of a world, cosmos, and environment in Aristotle, we can understand how the totality of beings is constituted as a singular totality by further considering the organism as microcosm. To this end, a comment of Heidegger is helpful. He

---

[31] On this point, see Taneli Kukkonen, "On Aristotle's world," Oxford Studies in Ancient Philosophy 45 (2014): 329–330.

[32] Plato, *Timaeus*, 92c.

[33] See Thomas Johansen, "From Plato's *Timaeus* to Aristotle's *De Caelo*: The case of the Missing World Soul" in *New Perspectives on Aristotle's De Caelo*, Alan C. Bowen and Christian Wildberg, eds. (Leiden, Boston: Brill, 2009), 10, 26.

[34] Kukkonen, "On Aristotle's World," 320.

says of αἴσθησις and κίνησις that "[w]hat lives is always surrounded, related to its surroundings, where what surrounds presents itself in some way or another, and in such a way that admittedly, its determination presents the utmost difficulty and is exposed to the danger of being overdetermined."[35] The surroundings of the living being are determined, and perhaps problematically "overdetermined," precisely because there is an overlapping of the kinds of Being that belong to those (many kinds of) beings in respect to which an organism senses, moves, grows, thinks, etc. An organism's surroundings, delimited by its capacities, are not an entity precisely insofar as the term designates the totality of beings occupying an ontological dimension. For this reason, the living being's surroundings may properly be called an "environment." An environment is that which reflects the living being's kind of potential in its surroundings. This potential surrounding the living being constitutes the Being of sensibles, knowables,

---

[35] Heidegger, *Aristoteles Metaphysik*: Θ *1-5 Von Wesen und Wirklichkeit der Kraft* in Gesamtausgabe, II. Abteilung: Vorlesungen 1923–1944, Band 33 (Frankfurt: Vittorio Klostermann, 1981/1931), 123. In this case, I have consulted the translation by Walter Brogan and Peter Warnek (Indianapolis: Indiana University Press, 1995), 104.

Notably and perturbingly, in the quotation Heidegger translates *dunamis* as *Kraft* (force) and *logos* as *Reden* (talk). For this reason, he misses that all *dunameis* of Psyche fall under the notion of *logos* for Aristotle, not just speaking or talk, but that what is being considered is a commensurability of *dunameis*, so that Psyche, insofar as it has *logos* (*Reden hat*, in Heidegger's translation) is a measure of itself; but insofar as Psyche is not *logos* (*redelos*) it cannot be measured up by *logos*.

The critical difference, then, is that Aristotle is referring to Psyche, not so much in terms of the power of speech, but in terms of the speak-ability of powers. Heidegger, in deferring (however critically) to the definition of human beings as *zoon logon echon*, and taking *logos* as a power (which it is) rather than a measure of all powers of Psyche (which it *also* is) cannot but think of the ontology of life, besides in the case of human life, except through a privative set of concepts.

etc., in the environment, which is the outward manifestation of an inward potentiality for Being alive, and which we have previously designated by the common phase "way of life." And yet, as stated above, the surroundings as such abide in a kind of negativity – they are not a being. A startling conclusion arises: if there were no living beings, there would be no environmental possibilities, no shape to the surroundings, and consequently, no surroundings at all. That is, in our estimation, the surroundings and the environment are identical in respect to entities, but very different with respect to Being. The former is a certain nothing, while the latter is the compass of all of the beings.[36]

But whence the environment? Psyche *is* potentially all of the beings—not in themselves, but as the form,[37] and she is the place

---

[36] The purpose of this paragraph is stipulation, not proof. The "proof" that the living being mediates the ontological difference that makes a surroundings an environment lies in the concept of "making-possible." If a possibility can come into Being through life, then this shows what is environmental about an environment. And if a possibility must come into Being—not as a matter of change arising in beings simply—this shows that life must wrest said possibility from a surrounding nothingness—from the prior nothingness that surrounds life on all sides.

[37] The Greek "εἶδος" and, by way of translation, the English word, "form," are historically and metaphysically loaded terms. Fundamental psychology, in a manner of speaking, is a "theory of forms." And yet, it admits, first of all, that forms are not beings, and that they *have* no reality. That is, fundamental psychology is not a theory of the reality *of* forms, or a theory of a certain domain of beings. There is no ascent to forms. We must look to the low places. This means first recognizing that forms are quite unlike the stars. They are not a static and immutable likenesses of a moving reality (a patent absurdity to anyone who thinks on the matter). In fact, they can be drawn up just about in any possible way. Life, in its course, is constantly reformulating Being. And in this aspect of reformulation, Psyche and Being coincide—although they may still be logically or nominally distinguished. In any case, the forms that life designs in Being have about as much decisiveness as a scissors or a hacksaw in cutting shapes out of paper or wood, which is to say, quite a bit when we consider that these tools bring out what does not otherwise exist

of forms as the intellect. The form, here, is a living being's potentiality for Being alive, displayed in the shape and direction of life's stretching out to insinuate its surroundings with possibilities for nourishment, for sensing, for thinking, etc.,[38] that is, to make its environment possible. It is our task to display the psychological structure of life's insinuation into its surroundings. This task is left as a result of Aristotle's not having attempted to do so himself (at least not in any extant work). After Heidegger, we might call the living being's stretching out into possibilities a primary *existentiale* of living beings,[39] i.e., a characteristic appropriate to a

---

in the material. But just as we have misunderstood forms as self-standing eternalities, we have also missed something important about things: they are not so ephemeral as might be supposed (we need not attribute a theory of forms—beings that always are, *aei*—to Plato himself. See Drew Hyland, "Against a Platonic Theory of Forms," in *Plato's Forms: Varieties of Interpretation*, William A. Welton, ed. (Lexington Books, 2003), 263; but also, Hyland has made this clear to me in comments on his unpublished work on Heraclitus). Just as life—supposing it evolves, can insinuate itself into Being to constitute new ontological dimensions, the things we do and make are constantly altering Being through and through, that is, for all time, that is, for eternity (as is becoming clearer in the "idea" that finite human action might outstrip the capacity of the Earth to any longer accommodate life, so that a new dimension of "environmental responsibility" is coming into Being in the face of our utter extinction and collective finitude. For an illuminating take on the justification for treating extinction as an "end of the world," where world is meant existential-phenomenologically, see Ted Toadvine, "Thinking After the World: Deconstruction and Last Things" in *Eco-Deconstruction: Derrida and Environmental Philosophy*, Matthias Fritsch, Philippe Lynes, and David Wood, eds. (New York: Fordham Press, 2018), 56.

[38] Cf. *De Anima* 431b28. The form of the stone is in the soul. Aristotle does not explicitly make the form in the soul a likeness of the form in the stone itself; rather, what he seems to imply is that the form in the soul and in the stone are *the same*. See fn. 4 above.

[39] *SZ*, 44. Heidegger says, "Alle Explikate, die der Analytik des Daseins entspringen, sind gewonnen im Hinblick auf seine Existenzstruktur. Weil sie sich aus der Existenzialität bestimmen, nennen wir die Seinscharak-tere des Daseins *Existenzialien*." "All *explicata* that spring up from the analytic of

being with existence as its kind of Being. This means that the living being does more than interact with its environment; rather, in interacting, each living being is the foremost existential condition of environmental Being as such – of the possibility of a 'going-about' with and in the midst of beings. In this sense, therefore, we say again that the living being *is* its surroundings – forming them up as a complex of possibilities, as an environment in which a living organism occurs as wresting the environment from a certain nothing that surrounds it.

In this sense, Psyche is best understood as the consistency of the place that living beings take in terms of what they themselves make possible as organisms. Not only is this thesis true to the sense in which Aristotle borrows the phrase "place of forms," but it can also be applied to the psychology of capacities that preoccupies Aristotle in *De Anima*. Undeniably, beings are intelligible or sensible—they are that towards which a living being can orient itself; they may also be living bodies or the parts of such, i.e., organisms and their organs, as that through which life acts and in which it moves; additionally, beings may be sustenance—that from which living beings live, growing and reproducing. This list is certainly not exhaustive; however, it does indicate some of the dimensions that life lays out by way of a psycho-logos: the "towards which," the "in or through which," and the "from which" that we understand in the above cases are all indications of the psychological articulation of Being. The living being surrounds itself with an environment of possibilities for sense, for being in a different location, for nourishment. Psyche is just the togetherness of these possibilities—all of them. In precisely this sense, she is

---

Dasein are obtained in view of Dasein's existence-structure. Because Dasein's Being-characteristics are defined in terms of existentiality, we call them *existentiales*." Cf. *SZ*, 117. "[D]ie »Essenz« des Daseins in seiner Existenz gründet." "The 'essence' of Dasein is grounded in its Existence" (trans., mine.).

not a being, but rather the way, in each case, of a certain kind of life. In the intellectual form of life, it may be said, Psyche is able to know these other ways or forms of life, which knowing we call thinking. And if the last point is right, thinking is the same activity as knowing Psyche first and foremost. Or rather, anything that is not a way of knowing Psyche may not appropriately be called thinking, but must be called sensing or desiring or by the name of some other way of life.

Bibliography

Agamben, Giorgio. *Homo Sacer: Sovereign Power and Bare Life*. Translated by Daniel Heller-Roazen. Redwood City: Stanford University Press, 1995/1998.

Aristotle. *On the Soul. Parva Naturalia. On Breath. Loeb Classical Library 288*. Translated by Walter S. Hett. Cambridge: Harvard University Press, 1957.

Aquinas. *Commentary on Aristotle's De Anima*. Translated by Kenelm Foster and Sylvester Humphries. New Haven: Yale University Press, 1951.

———. *Commentary on the Posterior Analytics*. Translated by Fabian R. Larcher. New York: Magi Books, 1970.

Goetz, Charles and Stuart Taliaferro. *A Brief History of the Soul*. West Sussex: Wiley-Blackwell, 2011.

Gonzales, Francisco. "Movement Versus Activity: Heidegger's 1922/23 Seminar on Aristotle's Ontology of Life." *The British Journal for the History of Philosophy* 27, no. 3 (2019): 615–634

Heidegger, Martin. *Aristoteles Metaphysik: Θ 1-5 Von Wesen und Wirklichkeit der Kraft* in *Gesamtausgabe, II. Abteilung: Vorlesungen 1923–1944*, Band 33. Frankfurt: Vittorio Klostermann, 1981.

———. *Basic Concepts of Ancient Philosophy*. Translated by Richard Rojcewicz. Bloomington: Indiana University Press, 2008.

———. *Sein und Zeit*. Max Niemeyer Verlag, Tübingen: 1927/1967.

Hyland, Drew. "Against a Platonic Theory of Forms," in *Plato's Forms: Varieties of Interpretation*. Edited by William A Welton. Lanham MD: Lexington Books, 2003.

Johansen, Thomas. "From Plato's *Timaeus* to Aristotle's *De Caelo*: The case of the Missing World Soul," in *New Perspectives on Aristotle's De Caelo*.

Edited by Alan C. Bowen and Christian Wildberg. Leiden, Boston: Brill, 2009.

Johnston, Rebekah. "Aristotle's De Anima: On Why the Soul is Not a Set of Capacities," *British Journal for the History of Philosophy British Journal for the History of Philosophy* 19, no. 2 (2011): 185–200.

Kukkonen, Taneli. "On Aristotle's world." *Oxford Studies in Ancient Philosophy* 45 (2014): 329–330.

Manoussakis, John P. *God after Metaphysics: A Theological Aesthetic*. Bloomington: Indiana University Press, 2007.

Marren, Marina. *Plato and Aristophanes: Comedy, Politics, and the Pursuit of a Just Life*. Evanston: Northwestern University Press, 2021.

Menn, Stephen. "Aristotle's Definition of Soul and the Programme of the De Anima," *Oxford Studies in Ancient Philosophy* 22 (2002): 83–139.

Plato. *Euthyphro. Apology. Crito. Phaedo. Loeb Classical Library 36*. Edited and translated by Christopher Emlyn-Jones William Preddy. Cambridge, MA: Harvard University Press, 2017.

Plato. *Timaeus. Critias. Cleitophon. Menexenus. Epistles. Loeb Classical Library 234*. Translated by Robert G. Bury. Cambridge: Harvard University Press, 1929.

Toadvine, Ted. "Thinking after the World: Deconstruction and Last Things." In *Eco-Deconstruction: Derrida and Environmental Philosophy*. Edited by Matthias Fritsch, Philippe Lynes, and David Wood. New York: Fordham Press, 2018. 50–80.